# Security and Privacy Trends in Cloud Computing and Big Data

# Security and Privacy Trends in Cloud Computing and Big Data

Edited by
Muhammad Imran Tariq
Valentina Emilia Balas
Shahzadi Tayyaba

CRC Press
Taylor & Francis Group
Boca Raton  London  New York

CRC Press is an imprint of the
Taylor & Francis Group, an **informa** business

First edition published 2022
by CRC Press
6000 Broken Sound Parkway NW, Suite 300, Boca Raton, FL 33487-2742

and by CRC Press
4 Park Square, Milton Park, Abingdon, Oxon, OX14 4RN

CRC Press is an imprint of Taylor & Francis Group, LLC

ISBN: 9780367619626 (hbk)
ISBN: 9781032261690 (pbk)
ISBN: 9781003107286 (ebk)

DOI: 10.1201/9781003107286

Typeset in Sabon
by codeMantra

# Contents

v

# Preface

Cloud computing and big data are two emerging paradigms in the recent developments of information technology. The big data paradigm is applied to complex data and to the dataset whose size is beyond the competency of traditional computing services. Due to the innovation of big data, this technology is exposed to vulnerabilities, new risks, and threats due to a substantial volume of data and also different types of data. Cloud computing provides IT services in a pay-per-use fashion with great other benefits. Although there are many benefits of cloud computing and big data, there are many significant roadblocks to adoption. In today's era of cloud computing and big data, the most significant barriers to adoption are security and privacy, followed by other issues such as vendor lock-in, portability, and scalability.

An organization needs to know before getting involved in cloud computing and big data, what are the key security requirements, aspects to ensure high security to applications, and data processing. Big data and cloud computing are integrated in practice. Cloud computing offers massive storage, high computation power, and distributed capability for the support of processing big data. Therefore, organizations are demanding to investigate the security and privacy of both cloud computing and big data.

This book is written for a computer scientist, a practitioner who is working on cloud computing and big data, a research community working on cloud computing and big data, security and privacy and risk mitigation techniques. This book was developed to introduce cloud developers, data mining engineers, and system programmers to new approaches to deal with threats, risks, and vulnerabilities inherent in cloud computing and big data. The book is handy for working professionals, managers, researchers, academicians, research scholars, and industry experts to deal with cloud and big data security challenges. The rationale of the study is to provide useful information gleaned from research to stakeholders of cloud computing and big data and their security. These are very broad topics and it is difficult to cover each aspect of these topics. We described the virtualization of cloud computing, cloud service and development models, protocols used in the cloud and big data, face recognition, bandwidth issues, security and privacy challenges, cloud storage issues, mobile cloud computing, the impact of cloud computing, and big data on healthcare, data mining security issues, roles of big data in the Internet of Things, as well as the cloud security framework.

The key features of the book are current security and privacy challenges and their countermeasures, which will help readers select the best security mitigation techniques and apply them. The editors and contributing authors tried and their level best to cover many of the topics related to the security and privacy of cloud computing and big data, plus much additional information. However, this book attempts to provide readers with at least the basic information needed on all relevant topics, as well as references to additional sources of information. In recent years, many books on cloud computing and big data security and privacy have been published, each focusing on a specific topic. The editors are confident that this book will provide vital information to readers.

# Editors

**Dr. Muhammad Imran Tariq** is working at Higher Education Department, Lahore, Pakistan, where he has been since 2006. He earned a Bachelor of Computer Science from Allama Iqbal University, Islamabad in 2003, M.Sc Computer Science from Preston Institute of Management Science and Technology in 2008, Master of Science in Computer Science from the University of Lahore in 2013, and finally Ph.D. in Computer Science from Superior College, Lahore in 2019. Moreover, he has MCSE, MCP+I, A+, and CCNA certifications. His research interests include Cloud Computing, Information Security standards, Service Level Agreement, Information Security Metrics, Cloud Risks and mitigation techniques, Wireless Network Security, Image Processing, Deep Learning, Artificial Intelligence, Sensor Networks, Multicriteria Decision Making, Fuzzy Logic, and Risk Management. Dr. Tariq is the author of many impact factor research papers and conference papers. He is also the author of two books on Cloud Security. He is a reviewer of internationally renowned impact factor journals and the Associate Editor of *IEEE Access* journal and a member of the editorial board of *SCIREA Journal of Computer*. He is also a member of the research group of Cloud Security Alliance.

**Prof. Dr. Engr. Valentina Emilia Balas** is currently a Full Professor in the Department of Automatics and Applied Software at the Faculty of Engineering, of Aurel Vlaicu University of Arad, Romania. She earned a Ph.D. in Applied Electronics and Telecommunications from the Polytechnic University of Timisoara. Dr. Balas is the author of more than 300 research papers in refereed journals and international conferences. Her research interests are in Intelligent Systems, Fuzzy Control, Soft Computing, Smart Sensors, Information Fusion, Modeling, and Simulation. She is a member of EUSFLAT, SIAM, and a Senior Member IEEE, a member of TC—Fuzzy Systems (IEEE CIS), TC—Emergent Technologies (IEEE CIS), and TC—Soft Computing (IEEE SMCS). She is the Editor-in-Chief of the *International Journal of Advanced Intelligence Paradigms* (IJAIP) and *International Journal of Computational Systems Engineering* (IJCSysE), an Editorial Board member of several national and international journals.

Dr. Balas is the director of the Intelligent Systems Research Centre in Aurel Vlaicu University of Arad and Director of the Department of International Relations, Programs, and Projects in the same university.

**Prof. Dr. Engr. Shahzadi Tayyaba** earned her Bachelor of Science in Computer Engineering and Master of Science from the University of Engineering and Technology, Lahore, Pakistan in 2006 and 2008, respectively. She earned her Doctorate of Engineering (Microelectronics and Embedded System), AIT, Thailand in 2013. Her areas of interest are Simulation Modeling, MEMS, Nanotechnology, Material Processing, Fuzzy Logic, Cloud Computing, and Information Security. She is the author/co-author of more than 100 papers in national/international conferences and journals.

# Contributors

**M. Zain Abbas** is pursuing a Master's degree from the Departments of Computer Science & IT at the University of Balochistan, Quetta. He also worked as a research intern at Government Innovation Lab (GIL) on smart projects funded by UNDP, PnD, and UOB.

**Muhammad Arif** is a Research Scholar at the School of Computer Science, Guangzhou University, Guangzhou, China.

**Muhammad Waseem Ashraf** is an Assistant Professor in the Department of Physics (Electronics), The Government College University, Lahore, Pakistan.

**Dr. Junaid Baber** earned an MS and Ph.D. in computer science from the Asian Institute of Technology, Thailand. He spent one year as a research scientist at the national institute of informatics, Tokyo. Currently, he is working as a faculty member at the University of Balochistan, Quetta. His research interests are in machine learning, high-performance computing, and data analytics.

**Maheen Bakhtyar** is an Assistant Professor in the Department of Computer Science and Information Technology at the University of Balochistan, Pakistan. She completed her Master's and Ph.D. from AIT, Thailand, with 1-year research experience from the National Institute of Informatics, Tokyo, Japan. Her research interests include information/knowledge management and retrieval, natural language processing, sentiment analysis, text processing, language understanding, question-answering systems, and ontology processing.

**Dr. Abdul Hafeez Buller** is an Engineer in the Department of Project Directorates, Quaid-e-Awam University of Engineering, Science & Technology (QUEST). He earned his Ph.D. in Civil Engineering from Quaid-e-Awam University of Engineering, Science & Technology, (QUEST) Nawabshah in July 2019. His current research interest is the use of Artificial Intelligence in various fields of civil engineering.

**Shariq Aziz Butt** earned his master's degree from Superior University, Lahore, Pakistan, in 2016, and his Ph.D. from The University of Lahore, Pakistan. He has collaborations with the Pakistan Institute of Engineering and Applied Sciences and the Universidad De La Costa, CUC, Colombia. He receives a grant for this publication from the Universidad De La Costa at CUC, Colombia. His areas of interest include WSN security, eHealth applications, and software engineering. He has professional certifications in software project management. He is a reviewer of many reputed journals and conference papers.

**Muhammad Subhan Dar** is completing his MS from Gold Campus of Superior University, Lahore, Pakistan. He earned his BS in Information Technology from Superior Group of Colleges in 2020. His research interests are cloud computing, big data, security and privacy, human–computer interaction, and software engineering. He has written several journal articles, conference papers, and book chapters. He plans to earn his PhD in Computer Science.

**Shahra Asif Haafza** is working toward her MS from Gold Campus of Superior University, Lahore, Pakistan. She completed her BS in Software Engineering from the University of Gujrat in 2017. Her research interests are cloud computing, big data, security, and HCI. She has authored several book chapters and conference papers. Her next goal is to earn her Ph.D. in Computer Science and contribute to research.

**Syed Aamer Hussain** is an M.Phil. student at Razak Faculty of Technology and Informatics, Universiti Teknologi Malaysia (UTM). He completed his Bachelor of Electronics Engineering from NUST, Pakistan, in 2010. His main area of research is IoT communications with a focus on signal processing and channel coding.

**Ali Imran** is pursuing an MS from Gold Campus of Superior University, Lahore, Pakistan. He completed his M.Sc in Information Technology/Computer Science from Superior University in the year 2021. His research interests are cloud computing, big data, security, and privacy. He has contributed book chapters, journal articles, and conference papers. His goal is to earn his Ph.D. in Computer Science.

**Ahsan Imtiaz** is working toward his MS from Gold Campus of Superior University, Lahore, Pakistan. He completed his BS in Computer Science from Superior University in 2020. His research interests are cloud computing, big data, security, and privacy. He has written several conference papers, book chapters, and journal articles. His next goal is earning his PhD in Computer Science.

**Dr. Muhammad Waseem Iqbal** is an Assistant Professor in the Department of Software Engineering at The Superior University, Lahore, Pakistan.

He has completed his PhD from The Superior University, Lahore, Pakistan. His research focuses on human–computer interaction, adaptive user interfaces for mobile devices, interfaces for visually impaired people, semantic relationing, and ontological modeling.

**Muhammad Arfan Jaffar** is a Professor in the Department of Computer Science, Superior University, Lahore, Pakistan.

**Dr. Akhtar Hussain Jalbani** is an Associate Professor in the Department of Information Technology, Quaid-e-Awam University of Engineering, Science & Technology, Nawabshah Sindh, Pakistan. He earned his Ph.D. (Computer Science) in 2012 from the Asian Institute of Technology, Bangkok, Thailand, Master of Science (Computer Science) in 2009 from Asian Institute of Technology, Bangkok, Thailand, and Bachelor of Science (Computer Science) in 2003 from Quaid-e-Awam University of Engg. & Tech., Nawabshah, Pakistan).

**Khowla Khaliq** is a writer. She graduated in Information Technology and currently pursuing her MS in Information Technology. She is a teacher of computer sciences. She a native of Sialkot. She has worked in the domain of Cloud Computing and IoT-based Smart Cities. She is passionately devoted to her work. When she is not busy in her world of writing, she enjoys reading, cooking, gardening, exploring the world, and catching up on her interesting series. Her personality is charming and kind as well as an avid learner.

**Azam Khan** is PhD scholar in University of Balochistan. His research interests are in machine learning, imbalance dataset learning, and computer vision. He is also a faculty member in Department of CS and IT, University of Balochistan.

**Muhammad Salman Mushtaq** earned a B.S. degree in Economics and a master's degree in Marketing. In 2016, he moved to Australia and started his master's degree in information technology from The University of Queensland. His postgraduate thesis was based on authentic e-learning education systems. Mr. Mushtaq is providing consultancy in Brisbane CBD in Software Development and QA Testing industry. Mr. Mushtaq is the recipient of the UQ Employability Grant and UQ Employability Award. His research interest areas include the use of technology in health and education, IoT, prime numbers (number theory), ubiquitous computing, and machine learning.

**Muhammad Yousaf Mushtaq** is an Assistant Director (IT) in Education Department as well as visiting Lecturer at The Islamia University of Bahawalpur for 15 years. He is a Ph.D. scholar in the Department of Computer Science & IT at The Superior University, Lahore, Pakistan. His research focuses on human–computer interaction, software engineering, IOT, and data science.

**Maryam Rani** completed her MS from Gold Campus of Superior University, Lahore, Pakistan. She earned her MCS in Computer Science from the University of Lahore Sargodha Campus in 2019. Her research interests are cloud computing, deep learning and machine learning, security and privacy. She has written several journal articles, book chapters, and conference papers. She looks forward to earning her PhD and contributing to research.

**Maryam Rasheed** is working on her MS from Gold Campus of Superior University, Lahore, Pakistan. She completed her MCS in Computer Science from GC University Faisalabad in 2020. Her research interests are cloud computing, big data, security, and privacy. She enjoys reading journal and conference articles and has authored several journal articles, conference papers, and book chapters. She plans to complete her Ph.D. in Computer Science from abroad and make her contribution to research.

**Adnan Saeed** is working in SLI in Pakistan and pursuing his Master's degree from University of Balochistan. His research interests lie in machine learning and imbalance dataset learning.

**Maryam Saleem** is pursuing her MS from Gold Campus of Superior University, Lahore, Pakistan. She completed her M.Sc in Computer Science from Government College University Faisalabad, Pakistan in 2019. Her research interests are cloud computing, big data, security, and privacy. She has authored several journal articles, conference papers, and book chapters. She plans to complete her Ph.D. in Computer Science from abroad.

**Anam Naz Sodhar** is pursuing a post graduate degree (M.E) from Quaid-e-Awam University of Engineering, Science & Technology (QUEST) Nawabshah in Computer Communications & Networking. He earned his Bachelor degree in Telecommunication Engineering in 2018 from QUEST, Nawabshah.

**Dr. Irum Naz Sodhar** is a Lecturer in the Department of Information, Shaheed Benazir Bhutto University, Shaheed Benazir Abad (SBBUSAB) Sindh, Pakistan. She earned her Ph.D. in Information Technology from Quaid-e-Awam University of Engineering, Science & Technology, (QUEST) Nawabshah in July 2021, Master of Science in Software Technology in 2016 from QUEST, Nawabshah and Bachelor degree in Computer Science in 2013 from QUEST, Nawabshah.

**Muhammad Arslan Yousaf** is pursuing his MS from Gold Campus of Superior University, Lahore, Pakistan. He completed his MCS in Computer Science from Government College University Faisalabad, Pakistan in 2020. His research interests are cloud computing, big data, and deep learning. He enjoys reading journal and conference articles and has authored several journal articles, conference papers, and book chapters. He plans to complete his Ph.D. in Computer Science from abroad and make his contribution to research.

**Muhammad Tahir Zaman** earned his MS from Gold Campus of Superior University, Lahore, Pakistan. He completed his BS in Computer Science from Superior University Lahore Campus in 2019. His research interests are in cloud computing, big data, cyber security, and privacy. He has authored several book chapters, journal articles, and conference papers. His next goal is to earn his PhD.

Chapter 1

# Information security framework for cloud and virtualization security

*Muhammad Imran Tariq*
Superior University of Lahore

*Shahzadi Tayyaba*
University of Lahore

*Muhammad Arfan Jaffar*
Superior University of Lahore

*Muhammad Waseem Ashraf*
Government College University Lahore

*Shariq Aziz Butt*
The University of Lahore

*Muhammad Arif*
Guangzhou University

**CONTENTS**

DOI: 10.1201/9781003107286-1

1

## 1.1 INTRODUCTION

Cloud computing is new technology as compared to other technologies that provide pay-per-use services over the Internet. It allows its consumers to dynamically allocate, configure and reconfigure resources according to their needs [1–5]. The core theme of cloud computing is its virtualization that users cannot see; however, the user can deploy their application and tools as per desire by utilizing the benefits of virtualization [6–8]. Virtual machines are permitted to share the assets of the host machine and at the same time can give disconnection among virtual machines and and the host. Virtual machine escape is one of the bugs that occurs if the confinement between the host machine and between the virtual machines is undermined. On account of virtual machine escape, the program running in VMs can totally sidestep the virtual machine layer and gain admittance to the host machine. Since the host machine is the base of security of a virtual framework, the program that accesses the host machine additionally gains the root benefits from the virtual machine [5,9,10].

The Cloud structure is celebrated because of its administrations that have drawn broad consideration from academicians and associations. The cloud assets are given as administrations over the web. Distributed computing is additionally confronting numerous detours in its sending and on the off chance that these barriers won't resolve at the appointed time of time, at that point numerous issues will resolve and innovation will develop quickly [11,12]. Security is one of the incredible worries of clients particularly when they moved classified and delicate data on the cloud server. The reality behind the said worry is that the vast majority of the cloud servers are taken care by business suppliers who are not heavily influenced by the client. In addition, the classification factor additionally emerges when the client redistributes its information in the cloud. The aftereffect is that the cloud clients feel uncertain when compared with different conditions [13]. Honestly speaking, it is not easy to resolve the security, privacy and confidentiality issues [4,14,15].

Cloud computing has already been taking leverages of virtualization for load balancing. Virtualization also provides security tools that not only allow the monitoring of virtual machines and management of compound clusters.. There have been various researches and discussions on virtualization security about different points of view but still, virtualization security is a big question mark in virtualization performance [16,17]. The structure of the chapter is the following: Section 1.2 is about virtualization. Cloud security issues regarding virtualization are discussed in Section 1.3, and cloud and security issues in virtualization are also discussed in detail in the same section. Section 1.4 is about the information security framework for cloud computing. The authors concluded all discussion in the conclusion section of this chapter.

## 1.2 VIRTUALIZATION

Virtualization allows more than one application to get maximum access to the hardware and software resources of the machine installed on it. It is a layer between the hardware and operating system and allows the sharing of the physical devices among virtual machines [18,19]. The hypervisor is a software and acts as a virtual machine monitor, it manages multiple operating systems or we may say multiple instances of operating systems [20]. The basic block diagram of Virtualization is shown in Figure 1.1.

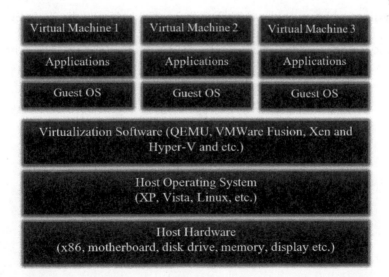

Figure 1.1 Basic virtualization block diagram.

For a better understanding of virtualization, it is necessary to know about the two types of the hypervisor listed below:

### 1.2.1 Type-I hypervisor

The applications run directly above the host machine. It means the hypervisor will act as an operating system and can be directly installed on the physical layer of the machine. The core benefit of the Type-I hypervisor is that it directly communicates with the underlying physical server hardware [21].

The resources are para-virtualized and virtual machines can use them. It also monitors the smooth running of both operating systems installed on the guest machine and the operating system installed on the hypervisor as shown in Figure 1.2. Type-I hypervisors are also called native, bare metal and embedded hypervisors.

### 1.2.2 Type-II hypervisor

Type-II hypervisor is renewed as a hosted hypervisor. It is installed on the existing host operating system. The guest operating system is installed above the hypervisor as shown in Figure 1.3. If any problem arises in the host operating system, then it directly affects the hypervisor and guest operating system that is installed on hypervisor [22]. The host operating system provides security to the hypervisor which is why it is secured, but the guest operating system would not be. The host operating system also manages the physical resources and device support to hypervisor [23].

### 1.2.3 Virtualization benefits

Virtualization brings a drastic change in Information Technology by providing huge capabilities and efficiencies that simply are not possible when roadblocks exist [24]. Virtualization itself continued its advancement and

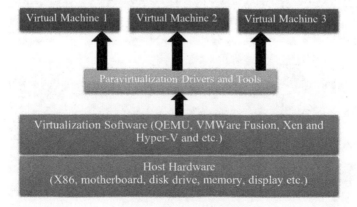

*Figure 1.2* Type-I hypervisor.

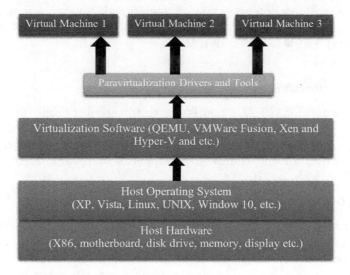

*Figure 1.3* Type-II hypervisor.

matureness, but few organizations that are using virtualization are still not taking full benefits/advantages that virtualization offers to its users [25]. Here we will discuss some major benefits of virtualization to brief the reader about its importance.

### 1.2.3.1 Low cost/save energy

Migrating physical servers over to virtual machines and then combining them into fewer physical servers generate marvelous results in the form of reducing capital cost, power consumption and cooling costs in the organization [26]. This thing will also increase the life of the Data Centre and fatter the bottom line.

### 1.2.3.2 Small footprints

In addition to power-saving and minimizing cooling costs, another advantage of virtualization is to reduce the overall footprints of the data center. It means few servers, networking devices, cables and racks are required in the data center. It will also reduce the cost of the data center in addition to saving energy [27].

### 1.2.3.3 Fast lab provisioning

Server virtualization provides the elastic ability to its users to deploy the system at any time. Users can speedily clone a master template image of an existing virtual machine to obtain an operational server in minutes. Next time when a user is required to build the same lab, he will just wait for hardware and its installation time [28].

### 1.2.3.4 Abstraction

The key feature of virtualization is the abstraction between software and hardware. It means that the user need not be linked to a particular provider [29,30]. Virtualized servers or machines do not care what hardware is running, so the user is not dependent on one supplier, server type or even platform.

### 1.2.3.5 Disaster recovery

Virtualization offers very important features when a disaster recovery solution is required. The first ability is reduced hardware lock-in. By eliminating vendor lock-in, particularly hardware or server model, a disaster recovery site do not require identical hardware to match the environment, and you can save money by purchasing more cheap equipment. Second, by consolidating servers, organizations can easily create an affordable replication site [31]. And third, most corporate server virtualization platforms have software that automates failover when disaster does strike. The same software usually provides a way to test failover disaster recovery as well [32].

### 1.2.3.6 Application isolation

In a physical world, different applications are installed on different servers to maintain their isolation, but this increases server and networking cost, power consumption, underutilization of servers, etc. But virtualization provides application isolation without compatibility issues installed on different physical servers [33]. Through virtualization, the user can fully utilize the resources of the virtual machine.

### 1.2.3.7 Easy migration to cloud

By moving from the physical world to the virtual machine, the user becomes closer to enjoy a cloud environment [34]. The user may even get to the point where its virtual machine is deployed to and from the user data center to create a powerful cloud infrastructure.

### 1.2.3.8 Better testing

Virtualization provides a better testing environment for its users. If a user unconsciously makes any mistake then he can revert to the previous snapshot and continue his work as he is not aware of the mistake [35,36].

Through virtualization, the user can isolate other applications and environments while working on his work. After the satisfaction of the user, he can deploy it live [37].

## 1.3 CLOUD AND SECURITY ISSUES IN VIRTUALIZATION

Cloud computing has various issues and one of the core issues with Cloud is a loss of control over data. The cloud user in a cloud environment does not exactly know where its sensitive data is located and processed [38,39]. Sometimes, cloud vendors perform computation in their third-party servers and transfer data to a location that is not directly under the control of cloud users. The data over the cloud is stored overseas/across international borders, which creates security and privacy issues. The cloud user is paying the amount of the services in which details are not in his knowledge.

Cloud has numerous security issues and few are listed below:
- Lock-in
- Loss of governance
- Regulatory requirements
- Privilege escalation
- Subpoena and e-discovery
- Data jurisdiction is not controlled by the customer
- Isolation failure

## 1.3.1 Virtualization issues

Nothing about virtual computing is inherently insecure; it's just a new security attack vector. The virtual layer of the machine is safer than any operating system due to its ease and secured access control [40,41]. In case of a compromised hypervisor, the attackers could get access to all virtual machines directly and indirectly running on it and perhaps the host, so the hypervisor may become an irresistible target. It is a violation of the basic principle of hypervisor's isolation when unauthorized communication occurred among clients through shared memory [35]. This section will discuss virtualization-related security issues and attacks that virtualization is facing today and required to be addressed.

### 1.3.1.1 Virtualization based malware

Virtualization-based malware is categorized as software-based malware and hardware-based malware. Blue Pill toolkit is a distinct type of malware that acts as a hypervisor to get control of the machine resources. It allows the hacker/attacker to get the full privilege of the machine, while the operating system that recognized it is directly running on the physical machine [42]. The Blue Pill takes control of the host operating system and is undetectable by the virtual machine manager (VMM).

The Red Pill is another type of malware that operates in the reverse manner of the Blue Pill. It facilitates the operating system to detect the presence of a hypervisor. When Red Pill works in virtual machine, it emphasizes the identification of virtual machine usage without attempting file system artifacts. We may say, it can conclude whether it is running on a virtual platform or an actual physical platform.

Vitriol and SubVirt are also toolkits malware. SubVirt is a software-based toolkit that works under an existing operating system and switches the host operating system to act as a guest operating system. It can change the machine boot sequence and emulates a set of different virtual machines. The Vitriol is a hardware based-toolkit that can swap the entire operating system state including processor state in and out of memory; thus, virtual machines can gain direct access to memory contents and devices [43].

### 1.3.1.2 Mobility

The theft of a virtual machine is possible without the theft of the physical machine. The hypervisor stores the contents of the virtual disks as a file to allow the virtual machines to run on another physical machine. Although it is a facilitating feature, it has security issues. The intruder may copy the file to a portable storage device and can gain access to the data through their machine. Once the intruder gets the file, he/she has also unlimited time to steal the passwords and other sensitive data and use the same to attack virtual machine [44,45].

The second security issue is that an attacker may disrupt the virtual disk or external file and the virtual machine online could change. The integrity of a virtual machine can be challenged if it is not protected adequately. The organization has to implement modern encryption algorithms in hypervisors to ensure the integrity of the machine [46].

### 1.3.1.3 Denial of service attack

DoS attacks are a threat to all of the client and server computers, but if a hypervisor is misconfigured, it will grant permission to a single virtual machine to consume all available resources, depriving other VMs running on the same physical machine. DoS attacks do not allow the host operating system to run till the availability of physical resources. Moreover, if the DoS attacker becomes capable of getting control over one guest virtual machine, it will also be able to gain control of the physical resources of the other guest virtual machines running on the same host operating system [35,47].

One of the solutions to prevent DoS attacks is to not grant permission to host computers to use 100% physical resources. The second solution is to configure the hypervisor in such a manner that if it detects 100% utilization of the resources, it can be evaluated whether it is an attack and if yes, then automatically reset the virtual machine. Virtual machines are usually started much faster than physical machines as their boot sequence does not require hardware verification [41,48,49].

### 1.3.1.4 Communication attack among guest VMs and hosts

Isolation is one of the features of virtualization through which each guest virtual machine can execute its tasks in its own allocated space and protect it from other guest virtual machines to interfere in its space. Therefore, it is very important for the network administrator to carefully configure the isolation and monitor it closely and regularly to avoid any interference or undesirable accessibility of data among themselves and between host machines [35,50].

A virtual machine has a feature of the shared clipboard to allow the guest virtual machines to share the data among guest virtual machines, and the host physical machine creates security challenges. A potentially malicious virtual machine may access other virtual machines through shared memory and resources [51]. For example, if a potentially malicious virtual machine comes to know in which area of memory is assigned to it then it could read and write at that location and even disturb the functions of the other guest virtual machine.

### 1.3.1.5 Virtual machine escape

In virtual machine escape, the attacker runs malicious codes on the virtual machine that allow the guest operating system to directly interact with the virtual machine manager (VMM). The attacker may gain access to the host operating system and all guest operating systems running on that virtual machines [52]. Virtual machine escape is a very serious threat to virtualization security. As we discussed above, every machine in virtualization is self-contained and isolated from other host OS and even other guest virtual machines [53].

To avoid virtual machine escape, the VM software should be patched, share only resources that are actually required and install limited software as every software bring its own risk [54].

### 1.3.1.6 Inter-VM attacks and network blind spots

Network Blind spots refer to the condition when traditional network security does not notice the malicious codes in the network and any undue behavior of the system. Such a critical situation brings significant security issues for virtualization [55,56].

Inter virtual machine attacks can happen in two different ways. First, if the guest virtual machines are compromised, the attacker may easily compromise all the guest hosts installed/running on the same physical hardware [57,58].

In the second case, if the hypervisor is compromised, the attacker may gain access to all the guest operating systems and even the host operating system installed on the same physical hardware. Virtual machine–based rootkits (VMBR) is the famous attack that through hypervisor's system call all the host operating system to run malicious code in the system. Once malicious code run in the guest operating system, it could gain access to it [59,60]. There are several methods to prevent hypervisor modification. A trusted platform module (TPM) can be used to build a trusted relationship with the hypervisor.

## 1.4 INFORMATION SECURITY FRAMEWORK FOR CLOUD COMPUTING

The information security systems of the organizations are resource allocation, resource optimization, concurrency demands, storage growth, memory and process management, and cost control. In this chapter, we will discuss the information security framework based on cloud computing. The core components and the architecture of the proposed framework are introduced. In this cloud framework, all the physical machines of the organizations are virtualized, and resources are allocated on demand to the users.

Furthermore, the proposed information security framework is also connected with middleware functions like load balancing and caching to make the proposed framework more reliable, scalable and efficient viz-a-viz users may use more services easily. The proposed framework also meets the current challenges and defends the users against all types of security attacks and risks.

The information security framework for cloud computing is shown in Figure 1.4. The proposed framework consists of four basic layers, namely user Network, Security Layer, Private Cloud and Public Cloud, as shown in the figure.

### 1.4.1 User network

It is the first layer of the proposed framework, users of the organizations will connect to the secured infrastructure through their laptops, mobile phone, desktop PC etc. These users will use their individual Internet connections to connect with the central secured infrastructure of the organization [61].

### 1.4.2 Security layer

The main purpose of the security layer is to authorize only legitimate users with the infrastructure, and they can access the education resources as per their provision. In this layer, the users will be connected to the server

*Figure 1.4* Information security framework for cloud computing.

computer through a firewall. It scans all inbound and outbound traffic, filter unnecessary connections and allows only legitimate traffic. Similarly, on the legitimate users, strong encryption algorithms will be applied to secure the transmission between client and server computers. Digital certificates will also be used on the same layer. This is the core layer of the framework wherein different security techniques will be applied like Firewall, authentication server, encryption and security keys. Multifactor authentication mechanisms will also be taken into consideration to provide secure authentication and communication between users and infrastructure.

### 1.4.3 Private cloud

The third layer of the proposed framework is the Private Cloud. It has further layers which are discussed as under:

#### 1.4.3.1 User interface layer

After the secure session and valid authentication, the user will get access to the User Interface. It is an entry-point into the proposed framework. This layer is comprised of further four components—Catalogue, User Portal, Stored Courses, and Web Portal. Each component has its own functionality that is assigned to it. The Catalogue as subcomponent offers many services and each service consists of detailed information regarding who can use these services and where data is located. The second subcomponent namely the user portal provides accessibility services to web applications that are accessed through the Internet after the successful uploading of the data. The store courses as the third subcomponent are used to store, sort and maintain an access list, and the fourth component is a web portal that provides web-related services.

#### 1.4.3.2 Platform layer

This layer will facilitate users to get access to various platforms (databases, operating systems and middleware) according to their requirements. Suppose, if a user wants to perform database practical, this layer will enable the user to build more advanced systems and distributed database systems. Similarly, this layer will provide various services to the users according to their requirements obtained after the pilot survey.

#### 1.4.3.3 Software layer

The software layer will enable users to enjoy the applications and tools hosted by the Private Cloud. These applications and tools will be selected on the basis of requirements during the pilot survey.

#### 1.4.3.4 Management layer

This layer will perform resource management–related tasks. Optimized resource allocation algorithms will be used to get maximum performance of the resources. This layer will also maintain and manage storage, networks, and power management using an Open Source called OpenStack. Load Balancing will also be used in this layer.

### 1.4.4 Public cloud

The Public Cloud will provide a basic software, platform and infrastructure services to the students that are not available in the Public Cloud. The framework will enable users to use these services securely and reliably.

Information Security Management

To make the framework more effective and keep it secure, different information security techniques, risk management techniques, vulnerability management, incident management, monitoring, governance and related techniques shall be implemented [62–64, p. 27], [65, p. 3], [66].

## 1.5 CONCLUSION

Cloud computing is a more useful technology in the organizations to utilize their resources more efficiently and also save the cost of IT resources by getting public cloud services over the Internet. The present economic crises are compelling organizations to move and adopt cloud computing services. Small and Medium Enterprises (SMEs) have taken initiative to adopt cloud computing services and it's proven that after the adoption of cloud services, organizations realized a significant decrease in their IT expenses. The purpose of this work is to identify virtualizations security issues and the countermeasures techniques especially related to cloud computing. Mainly, we find out risks, vulnerabilities and threats to cloud computing and propose an information security framework. In this chapter, the authors proposed an information security framework for cloud computing. It ensures the security and privacy of the organization and offers reliable and scalable services for organizations. The cloud organizations by using a proposed framework can develop systems through proposed services without worrying about reliability, scalability, resource management, security and privacy issues. The proposed framework allocates resources to cloud users on demand, which resolves dynamic workload problems for information security systems. This work is just a road map to secure cloud virtualization resources and service delivery ecosystem. After the development of the system, the performance of the system will be a comparison study that shall be conducted on the prevailing security system of the organization and the proposed security system. The organizations may test this framework at the department level first and then further implement it to the whole organization.

## REFERENCES

1. M. I. Tariq, "Towards information security metrics framework for cloud computing," *International Journal of Cloud Computing and Services Science*, vol. 1, no. 4, p. 209, 2012.
2. M. I. Tariq, S. Tayyaba, H. Rasheed, and M. W. Ashraf, "Factors influencing the Cloud Computing adoption in Higher Education Institutions of Punjab, Pakistan," *2017 International Conference on Communication, Computing and Digital Systems (C-CODE)*, Islamabad, Pakistan, 2017, pp. 179–184.
3. M. I. Tariq et al., "Prioritization of information security controls through Fuzzy AHP for cloud computing networks and wireless sensor networks," *Sensors*, vol. 20, no. 5, p. 1310, 2020.
4. M. I. Tariq, S. Tayyaba, M. W. Ashraf, and V. E. Balas, "Deep learning techniques for optimizing medical big data," In: *Deep Learning Techniques for Biomedical and Health Informatics*, S. Dash, B. R. Acharya, M. Mittal, A. Abraham, A. Kelemen (Eds). New York: Springer Nature, 2020, pp. 187–211.
5. M. I. Tariq, "Towards information security metrics framework for cloud computing," *International Journal of Cloud Computing and Services Science*, vol. 1, no. 4, p. 209, 2012.
6. M. I. Tariq, "Agent based information security framework for hybrid cloud computing.," *KSII Transactions on Internet & Information Systems*, vol. 13, no. 1, pp. 406–434, 2019.
7. M. I. Tariq, "Analysis of the effectiveness of cloud control matrix for hybrid cloud computing," *International Journal of Future Generation Communication and Networking*, vol. 11, no. 4, pp. 1–10, 2018.
8. M. I. Tariq, "Providing assurance to cloud computing through ISO 27001 certification: How much cloud is secured after implementing information security standards," 2015.
9. S. A. Butt, M. I. Tariq, T. Jamal, A. Ali, J. L. D. Martinez, and E. De-La-Hoz-Franco, "Predictive variables for agile development merging cloud computing services," *IEEE Access*, vol. 7, pp. 99273–99282, 2019.
10. A. Sohail, K. Shahzad, M. Arif Butt, M. Arif, M. Imran Tariq, and P.D.D. Dominic, "On computing the suitability of non-human resources for business process analysis," *Computers, Materials & Continua*, vol. 67, no. 1, pp. 303–319, 2021. doi: 10.32604/cmc.2021.014201.
11. I. U. Haq, I. Brandic, and E. Schikuta, "SLA validation in layered cloud infrastructures," *Economics of Grids, Clouds, Systems, and Services*, vol. 6296, pp. 153–164, 2010.
12. I. U. Haq, R. Alnemr, A. Paschke, E. Schikuta, H. Boley, and C. Meinel, "Distributed trust management for validating sla choreographies," In: *Grids and Service-Oriented Architectures for Service Level Agreements*, P. Wieder, R. Yahyapour, W. Ziegler (Eds). New York: Springer, 2010, pp. 45–55.
13. K. Kofler, I. U. Haq, and E. Schikuta, "User-centric, heuristic optimization of service composition in clouds," 2010, pp. 405–417.
14. M. I. Tariq, J. Diaz-Martinez, S. A. Butt, M. Adeel, E. De-la-Hoz-Franco, and A. M. Dicu, "A learners experience with the games education in software engineering," In: *Soft Computing Applications*, vol. 1222, V. E. Balas, L. C. Jain, M. M. Balas, and S. N. Shahbazova (Eds). Cham: Springer International Publishing, 2021, pp. 379–395. doi: 10.1007/978-3-030-52190-5_27.

15. M. I. Tariq et al., "Combination of AHP and TOPSIS methods for the ranking of information security controls to overcome its obstructions under fuzzy environment," *Journal of Intelligent & Fuzzy Systems*, vol. 38, pp. 6075–6088, 2020.

16. M. I. Tariq, D. Haq, and J. Iqbal, "SLA based information security metric for cloud computing from COBIT 4.1 framework", *International Journal of Computer Networks and Communications Security*, vol. 1, no. 3, pp. 95–101.

17. B. Pittl, I. Ul-Haq, W. Mach, and E. Schikuta, "Towards self-organizing cloud markets fostering intermediaries," *2017 IEEE 26th International Conference on Enabling Technologies: Infrastructure for Collaborative Enterprises (WETICE)*, Poznan, Poland, 2017, pp. 131–136.

18. S. R. Krishna and B. P. Rani, "Virtualization security issues and mitigations in cloud computing," In: 2017, pp. 117–128.

19. M. I. Tariq, S. Tayyaba, M. U. Hashmi, M. W. Ashraf, and N. A. Mian, "Agent Based Information Security Threat Management Framework for Hybrid Cloud Computing," *IJCSNS*, vol. 17, no. 12, p. 57, 2017.

20. A. M. Alwakeel, A. K. Alnaim, and E. B. Fernandez, "A survey of network function virtualization security," In: *Proceedings of the First International Conference on Computational Intelligence and Informatics*, 2018, pp. 1–8.

21. Z. Li, M. Kihl, Q. Lu, and J. A. Andersson, "Performance overhead comparison between hypervisor and container based virtualization," S. C. Satapathy, V. K. Prasad, B. P. Rani, S. K. Udgata, and K. Srujan Raju (Eds). New York: Springer 2017, pp. 955–962.

22. M. S. Dildar, N. Khan, J. B. Abdullah, and A. S. Khan, "Effective way to defend the hypervisor attacks in cloud computing," In *Proceedings of the 2nd International Conference on Anti-Cyber Crimes, ICACC*, Abha, Saudi Arabia, 2017, pp. 154–159.

23. Z. Jiang, N. C. Audsley, and P. Dong, "Bluevisor: A scalable real-time hardware hypervisor for many-core embedded systems," 2018, pp. 75–84.

24. Y. Cho, J. Shin, D. Kwon, M. Ham, Y. Kim, and Y. Paek, "Hardware-assisted on-demand hypervisor activation for efficient security critical code execution on mobile devices," *USENIX ATC'16: Proceedings of the 2016 USENIX Conference on Usenix Annual Technical Conference*, 2016, pp. 565–578.

25. G. Rastogi, S. Narayan, G. Krishan, and R. Sushil, "Deployment of cloud using open-source virtualization: Study of vm migration methods and benzefits," In: *Big Data Analytics*, G. Sudha Sadasivam, R. Thirumahal (Eds). New York: New Springer, 2018, pp. 553–563.

26. D. Mishra, P. Kulkarni, and R. Rangaswami, "Synergy: A hypervisor managed holistic caching system," *IEEE Transactions on Cloud Computing*, vol. 7, pp. 878–892, 2017.

27. N. Ahmad, "Cloud computing: Technology, security issues and solutions," 2017, pp. 30–35.

28. F. Sabahi, "Secure virtualization for cloud environment using hypervisor-based technology," *International Journal of Machine Learning and Computing*, vol. 2, no. 1, p. 39, 2012.

29. J. Szefer and R. B. Lee, "Architectural support for hypervisor-secure virtualization," *ACM SIGPLAN Notices*, vol. 47, no. 4, pp. 437–450, 2012.

30. S. U. Malik, S. U. Khan, and S. K. Srinivasan, "Modeling and analysis of state-of-the-art VM-based cloud management platforms," *IEEE Transactions on Cloud Computing*, vol. 1, no. 1, pp. 1–1, 2013.

31. D. L. Q. Brown, S. F. Crowell, J. A. Nikolai, and A. T. Thorstensen, "Management of addresses in virtual machines," US9634948B2, April 25, 2017. Accessed: February 15, 2020. [Online] Available: https://patents.google.com/patent/US9634948B2/en.

32. P. Ganeshkumar and N. Pandeeswari, "Adaptive neuro-Fuzzy-based anomaly detection system in cloud," *International Journal of Fuzzy Systems*, vol. 18, no. 3, pp. 367–378, 2016. doi: 10.1007/s40815-015-0080-x.

33. S. Manavi, S. Mohammadalian, N. I. Udzir, and A. Abdullah, "Hierarchical secure virtualization model for cloud," In *2012 International Conference on Cyber Security, Cyber Warfare and Digital Forensic (CyberSec)*, June 2012, pp. 219–224. doi: 10.1109/CyberSec.2012.6246117.

34. J. H. Park, "A virtualization security framework for public cloud computing," In: *Computer Science and its Applications*, J. J. Park, I. Stojmenovic, H. Y. Jeong, G. Yi (Eds). Dordrecht: Springer. 2012, pp. 421–428. doi: 10.1007/978-94-007-5699-1_41.

35. D. Hyde, "A survey on the security of virtual machines," Department of Computer Science, Washington University in St. Louis, Technical Report, 2009.

36. H.-Y. Tsai, M. Siebenhaar, A. Miede, Y. Huang, and R. Steinmetz, "Threat as a service? Virtualization's impact on cloud security," *IT Professional*, vol. 14, no. 1, pp. 32–37, 2011.

37. P. H. Shah, "Security in live virtual machine migration," 2011.

38. G. Z. Santoso, Y.-W. Jung, and H.-Y. Kim, "Analysis of virtual machine monitor as trusted dependable systems," 2014, pp. 603–608.

39. R. Erlandsson and E. Hedrén, "Improving software development environment: Docker vs virtual machines," 2017.

40. S. Manavi, S. Mohammadalian, N. I. Udzir, and A. Abdullah, "Secure model for virtualization layer in cloud infrastructure," *International Journal of Cyber-Security and Digital Forensics (IJCSDF)*, vol. 1, no. 1, pp. 32–40, 2012.

41. P. R. Kumar, P. H. Raj, and P. Jelciana, "Exploring security issues and solutions in cloud computing services–a survey," *Cybernetics and Information Technologies*, vol. 17, no. 4, pp. 3–31, 2017.

42. R. Ashalatha, J. Agarkhed, and S. Patil, "Network virtualization system for security in cloud computing," 2017, pp. 346–350.

43. F. Bazargan, C. Y. Yeun, and M. J. Zemerly, "State-of-the-art of virtualization, its security threats and deployment models," *International Journal for Information Security Research (IJISR)*, vol. 2, no. 3/4, pp. 335–343, 2012.

44. M. García-Valls, T. Cucinotta, and C. Lu, "Challenges in real-time virtualization and predictable cloud computing," *Journal of Systems Architecture*, vol. 60, no. 9, pp. 726–740, 2014.

45. K. Janjua and W. Ali, "Enhanced secure mechanism for virtual machine migration in clouds," In *2018 International Conference on Frontiers of Information Technology (FIT)*, Islamabad, Pakistan, 2018, pp. 135–140.

46. E. Bauman, G. Ayoade, and Z. Lin, "A survey on hypervisor-based monitoring: Approaches, applications, and evolutions," *ACM Computing Surveys (CSUR)*, vol. 48, no. 1, pp. 1–33, 2015.

47. J. Sahoo, S. Mohapatra, and R. Lath, "Virtualization: A survey on concepts, taxonomy and associated security issues," In: *2012 International Conference on Communications and Information Technology (ICCIT)*, 2010, pp. 222–226. DOI: 10.1109/ICCITechnol.2012.6285775.

48. M. A. Khan, "A survey of security issues for cloud computing," *Journal of Network and Computer Applications*, vol. 71, pp. 11–29, 2016. doi: 10.1016/j.jnca.2016.05.010.

49. M. I. Tariq, N. A. Mian, A. Sohail, T. Alyas, and R. Ahmad, "Evaluation of the challenges in the Internet of medical things with multicriteria decision making (AHP and TOPSIS) to overcome its obstruction under fuzzy environment," *Mobile Information Systems*, vol. 2020, p. e8815651, 2020. doi: 10.1155/2020/8815651.

50. L. M. Vaquero, L. Rodero-Merino, and D. Morán, "Locking the sky: A survey on IaaS cloud security," *Computing*, vol. 91, no. 1, pp. 93–118, 2011, doi: 10.1007/s00607-010-0140-x.

51. W. Yang and C. Fung, "A survey on security in network functions virtualization," *In 2016 IEEE NetSoft Conference and Workshops (NetSoft)*, June 2016, pp. 15–19. doi: 10.1109/NETSOFT.2016.7502434.

52. G. Pék, L. Buttyán, and B. Bencsáth, "A survey of security issues in hardware virtualization," *ACM Computing Surveys*, vol. 45, no. 3, pp. 1–40, 2013. doi: 10.1145/2480741.2480757.

53. C. Modi, D. Patel, B. Borisaniya, A. Patel, and M. Rajarajan, "A survey on security issues and solutions at different layers of Cloud computing," *The Journal of Supercomputing*, vol. 63, no. 2, pp. 561–592, 2013. doi: 10.1007/s11227-012-0831-5.

54. A. Blenk, A. Basta, M. Reisslein, and W. Kellerer, "Survey on network virtualization hypervisors for software defined networking," *IEEE Communications Surveys Tutorials*, vol. 18, no. 1, pp. 655–685, Firstquarter 2016. doi: 10.1109/COMST.2015.2489183.

55. D. A. B. Fernandes, L. F. B. Soares, J. V. Gomes, M. M. Freire, and P. R. M. Inácio, "Security issues in cloud environments: A survey," *International Journal of Information Security*, vol. 13, no. 2, pp. 113–170, 2014. doi: 10.1007/s10207-013-0208-7.

56. S. Basu et al., "Cloud computing security challenges solutions-A survey," *In 2018 IEEE 8th Annual Computing and Communication Workshop and Conference (CCWC)*, January 2018, pp. 347–356. doi: 10.1109/CCWC.2018.8301700.

57. R. Bhadauria and S. Sanyal, "Survey on security issues in cloud computing and associated mitigation techniques," arXiv preprint arXiv:1204.0764, 2012.

58. M. Arif and H. Shakeel, "Virtualization security: Analysis and open challenges," *International Journal of Hybrid Information Technology*, vol. 8, no. 2, pp. 237–246, 2015.

59. I. Ahmad, S. Namal, M. Ylianttila, and A. Gurtov, "Security in software defined networks: A survey," *IEEE Communications Surveys Tutorials*, vol. 17, no. 4, pp. 2317–2346, Fourthquarter 2015. doi: 10.1109/COMST.2015.2474118.

60. J. Lv and J. Rong, "Virtualisation security risk assessment for enterprise cloud services based on stochastic game nets model," *IET Information Security*, vol. 12, no. 1, pp. 7–14, 2017.

61. M. I. Tariq, S. Tayyaba, M. W. Ashraf, and H. Rasheed, "Risk based NIST effectiveness analysis for cloud security," *Bahria University Journal of Information & Communication Technologies (BUJICT)*, vol. 10, no. Special Is, 2017.
62. M. I. Tariq et al., "An analysis of the application of fuzzy logic in cloud computing," *Journal of Intelligent & Fuzzy Systems*, vol. 38, no. 5, pp. 5933–5947, 2020.
63. M. I. Tariq et al., "A review of deep learning security and privacy defensive techniques," *Mobile Information Systems*, vol. 2020, pp. 1–18.
64. M. I. Tariq and V. Santarcangelo, "Analysis of ISO 27001: 2013 Controls effectiveness for cloud computing," 2016, vol. 2, pp. 201–208.
65. M. I. Tariq, S. Tayyaba, M. W. Ashraf, H. Rasheed, and F. Khan, "Analysis of NIST SP 800-53 rev. 3 controls effectiveness for cloud computing," *Computing*, vol. 3, p. 4, 2016.
66. S. Tayyaba, S. A. Khan, M. Tariq, and M. W. Ashraf, "Network security and Internet of things," In: *Industrial Internet of Things and Cyber-Physical Systems: Transforming the Conventional to Digital*, P. Kumar, V. Ponnusamy, and V. Jain (Eds). Hershey, PA: IGI Global, 2020, pp. 198–238.

# Chapter 2

# Security, integrity, and privacy of cloud computing and big data

*Muhammad Salman Mushtaq*
The University of Queensland, ITEE

*Muhammad Yousaf Mushtaq and*
*Muhammad Waseem Iqbal*
Superior University

*Syed Aamer Hussain*
Universiti Teknologi Malaysia (UTM)

## CONTENTS

DOI: 10.1201/9781003107286-2

## 2.1 INTRODUCTION AND LITERATURE REVIEW

### 2.1.1 What is big data?

Big data was presented initially as the datasets, which could not be processed or analyzed with the methods, techniques, and models existing at the time [1]. However, the inability continues even today with existing datasets that are difficult to be processed with modern methods or techniques. Big data is an evolutionary term that will continue to challenge the human ability to handle masses of data being generated continuously and increasing exponentially with time. Big data characterizes itself with four traits: volume, variety, velocity, and veracity [2]. Any dataset exhibiting these traits is big data. It mainly comprises a large number of datasets in the form of structured, unstructured, and semi-structured data generated from healthcare, astronomy, social media, and geosciences [3]. Out of these, the significant sources identified are modern digital communication and the IoT domain [4].

The modern interconnected digital world generates volumes of data from data logging, emailing, social media networking, and search engines. The reason being that with the advent of web technologies, the transformation has taken place with user-created contents [5]. With the ease of creating content and modern knowledge, data generation has seen a considerable rise. Adding the recent social media boom has fueled the user content and now real-time content generation has transformed this domain into big data. Currently, more than a billion individuals are using social media, generating volumes of unstructured data in a short span. The main challenge behind this colossal data is its analysis and processing in the big data domain [6].

The other primary source of big data is the newly emerging IoT domain, where machines generate data from various sensors like healthcare devices, temperature sensors, and many additional software modules and digital devices [7]. These devices continually generate massively structured, unstructured and semi-structured data, which is beyond the handling capability of modern database systems [8].

To create an idea about the volume and speed of the generated data, Intel researched that almost 90% of the current data is created in the last 2 years. Also, the data generated till 2003 was five exabytes, whereas data generated till 2012 exceeds 2.7 zettabytes, estimated to be three times that in 2015. Additionally, the use of radio ID tags is estimated to increase from 12 million in 2012 to 209 billion in 2021 [9]. There is a need to manage and analyze massive data and devices in the coming years. In addition to speed and volume, the next challenge is the variety of data that exists. The customarily used relational databases are inappropriate to handle such conditions, data being raw, semi-structured, or unstructured. There is a need for database systems that can handle the velocity of big datasets, and conventional databases lack it. Apart from databases, the processing models need optimization since the data of interest is usually a minimal amount of the big total data (low-value density) [10].

## 2.1.2 Why big data?

After defining the big data, the next question that arises is why we need big data. The answer to this lies in the exponential growth of human civilization in the past decade or two. The knowledge and research challenges that are generated and solved in this period are incredible, and this is mainly because of our improved capability of extracting meaningful results from the datasets thanks to the big data-based technologies [11].

Considering astronomy, in 2019, the black hole image was released, created from the data collected over 7 days. The data gathered in this duration amounts to 5 petabytes which were analyzed to generate a single image of the black hole [12]. Specialized techniques were used to analyze the data and publish results that were otherwise difficult with conventional methods. Considering the healthcare industry, it generates an enormous amount of data in the form of records, submissions, supervisory requirements, and patient care. With the increasing trend of digitizing the data, in 2011, the data only in the United States reached 150 exabytes. At this pace, the data will reach to zettabytes scale and then to yottabytes [13].

Financially, according to statistics, the big data market generated USD 58.9 billion in 2017, with an increase of 29.1%. It is assessed that this will increase to USD 120 billion in 2020 [14]. So, there is a critical requirement of handling, processing, and analyzing the big data in all the fields to improve social supremacy and manufacturing efficiency, and help technical study [15]. Wikibon Big data project provides big data market prediction for 2026 with an estimate of USD 90 billion and a Compound Annual Growth Rate of 14.4%. The values are relatively high and show quite an open market share for the big data.

## 2.1.3 Datasets and processing in bigdata

Big data sets are considered based on the speed of the generating module. They can be static datasets that are generated in batch format or can be continuously generating a stream of data called dynamic datasets. In the case of static datasets, the data is extracted from the data source, which is then transformed and loaded into the database (called ETL Extract transform load) [16] as shown in Figure 2.1. In the initial phase of data extraction, the data is cleaned by transformation or connection. For ETL, the commonly used tools are a kettle, DataStage, and Informatica. But in the case of streaming dynamic datasets, the whole datasets are not stored [17]. The dataset is discarded and processed before it is stored, but due to the real-time reception, a module is required that can collect the data instantly and guarantee liability tolerance, constancy, and steadfastness in operation. Commonly used tools used for dynamic datasets are Flume, Kafka, and Scribe.

Flume is a distributed, consistent, and fault-tolerant service for data collection, accumulation, and moving a large amount of data. It has a simple

*Figure 2.1* Extract transforms load process.

architecture that is based on streaming data flow. It is commonly used with the Hadoop file system as a communicator between the data source and receiver [18,19]. The mechanism of flume is shown in Figure 2.2.

Kafka, used as the kernel for data streams, is originally a publish–subscribe messaging service. Architecturally it is a distributed system designed for streams, built with fault tolerance, high bandwidth, scalability and capability of geographically spread data streams and processing [20]. Kafka also implements queues to optimize the control and processing of data streams evading asynchronism in processing speed between data production and handling [21]. Amazon Kinesis also serves as a distributed data stream for real-time data. It can unceasingly acquire and stock a massive amount of data from multiple sources including website clickstreams, financial communications, social media sources, and location tracking services [18]. IBM Infosphere streams also have the capability of acquiring data from a large number of real-time sources with high throughput [22]. Additionally, Scribe, and Time Tunnel are also used for data streaming [23,24].

## 2.2 BIG DATABASES

Conventionally relational databases (SQL databases, RDBMS) have been used along with structure data management techniques [25]. However, these are useful in the case of small datasets with a specific type of data.

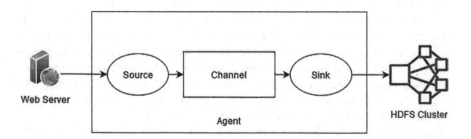

*Figure 2.2* Apache flume.

For the topic at hand, these databases are incapable of achieving the task. The traits of big data that is velocity, volume, and variety of data are beyond the capabilities of conventional relational databases. The other type of database used is a non-relational database that is NoSQL databases (not only SQL), NewSQL, and file systems. These databases are distributed in nature and are scalable. NoSQL is the term used for non-relational databases that include different models like key-value pair model, document model, and column-family model. The key-value pair model is a simple model with minimal data collision and a simple programming model. The document model is similar using a key to identify every document; however, unlike key-value model data in the document model can be queried. Compared to them, column models are developed based on Google Bigtable [26]. NewSQL is another kind of relational distributed databases with SQL capabilities and also has the scalability of NoSQL [27]. NewSQL include spanner and MemSQL databases [28,29]. In the file system category, Google has a scalable file system for distributed data storage named Google file system (GFS) [30] and Apache has its file system named Hadoop distributed file system (HDFS) [31]. GFS is meant for large-scale user data storage, while HDFS is the most used big data system that supports redundancy, consistency, and scalability in the case of parallel distributed architectures.

## 2.2.1  Big data processing

A large amount of data that falls in the big data domain needs to be prepared, gathered, and combined before data processing. The pre-processing enhances the processing capability of the big data systems and improves the services. After pre-processing the data is processed based on the type of datasets. In the case of static datasets, batch data processing techniques are used. Similarly, real-time data is processed through stream data processing, and hybrid techniques are used for both static and real-time data types.

Static data is usually in a substantial amount, and its processing is typically done with offline computing techniques with parallel processing capabilities. Commonly used computing model for this purpose includes MapReduce by Google, which is a distributed programming model capable of processing big data-keeping data management, consistency, and accessibility [32]. The process splits the big data into blocks that are processed by parallel map tasks. The reduced tasks eventually process the output of these tasks.

Dynamic data needs real-time processing; therefore, stream data processing models are used to handle such data. These models have low latency and are suitable for fast processing. Commonly used models for dynamic data are Storm and Samza. The storm is a Hadoop computing system capable of real-time processing based on simple scheduling, thereby reducing latency [33]. The model has a simple programming model, scalable, error-resilient, and reliable.

Samza is also commonly used for dynamic big data processing. Apache develops it, and its prominent deployment is by LinkedIn, where it manages a massive number of messages [34]. As claimed, Samza and Kafka are used with enhanced performance extracting the best traits of both the models.

In the case of tasks where both static and dynamic datasets are present, hybrid data processing models are incorporated. While most of the frameworks support hybrid processing by combining the components of the two and adding functionalities through APIs, some specialized models for hybrid processing are Spark and Flink. Spark is Apache developed static data processing model with the capability of stream data processing [35]. Spark, being a batch data processor, uses a resilient distributed dataset method for batch data processing by putting the whole process in memory. It uses the same batch processing mechanism to handle the dynamic data by treating it as a continuous flow of micro-batches referred to as Micro-batch and handles it continuously [36,37]. The technique has its consequences in the form of reduced performance for stream data processing; however, Spark has a better tolerance for faults and load sharing. Another model or framework for hybrid data processing is Flink, also developed by Apache [38]. Flink uses persistent message queue for stream data processing by processing it at different points [39]. Due to the persistent nature of its processing, its performance is much better than Spark, where micro-batch processing causes latency in completing the task [40].

## 2.2.2  Big data analytics

Why is technology focusing so much on processing big datasets, and what is so important about it? The aim is to mine the critical information in the massive datasets and use it for carrying out predictions and analysis of future trends and patterns. The possible use of massive information allows the technology to make improvements in the modern smart cities and use the big data in modern research, business development, and numerous other applications that are emerging in medicine, transportation, and banking [3,41]. The integration of results from the considerable knowledge bank of big data in research can take in further in several ways. Like in the field of medicine, big datasets can be helpful in the identification of indications and patterns of diseases. It can also be helpful in pandemics and modem health issues, can be useful in providing a sizeable ground-truthing database for scientific research, and most importantly it can provide useful computing capabilities which are needed for a large amount of data processing in the case of successful model and techniques creation. Figure 2.3 shows the processing stages of big datasets to extract useful information.

The business sector can also benefit from the analytical power of big data. It can be beneficial in the context of smart cities, smart devices, and better user services. With the extensive use of social media networks and smart devices, the data generated by user interaction is quite valuable in

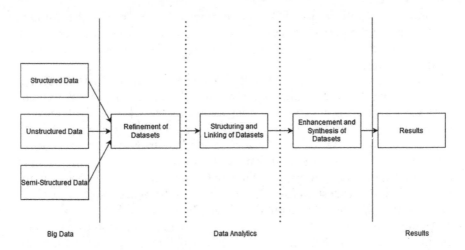

*Figure 2.3* Big data processing stages.

identifying the user preferences, gathering the unsatisfactory service situations, and improving the relationship with the user. This allows improvement and development in user-centric services and products. In the modern competitive market, the insight into the user preferences and requirements is very beneficial for organizations in creating an edge over competitors [42]. Currently, big data in the corporate sector is treated as an asset with a crucial economic input and backbone of new business models [43]. It's been a significant contributor along with ICT technologies and communication protocols in shaping the modern e-business and extensive connectivity [44]. The inclusion of big data analytics in the public sector helps in improving the healthcare sector, public transportation, education sector, and social services leading to an improved and efficient modern society. Individually, IoT applications of big data, including smart homes, wearable devices, and smart cities are considered the main contributing factors in the economic and social development of cities [45].

### 2.2.3 Big data techniques and visualization

With the importance of big data analytics in different sections of society, it is to be considered to how the information will be processed and presented to the user or decision-maker and what modes of presentation can be referred to for a better understanding of analysis results. With the advancement of the machine-learning domain, it is widely used in the analysis of big datasets [46]. It has been incorporated in healthcare delivery, flight planning, smart traffic management, and clinical procedures [47–49]. For analysis of big image data, various models are presented including multi-scale depth model for extracting features [50], unsupervised feature learning for encoding pixel reflectance [51], and an efficient image retrieval technique for improving the performance [52]. Audio big data processing is proposed to be processed through unsupervised learning, estimating the sound model of speech recognition [53].

Based on the processing, the results need to be visualized inefficiently for understanding and concluding. Commonly, tables and images are used for data visualization and to present information to users. To study data thoroughly, analysts can use data visualization techniques. It gives an opportunity of creating data trends, patterns, and relationships from various perspectives and improve analysis results. Commonly, data visualization tools used are charting tools like D3, RawGraphs, and Google charts; mapping tools like Modest Maps, Opeheatmap, and ColorBrewer; and time-dependent tools like Cube, TimeFlow, and Dipity.

An enormous increase in the scale of data or big data produced through cloud computing has been detected. Tackling big data is a time-demanding and challenging assignment that requires a broad computational infrastructure to ensure successful data processing and analysis. Owning such a vast infrastructure is not only expensive but also redundant. The other way to resolve this problem is to share the resources with other parties working with similar or related tasks and need computational power to complete them. The sharing not only reduces the cost but also allow more computational power to be used by a client in case of single usage. In a practical scenario, such a task is handled by cloud computing.

## 2.3 WHAT IS CLOUD COMPUTING?

Conferring to the National Institute of Standards and Technology (NIST), cloud computing is demarcated as, "a model for allowing suitable, on-demand network admittance to a shared pool of configurable computing resources that can be rapidly provisioned and released with negligible administration effort or facility provider contact" [54]. From the definition, cloud computing is primarily composed of on-dammed self-service, network access, resource sharing, scalability, and measured service [55]. Figure 2.4 shows the primary services that cloud platforms provide to their clients.

The on-demand resource service trait of cloud computing is primarily required to present automated computing or network resource to the consumer instantaneously at a time. Similarly, the network access trait is required to provide computing resources to the consumer through the network, which is used by client applications like mobile phones, PDA, and laptops at the consumer site. The cloud platform is also required to have sharing capability by pooling resources among multiple users using multitenancy or virtualization of resources where resources are dynamically designated and relocated according to end-user requirements. With pooling, the physical computing resource becomes invisible, and computing resource

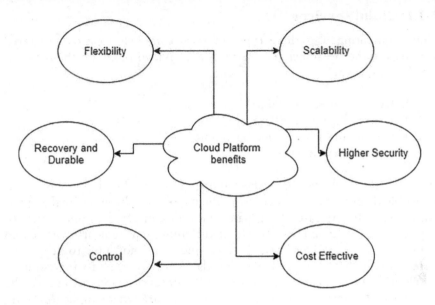

*Figure 2.4* Cloud computing benefits.

is shared according to the requirement without specifying itself. This keeps the users from knowing where the data is stored in the cloud [56]. The scalability of the computing resource allows a user using a specific computing resource to scale up and use more resources or to scale down and release the resource like in the case if the task is finished. To a user, the provisioning is infinite, and the resource allocation can rise rapidly to meet the requirement at any given time. The cloud is also required to measure services provided to the consumer by metering the usage [57]. Figure 2.5 gives the services and cloud types that exist commonly in cloud infrastructures.

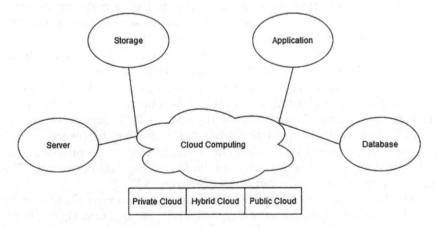

*Figure 2.5* Cloud services and types.

### 2.3.1  Cloud services

Cloud computing uses three types of service models to provide shared resources to the consumer. The services are divided based on the resource type being shared:

1. Software as a Service (SaaS),
2. Platform as a Service (PaaS),
3. Infrastructure as a Service (IaaS) and
4. Data as a Service (DaaS)

In SaaS, the cloud user hosts their application on a hosting environment accessible through the network using clients like web browser by the application users. In the case of big data, the user can get the opportunity to acquire processing models, fulfilling different requirements with cloud computing services. This way, the consumer does not have to keep software with them, but the big data needs to be provided to the computing cloud to be processed by the specific SaaS services [58]. However, the users have no control over the cloud infrastructure where applications are organized in a rational situation on the SaaS cloud. The organization is done to achieve the parsimonies of scalability and optimization. From a big data perspective, already optimizations have been carried out for the improvement of the data collection process [59]. Additionally, a new tenet replication protection mechanism has also been presented to improve SaaS services [60]. Major frameworks listed under SaaS are SalesForce.com, Google Mail, and Docs.

PaaS has more flexibility in terms of functionalities and supports complete software development and deployment cycle. Using PaaS services, the users can develop cloud services along with applications on the PaaS cloud itself. To fulfill this, the PaaS supports the development of infrastructure in addition to application hosting. Summarizing the PaaS system provides scalability, fault resilience, and tolerance in cloud services along with the programming platform for big data processing [61].

IaaS provides further freedom to the consumers by providing direct access to the IT infrastructure, i.e., storage, network, and computing services under the IaaS cloud. It uses virtualization to accomplish the task by encapsulating the real assets in an ad-hoc fashion to fulfill the extended or reduced resource requirement of the user [62]. Independent virtual machines (VMs) provide isolation from the underlying hardware as well as from the other users sharing the IaaS infrastructure. IaaS provides variability, scalability, and optimization in the case of big data operations. The main framework under this category is Amazon EC2.

DaaS goes hand in hand with the IaaS by providing virtualized storage to the consumers. Considered as a particular case of IaaS, DaaS allows organizations to get rid of the on-site database systems linked with keeping dedicated servers, licenses, services, and maintenance [63]. In DaaS, the consumers only must pay for usage rather than for the full license in the case of the on-site storage systems. For handling large datasets, some DaaS provides abstractions intended to level, store, and recover a large quantity of data inside a short time. Frameworks under DaaS are Amazon S3, Google Bigtable, and Apache HBase [64].

Figure 2.6 gives a perspective of what is covered under client and service provider considering the different cloud services.

## 2.3.2 Cloud deployment models

Cloud computing infrastructure can be deployed in many ways depending on the access services it is providing—it can be private, public, community, or hybrid clouds. Private clouds as the name points are deployed within or for a single corporation controlled by it or a third party, located within the premises or remote [65]. The advantage of keeping a private cloud is primarily for security and control of the data by keeping privacy and trust in place. Secondary advantage can be to optimize the usage of existing resources within the organization, to reduce the data communication cost in transferring data to public clouds [66]. Community clouds are a layer higher than private clouds in terms of control, where multiple organizations share the cloud infrastructure, where sharing means maintaining similar strategies, morals, and apprehensions. The infrastructure can be located at a remote site or on the sites of one of the shareholders. Public clouds are the most common type of cloud infrastructure used by the general users where the cloud owner has complete ownership of the cloud. The owner has their policies and morals and costings. Popular cloud infrastructures with public services are Amazon server and Google application engine [67]. Hybrid cloud is a grouping of any of the above three types of clouds (private, community, or public). Hybrid clouds have an independent existence but are bound with other clouds in terms of standardization or due to proprietary technology enabling data and application transferability. The concept of hybrid clouds arises from the business models where an enterprise intends to control the core activities on-premises using the private cloud; however, moving the secondary business functions onto the hybrid clouds. A prominent example of a hybrid cloud is Amazon virtual private cloud, where a single link is created between the organization infrastructure and Amazon public cloud [68]. So, the public cloud is used for private cloud computing by creating a secure link with the organization and virtually applying all the corporate policies on the cloud even though it is public, thus creating a hybrid approach. Figure 2.7 shows the link between the cloud service models and the cloud deployment models.

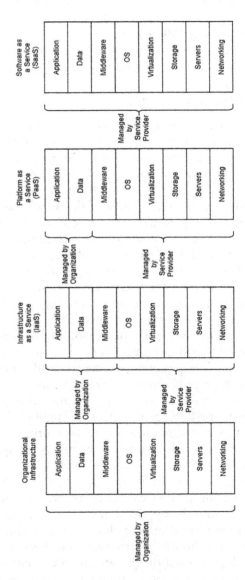

*Figure 2.6* Cloud services and their scope.

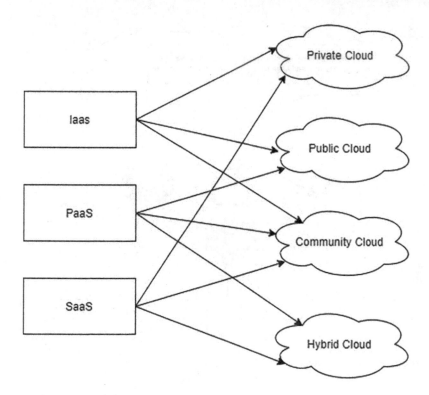

*Figure 2.7* Linking cloud service and deployment patterns.

## 2.4 SIGNIFICANCE OF CLOUD PROCESSING FOR BIG DATA

Big data is an ever-increasing domain with more and more datasets falling in this category ranging from finance [69], agriculture [70], medicine [71], and energy [72]. From the discussion of Section 2.1, big data cannot be processed with conventional processing techniques, and infrastructures and cloud computing serve as the best option. Even in the modern technological world, big data and cloud computing are inseparable. It can be realized from the fact that most of the modern cloud service providers like Amazon and Microsoft are integrating the data computation algorithms, data services, and development tools keeping in perspective the big data integration and development on the cloud [73]. Figure 2.8 shows the network link between the big data sources and the cloud infrastructure.

In the modern world, big data and cloud computing are interlinked. In this linkage, the big data provides the capability to the user to use the computing resource for processing complex queries in a distributed architecture on multiple datasets and getting results in a timely way.

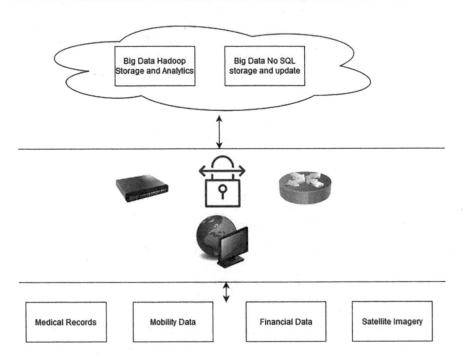

*Figure 2.8* Big data cloud access.

In contrast, cloud computing provides the necessary apparatus to execute these tasks using state-of-the-art distributed data processing platforms. The big, massive datasets are stored in the distributed error mitigated databases and processed using programming models based on parallel distributed algorithms in a cluster. So conveniently, it can be said that big data valuation is directly linked with the cloud-based application development using virtualization techniques, thereby serving as a service model for the big data [74–76].

Cloud computing is widely used with big data for processing and data storage. It has been found useful for addressing data storage requirements in the case of big data and can also manage complexity and diversity of data types concerning processing power for analyzing large datasets [77]. However, still, the complexity of processing big data is a challenging task, and multiple cloud-based technologies need to be combined to deal with the challenge [78]. A commonly used framework for big data processing in the cloud domain is MapReduce by Google [79]. It provides parallel processing for large datasets in clusters which provide higher performance in distributed environments considering power, storage, and network. The importance of cluster computing is also provided by researchers highlighting its abilities for data growth [80]. In the case of data acquisition, hybrid data acquisition along with batch and stream data acquisition techniques are used for big real-time data. In terms of data processing, the machine learning platforms provide an implementation of different algorithms supporting conventional techniques like classification, regression to deep learning frameworks like PyTorch, TensorFlow, and Caffe. For data management, the cloud service provides data maps that can search data information with ease in data management. Researchers are still progressing in developing new techniques and tools for handling the big data cloud services in an optimized manner. Like the development of a new data storage technique based on divide and conquer technique on tables [81], development of an energy-efficient storage technique for cloud datacenters using a hypergraph overlay model and many other similar approaches.

However, with all the advantages of cloud computing, the amount of control, confidentiality, and trust do create challenges of security and privacy. In the current technological age with data security being the prime concern in the corporate sector and frequent compromise of firewalls; the challenge has become even more significant.

## 2.5  CHALLENGES AND SOLUTIONS

### 2.5.1  Challenges: data security and integrity

With technological progress, more data has been generated with each passing time, and this growth is exponential. Currently, organizations are interested in the storage and analysis of big datasets existing in almost every industry. Cloud computing is viewed as a promising technology to handle such datasets. It can provide programming tools for assembly, connection, configuration, and visualization of resources. These services allow organizations to manage their datasets efficiently by deploying cloud computing services in any of the available structures [82,83]. However, as dependence on cloud-based architecture is increasing, it is bringing with itself the concerns of safety and security of data. These exist because of the traits of cloud architecture like multi-tenancy, loss of control, and liability. So, to safeguard the critical organizational data, cloud services need to be secured, and multi-layered safety mechanisms need to be added to protect the assets [84]. Figure 2.9 gives additional security and privacy challenges that exist in storing and processing big datasets on cloud platforms.

Security issues are created mainly due to ambiguities, vulnerability, misconfiguration, or flaws within the system. A survey in 2017 [85] encapsulated all the protection concerns existing in the cloud infrastructure and divided them into eight categories based on the type of interface or subject involved in the risk—data and computing issues, virtualization issues, services issues, network issues, access issues, software issues, trust issues, and legal issues.

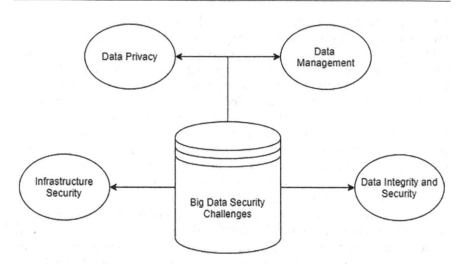

*Figure 2.9* Cloud security challenges.

## 2.5.2 Data and computing issues and mitigation

Several issues and challenges are presently related to data handling and computing resources. Prominent of these are related to data management and access. To ensure user trust, various measures are taken by the service providers in mitigating these issues [86]. The main challenge in this category is data control on the part of users. When storing big datasets on the cloud platform, the consumer is unsure about the actual placement, protection facilities, and safety processes of the cloud center in the case of remote platforms. That is why the excellence of service is a prominent factor in cloud storage, and service supplier needs to store data effectively and consistently in the cloud platform [87]. Within the dataset storage, the loss of control is a prominent concern. It occurs because the cloud provides a server pool for data storage which is distributed and remote with management provided by the service provider while the consumer is separated from the data, storage, and computing server [88]. To service provider mostly distribute the data on servers for redundancy with servers located at different locations. However, like Google and Amazon, which have servers in different countries having different legal and security policies, data control can be a challenging task. The mitigation is on the part of system managers who can ensure data centers are placed at a location that has better IT policies and a bridge of trust can be established with the clients regarding data control.

Data and cloud services availability is another main challenge within the security domain. Since cloud resources are required to be readily available to clients, any glitch in the availability can have drastic consequences for clients using these for big datasets. Since the magnitude of big datasets requires services to process the data and store results in real-time, any hindrance in this can cause the system to overload and even collapse [89]. The main reason for such an issue can be a denial of service (DoS) attack on the servers leading to blockage of services. Using multiple servers with multiple application instances can be deployed to handle DoS attacks [90]. Another reason for server unavailability is exceedingly demanding application tasks which are bound to require more power, resources, and time for execution. It causes application and computing resource to be booked. For handling such case service level agreements (SLA) are generated between the service providers and clients to define the level of services required by the client and draws matrices based on which the services will be measured along with penalties in case of non-conformance [91].

Since cloud assets are mostly virtual and allocated among the clients, allocation of the same data space to a different user after usage is a regular operation. To make the transition smooth, there is a need for data space refinement before assignment to another user. The data rectification is a critical step and needs to be performed very diligently since improper work can cause data leakage or removal of essential data leading to data loss [92]. Since most big datasets have sensitive information like medical records, financial information, and administrative data. These need to be protected, and their integrity needs to be ensured. A similar issue related to data rectification is data recovery. Since cloud assigns data using resource pooling and elasticity feature. This feature allows on-demand and dynamic allocation of resources. In the case same data resource is allocated to a different user after relieved by the earlier client; there is a possibility that the subsequent client could recover the previous user data since this will cause data breach and loss of confidentially [93]. There is a need to check the dynamic allocation of resources and keep a data rectification stage before assigning the data resource between the two users, thereby removing the chance of recovery.

Another issue with resource sharing occurs in data backups, which are used in cloud infrastructure by the providers for protecting user data in case of accidents or disasters [94]. Since the backups are frequently made, there is a chance of unauthorized access and data tampering in the cloud shared domain. Cloud service providers are encouraged to deploy authorization mechanisms in creation and access of backups to mitigate such a situation. A closely related issue to data handling is data privacy and integrity of users. Service providers with no user involvement manage cloud platforms. However, with an increase in the client's number, there is a risk of privacy and integrity breach by insecure entities by users [95].

In modern hacking trends, malware is the most common type of infection that is reported to be infecting every organization. It is mainly spread due to the inheritance of data across the cloud platform, infecting all the resources, resulting in deleting or corrupting the data [96]. Since antivirus systems are not very effective against the malware identification, there is a need to deploy separate monitoring systems to detect the malware and handle them before they spread and cause loss of precious data [97].

Cryptographic techniques are commonly used to secure the datasets on the cloud platforms. It encrypts the datasets into cypher text based on the key models. Recently quantum methods are also being deployed for data protection, but the most readily used method in cryptography is Rivest Shamir Adleman (RSA) based encryption [98]. However, the effectiveness of these cryptographic techniques is limited by their implementation. Weak implementation of such algorithms or incorporating weak keys in ciphering data can result in hacking. In cryptography, the main attack conducted is a brute force attack, where all the possible combination of keys is used to decrypt the data. Mitigation for such attacks can be to use high order encryptions like Advanced Encryption Standard and Message Authentication Code; which ensure data integrity by implementing 128-bit encryption keys as in case of AES [99].

## 2.6 SOFTWARE ISSUES AND MITIGATION

To process the big datasets on cloud platforms, developers need to create routines and applications for the tasks. Different cloud clients use different development platforms and various programming languages to create their applications; also, these applications are at times composed of complex algorithms and enormous coding. When executed on the cloud servers, bugs within these applications are a prime risk for the platform itself [100]. These development tasks can be divided into two categories, platform or PaaS related issues and user interface issues.

PaaS gives the capability of sharing platform services for establishing cloud applications. It supports various programming environments for cloud application development. Because of these implemented applications, there are chances of data leakage and information loss. So, the applications are implemented with isolation mechanisms [101]. In the case of Java-based applications, sandbox provides isolation and encryption in communication. Java VM is also used to achieve data isolation, but it has its security issues. In the case of applications that belong to different domains, common language runtime (CLR) provides protected segregation [102]. The other issue lies in the user interface that provides the window to retrieve the IaaS and SaaS services. Issues within this interface in the form of flawed configuration, low applications, unapproved access, and inducing wrapped codes can cause system security issues for firewalls and barricades. The condition needs to be addressed with better security SOPs and better management schemes.

## 2.7 VIRTUALIZATION ISSUES AND MITIGATION

In the cloud architecture, the services are mostly provided to the clients in a virtualized environment. It is beneficial in keeping privacy as well as the efficient sharing of hardware by inducing multi-tenancy. However, the virtualization is not entirely isolated, and there are chances of attacks by hackers. One possible reason for such a situation is the dynamic nature of the cloud where VMs are created, edited, and copied. Since these VMs are present in the database where they are saved in their existing operating condition, the hacker can use an active type of cloud to build a new VM or an existing VM to create a corrupted image with malware in the repository. These malicious VMs can track user activity and even perform data theft or breaching user privacy. The problem is aggravated because of the continuously increasing VMs on the cloud, and management is a complicated task. There is a need for strict management policies that need to be implemented on the part of the service provider to handle such cases [103]. VM monitors (VMM) are mostly used to isolate the VMs from each other and create a sense of trust among the clients. However, these come with their own set of vulnerabilities in terms of interposition and inspection [104].

Attacks like the blue pill, subvert and Direct Kernel Structure Manipulation (DKSM) can disrupt the monitor and extract the useful information [105]. Apart from separate VM and VMM vulnerabilities, there also exist VMs with malicious accesses through the VM-VM or VM-VMM attacks [106]. This can give a hacker access to system configuration, resource usage log, and can result in file leakage. Two types of attacks exist in VMs, side-channel attacks and active attacks [107]. The side-channel attacks inactively examine the data flowing between sender-receiver. While covert or active channel attack actively examines the data flowing and even induce bits in the data to gain important information. Machine learning techniques are used in the functional examination of data for decrypting data by training on it. Nevertheless, these attacks are not easy to be carried out and require expertise and skills beyond an average attacker. Robust policy implementation and management of machines can mitigate such attacks. However, they will require developers with exceptional capabilities. Closely related to this are another class of attacks referred as resetting attacks performed on VMware and virtual box machines. These attacks are possible by exploiting the previous instances of VMs. These attacks can also be mitigated by the implementation of better management schemes for VMs.

The other main issue that exists in the virtual domain is network virtualization. The issue causes the network to be unstable, having delays, and unstable throughput [108]. The performance gaps cause holes in the network, which can be exploited by hackers to gain limited administrative control or modifying network. Additionally, some clouds provide VMs with a public IP address bridging the access with an adapter to monitor the data. The attacks can cause further issues in case of privacy and integrity of data. So, it is compulsory to keep checks on VMs and not o compromise on the performance of the systems, including software or hardware to mitigate such scenarios [109].

## 2.8 WEB AND SERVICES ISSUES AND MITIGATION

Since the big datasets need to be communicated to the cloud servers through web services and infrastructure, the security issues associated with web technologies are another challenging domain for cloud data security. There exist several issues like IP spoofing, packet sniffing, and malware inclusion. Corporate and professional solutions for such issues exist which are to be implemented for mitigation of such attacks.

The primary issue in data transaction is with data integrity. A part of it is handled by using software-oriented architecture (SOA), but the use of insecure APIs can create data integrity issues across multiple cloud services [110]. Additionally, there can be XML signature wrapping attacks where the attacker injects the wrong messages in the Simple Object Access Protocol (SOAP) messages to get access to the web resources [111]. One such attack was observed with Amazon where the attacker accessed the SOAP messages and replaced it with the customized signature, thereby getting access to several AMAZON services. Specifying correct policies and their efficient implementation can mitigate such attacks in servers.

Another prominent issue in data transaction is through the denial-of-service attack. In the big data domain where service availability is a prime factor for cloud platforms, a DoS will cause massive congestion on the part of the data generator and network [112]. Apart from that, it affects the network bandwidth, the resources of the cloud, and processing resources. The attacks can be carried out both in downlink and uplink. In downlink mostly, the attacker can make many requests or can capture the link completely through fake requests, or they can present many processing data for routers to handle. In the uplink, the attacker can upload several packets to choke the network bandwidth [113]. A closely related attack is resource exhaustion where the resource consumption of the cloud resource is increased, preferably the memory access. There have been several solutions for such attacks including backup systems, bandwidth monitoring, and denial of requests for doubtful clients. However, further development in this domain is still needed.

## 2.9 NETWORK ISSUES AND SOLUTIONS

The processing of big datasets is directly dependent on the link between the source and cloud server. Considering the network link, it is the network deployed between the nodes. This layer is also prone to security issues and can be the cause of data alteration or even theft [114]. Since the cloud is composed of internal and external networks, mitigation steps need to be implemented at both levels. To check the security of these parameter static security protocols are implemented. For this network, security devices are deployed at the entry points of networks and the gateways. However, in the current dynamic networks where boundaryless connectivity for cloud services is required, further steps reinforcing the protocols need to be implemented [115].

## 2.10  CLOUD SECURITY ISSUES AND SOLUTIONS

Considering the sensitivity of different datasets that exist under big data domain, security and privacy are of prime concern. With the use of cloud and remote services, the data needs to be stored and entrusted to a third party. For better working of this scheme, the amount of trust is directly proportional to user satisfaction. This needs to be reflected from all the cloud services, including storage, access, processing, and VM use.

Human interventions are a prime reason for trust in the security domain of cloud computing. Since the development is done primarily to be humans, any fault or ambiguity can cause severe damage to the system. In addition, the client organization employees access the cloud resources repeatedly. In this case, there should be a trust link between the organization and the employees working for them. On the other hand, the cloud infrastructure is maintained by service provider employees and developers. Any negligence or deliberate action can cause much damage to the precious datasets as well as shatter the trust bridge between the client and provider. To mitigate such issues, checks must be in place on all the stakeholders, and iterative assurances are to be ensured.

To enhance the trust of the clients, the service providers repeatedly audit their resources and assets, making several tests to find the health of the assets [116]. This step can also have several issues due to human interventions—service providers might not give accurate or comprehensive info of their resources or the auditor compromise with the service provider giving fraudulent information in the generated report. The client and the service provider usually trust the third-party carrying out the audit, but mishaps do happen. To handle such issues, more transparency needs to be insured in the system. The client should be kept aware of the challenges and mitigations to develop the level of trust [117].

## 2.11  AUTHORIZED DATA ACCESS ISSUES AND SOLUTIONS

To access the cloud for various services, there needs to be authentication to avoid unauthorized read or write activity. This authentication can be implemented in many ways, either through login information, biometric authentication, or retinal identification. However, with the increase in the number of cloud users accessing the resources, the authentication mechanism becomes weak due to the use of various front-end interfaces, problems due to remote access of resources, and other identification challenges [118]. A primary mitigation step to be implemented is to separate the access for a different level of authorization, where this separation can be created at the logical or physical level [119].

Considering access challenges in detail, the first and foremost problem in data centers is their physical security. Since they are mostly owned by third-party organizations and provide services to many other organizations based on contracts, physical security is the responsibility of the owner. However, it is noted that the focus of data centers is mostly on the software domain considering data leakage and theft. However, the more significant challenge is to manage the developer working in the data centers and have the capability of cold boot attacks or hardware tempering [120]. To identify the attacker, the platform needs to implement individual access control lists, and checks need to be enforced to protect the physical asset. Another issue related to authentication is the protection of user identity. Since many clients from single organization access the cloud resources, compromise of user identity can be fatal since an attacker can use the credentials to take complete access to data and can delete or alter the sensitive information. Strict security checks and responsible behavior on the part of clients can lead to a safer environment. In addition to that, authorization and checks are also advised to be in place so that malicious software or individuals cannot gain access to the cloud data.

Authentication data is stored on the cloud platforms through identity management systems (IDM). They provide authentication for resource access. They have a configurable architecture providing credential synchronization ability to the service provider allowing a user to link a single account to multiple IDMs [121]. For this, the system permits replication of user account information which can create a security risk in case of information leakage during replication of data. Restricting multi-service access and following strict policies can reduce the effect of such issues [122].

In the case of sensitive medical records or secret information, anonymity is a prime factor of concern [123]. However, a breach in such a case has been observed where an attacker either delinks data from a specific client by removing tracking information or track the origin of datasets to identify the client. In the former case, loss of data occurs but in the trailing event privacy of the client is at risk. The situation can be handled by implementing security layers in the cloud architecture and enforcing anonymization systems keeping client privacy at priority [124].

## 2.12  LEGAL ISSUES AND MITIGATION

To avoid the legal challenges between the clients and providers SLA plays a vital role. The SLA specifies all formalities and mitigations in the cloud services along with terms and conditions to exercise clauses presented in the document. Apart from these user-level agreements, the cloud platforms must consider several legal scenarios in the execution of their operations [125]. Sine the cloud platforms operated in various countries where the cyber laws are quite different in implementation, so it must take it into account in case of any breach. For example, the cyber laws mentioned as Personal Information Protection and Electronic Document Act [126] in Canada clash with the cyber law of the United States called the USA Patriot Act [127]. In addition to that, various old privacy laws, regulations, and rules also hinder the operations in case of data leakage. All these legal issues need to be taken into consideration in developing the SLA document. There is also a need to update the existing data protection and privacy laws and give them an international look to streamline the execution of operations globally. In addition to the privacy laws conflicting between nations, there are also data sharing laws that exist in some countries restricting access. In the case of cloud platforms existing in such countries, it is difficult to point out the responsible if any accident happens [128].

Concerning SLA there exist several issues, like non-conformance, fraud, and deception. SLA is a legal document between the parties' providing directives on the level and quality of services to be provided. Non-conformance to the document happens due to unintended resource allotment, fraudulent computing, and data loss. The conflict between parties can also arise due to external attacks like in the case of fraudulent resource consumption (FRC) attacks. Since resources are allocated to the client on a usage basis and charged accordingly, the attacker can generate many requests from the client for the consumption of bandwidth since these attacks are tough to identify, creating confusion in billing on the part of the client. Strong accountability on the resources can keep a check on such issues that are still hard to mitigate.

Governance is another prime issue in the legal domain. It includes problems like loss of admirative access, functioning, and protection control over the cloud for the user. It also includes various governmental policies between the clouds that are facing standardization issue from security and privacy perspective. It also encapsulates the service quality, validity, pricing increase, reliability, and business strategies that are all hard to handle issues in the operation of cloud infrastructure [129].

## 2.13 DISCUSSION AND OPEN CHALLENGES

As already presented cloud architecture and communication have several safety problems associated with the network, confidentiality, software applications, and net services that clouds provide. Innovative security challenges arise due to the multitenancy, virtual domain, and sharing of cloud resources. Cloud platforms provide several services and resources, but the security of these resources depends on the importance and sensitivity of the resource. To deal with different security and privacy scenarios, many solutions are provided, some of which are already discussed in the previous section. However, even now, many open issues are existing in the security domain that needs to be catered to provide resilient cloud infrastructure.

The most prominent of the existing open issues is the absence of an integrated and complete solution that can handle all the leading security needs of the cloud platform. In the existing technology, most of the solutions are designed, keeping in view a single aspect or a specific criterion. It results in several techniques and solutions to mitigate all the problems, creating confusion and complexity. The integration will provide even better results and can handle hidden problems in a much better way than dealing with them individually.

The sharing environment in cloud computing because of multi-tenancy is another prime challenge in the way of security and privacy. The security protocol in the multi-tenancy environment is an open research area in the cloud environment. Many solutions exist in this domain as already discussed but still they fail to handle all the problems that exist concurrently.

Access control is another problem in the shared pool of resources. It is fueled by the complexity of the services and runtime allocation of resources that makes it challenging to manage the access protocols. In addition to access control, the protection of client individuality and privacy is also a complicated matter in the cloud domain. The topic is quite relevant in the current research, and new tools are being developed to mitigate the issue, but still, it is an available domain.

Another gray area in the security domain is the processing mechanism of the cloud data. Big datasets in the cloud databases need to be processed, and the output data is again stored in the databases. Since data is encrypted in debases, it needs to be decrypted in temporary memory for processing, and that poses a threat to its integrity and security. The solutions to handle this aspect of security are an available domain and need to be explored.

The security of cloud platforms from insider attacks is also an open research area. The existing solutions for cloud security are not adequate to handle insider threats. The main research objective is to make indicators to identify the insider attacks which will serve as a measure to secure the cloud system. Additionally, the identification of a genuine user from a malicious user is another area of development in the cloud environment.

Legal issues related to SLA need considerable improvements in cloud computing. The auditing mechanism also needs to be improved, and modern techniques need to be incorporated to make it more trustable and long-lasting. The auditing mechanism by the cloud service provider is not a viable option in the case of many cloud clients.

## 2.14 CHAPTER SUMMARY

In the modern world, the data is increasing at an exponential rate, and more datasets are going in the domain of big datasets. Storage and analysis of these datasets is a technical issue from hardware, software, and economic point. In this domain cloud, computing serves the primary purpose. Cloud computing offers the advantage of expense-effectiveness, massive storing capability, effortless availability of resources, and on-demand processing resources. However, with these advantages, there are a few shortcomings in the form of data security and privacy. The chapter discusses the various security and privacy challenges considering each block of the architecture. Mitigation steps for these challenges have been suggested along with practical solutions. However, there are still many avenues to be explored, and challenges concerning these are still awaiting appropriate solutions. Since cloud computing incorporates many novel technologies, managing all the aspects of technology is not an easy task. It is expected that further research will cover the leftover gaps, and the computing world can progress to a newer era.

## REFERENCES

1. F. Frankel and R. Reid, "Big data: Distilling meaning from data," Nature, vol. 455, no. 7209, pp. 30–30, 2008.
2. A. Oguntimilehin and E. Ademola, "A review of big data management, benefits and challenges," A Review of Big Data Management, Benefits and Challenges, vol. 5, no. 6, pp. 1–7, 2014.
3. I. A. T. Hashem, I. Yaqoob, N. B. Anuar, S. Mokhtar, A. Gani, and S. U. Khan, "The rise of "big data" on cloud computing: Review and open research issues," Information Systems, vol. 47, pp. 98–115, 2015.
4. M. Mohammadi, A. Al-Fuqaha, S. Sorour, and M. Guizani, "Deep learning for IoT big data and streaming analytics: A survey," IEEE Communications Surveys & Tutorials, vol. 20, no. 4, pp. 2923–2960, 2018.
5. B. Alexander, "Web 2.0: A new wave of innovation for teaching and learning?" Educause Review, vol. 41, no. 2, p. 32, 2006.
6. A. Oboler, K. Welsh, and L. Cruz, "The danger of big data: Social media as computational social science," First Monday, 2012.
7. K. Kambatla, G. Kollias, V. Kumar, and A. Grama, "Trends in big data analytics," Journal of Parallel and Distributed Computing, vol. 74, no. 7, pp. 2561–2573, 2014.
8. M. M. Gobble, "Big data: The next big thing in innovation," Research-Technology Management, vol. 56, no. 1, pp. 64–67, 2013.
9. K. A. I. Hammad, M. Fakharaldien, J. Zain, and M. Majid, "Big data analysis and storage," in International Conference on Operations Excellence and Service Engineering, Orlando, FL, September 10–11, 2015, pp. 10–11.
10. A. Labrinidis and H. V. Jagadish, "Challenges and opportunities with big data," Proceedings of the VLDB Endowment, vol. 5, no. 12, pp. 2032–2033, 2012.
11. C. P. Chen and C.-Y. Zhang, "Data-intensive applications, challenges, techniques and technologies: A survey on Big Data," Information Sciences, vol. 275, pp. 314–347, 2014.
12. E. Landau. "Black hole image makes history; NASA telescopes coordinated observations." NASA. https://www.nasa.gov/mission_pages/chandra/news/black-hole-image-makes-history.

13. M. I. Pramanik, R. Y. Lau, H. Demirkan, and M. A. K. Azad, "Smart health: Big data enabled health paradigm within smart cities," Expert Systems with Applications, vol. 87, pp. 370–383, 2017.

14. V. Snášel, J. Nowaková, F. Xhafa, and L. Barolli, "Geometrical and topological approaches to Big Data," Future Generation Computer Systems, vol. 67, pp. 286–296, 2017.

15. G. Bello-Orgaz, J. J. Jung, and D. Camacho, "Social big data: Recent achievements and new challenges," Information Fusion, vol. 28, pp. 45–59, 2016.

16. J. C. Nwokeji, F. Aqlan, A. Anugu, and A. Olagunju, "Big data ETL implementation approaches: A systematic literature review (P)," in 30th International Conference on Software Engineering and Knowledge Engineering, SEKE 2018, 2018, pp. 714–713.

17. P. Karunaratne, S. Karunasekera, and A. Harwood, "Distributed stream clustering using micro-clusters on apache storm," Journal of Parallel and Distributed Computing, vol. 108, pp. 74–84, 2017.

18. D. Namiot, "On big data stream processing," International Journal of Open Information Technologies, vol. 3, no. 8, pp. 48–51, 2015.

19. B. Shu, H. Chen, and M. Sun, "Dynamic load balancing and channel strategy for apache flume collecting real-time data stream," in 2017 IEEE International Symposium on Parallel and Distributed Processing with Applications and 2017 IEEE International Conference on Ubiquitous Computing and Communications (ISPA/IUCC), Guangzhou, China, 2017, IEEE, pp. 542–549.

20. N. Garg, Apache Kafka. Birmingham: Packt Publishing Ltd, UK, 2013.

21. H. Jafarpour, R. Desai, and D. Guy, "KSQL: Streaming SQL engine for Apache Kafka," in EDBT, 2019, pp. 524–533.

22. C. Ballard et al., IBM Infosphere Streams: Accelerating Deployments with Analytic Accelerators. IBM Redbooks, USA, New York 2014.

23. M. Castro, P. Druschel, A.-M. Kermarrec, and A. I. Rowstron, "SCRIBE: A large-scale and decentralized application-level multicast infrastructure," IEEE Journal on Selected Areas in communications, vol. 20, no. 8, pp. 1489–1499, 2002.

24. H. Notsu, Y. Okada, M. Akaishi, and K. Niijima, "Time-tunnel: Visual analysis tool for time-series numerical data and its extension toward parallel coordinates," in International Conference on Computer Graphics, Imaging and Visualization (CGIV'05), 2005, Beijing, China: IEEE, pp. 167–172.

25. C. A. Deagustini, S. E. F. Dalibón, S. Gottifredi, M. A. Falappa, C. I. Chesñevar, and G. R. Simari, "Relational databases as a massive information source for defeasible argumentation," Knowledge-Based Systems, vol. 51, pp. 93–109, 2013.

26. F. Chang et al., "Bigtable: A distributed storage system for structured data," ACM Transactions on Computer Systems (TOCS), vol. 26, no. 2, pp. 1–26, 2008.

27. A. Pavlo and M. Aslett, "What's really new with NewSQL?" ACM Sigmod Record, vol. 45, no. 2, pp. 45–55, 2016.

28. J. Chen, S. Jindel, R. Walzer, R. Sen, N. Jimsheleishvilli, and M. Andrews, "The MemSQL query optimizer: A modern optimizer for real-time analytics in a distributed database," Proceedings of the VLDB Endowment, vol. 9, no. 13, pp. 1401–1412, 2016.

29. J. C. Corbett et al., "Spanner: Google's globally distributed database," ACM Transactions on Computer Systems (TOCS), vol. 31, no. 3, pp. 1–22, 2013.
30. M. Wang, B. Li, Y. Zhao, and G. Pu, "Formalizing google file system," in 2014 IEEE 20th Pacific Rim International Symposium on Dependable Computing, 2014, Singapore: IEEE, pp. 190–191.
31. T. Yeh and T. Chien, "Building a version control system in the hadoop HDFS," in NOMS 2018-2018 IEEE/IFIP Network Operations and Management Symposium, 2018: IEEE, pp. 1–5.
32. Y. Guo, J. Rao, D. Cheng, and X. Zhou, "ishuffle: Improving hadoop performance with shuffle-on-write," IEEE Transactions on Parallel and Distributed Systems, vol. 28, no. 6, pp. 1649–1662, 2016.
33. H. Yan, D. Sun, S. Gao, and Z. Zhou, "Performance analysis of storm in a real-world big data stream computing environment," in International Conference on Collaborative Computing: Networking, Applications and Worksharing, 2017, Shanghai, China: Springer, pp. 624–634.
34. M. Kleppmann and J. Kreps, "Kafka, Samza and the Unix philosophy of distributed data," 2015.
35. A. Spark, "Apache spark: Lightning-fast cluster computing," http://spark.apache.org, pp. 2168–7161, 2016.
36. O. Backhoff and E. Ntoutsi, "Scalable online-offline stream clustering in apache spark," in 2016 IEEE 16th International Conference on Data Mining Workshops (ICDMW), 2016, Barcelona, Spain: IEEE, pp. 37–44.
37. D. Cheng, X. Zhou, Y. Wang, and C. Jiang, "Adaptive scheduling parallel jobs with dynamic batching in spark streaming," IEEE Transactions on Parallel and Distributed Systems, vol. 29, no. 12, pp. 2672–2685, 2018.
38. A. Flink, "Scalable batch and stream data processing," https://flink.apache.org, 2016.
39. E. Friedman and K. Tzoumas, Introduction to Apache Flink: Stream Processing for Real Time and Beyond. O'Reilly Media, Inc.: Newton, MA, 2016.
40. D. L. Quoc, R. Chen, P. Bhatotia, C. Fetze, V. Hilt, and T. Strufe, "Approximate stream analytics in apache flink and apache spark streaming," arXiv preprint arXiv:1709.02946, 2017.
41. T. B. Murdoch and A. S. Detsky, "The inevitable application of big data to health care," JAMA, vol. 309, no. 13, pp. 1351–1352, 2013.
42. S. Sagiroglu and D. Sinanc, "Big data: A review," in 2013 International Conference on Collaboration Technologies and Systems (CTS), 2013: IEEE, pp. 42–47.
43. D. D. Hirsch, "The glass house effect: Big Data, the new oil, and the power of analogy," Maine Law Review, vol. 66, p. 373, 2013.
44. F. F. Qureshi, R. Iqbal, M. Qasim, F. Doctor, and V. Chang, "Integration of OMNI channels and machine learning with smart technologies," Journal of Ambient Intelligence and Humanized Computing, vol. 8, pp. 1–17, 2017.
45. G. Song, S. Min, S. Lee, and Y. Seo, "The effects of network reliance on opportunity recognition: A moderated mediation model of knowledge acquisition and entrepreneurial orientation," Technological Forecasting and Social Change, vol. 117, pp. 98–107, 2017.

46. Y. Roh, G. Heo, and S. E. Whang, "A survey on data collection for machine learning: A big data-ai integration perspective," IEEE Transactions on Knowledge and Data Engineering, vol. 33, pp. 1328–1347, 2019.

47. K. Y. Ngiam and W. Khor, "Big data and machine learning algorithms for health-care delivery," The Lancet Oncology, vol. 20, no. 5, pp. e262–e273, 2019.

48. G. Gui, F. Liu, J. Sun, J. Yang, Z. Zhou, and D. Zhao, "Flight delay prediction based on aviation big data and machine learning," IEEE Transactions on Vehicular Technology, vol. 69, no. 1, pp. 140–150, 2019.

49. R. B. Rutledge, A. M. Chekroud, and Q. J. Huys, "Machine learning and big data in psychiatry: Toward clinical applications" Current Opinion in Neurobiology, vol. 55, pp. 152–159, 2019.

50. Y. Niu, Z. Lu, J.-R. Wen, T. Xiang, and S.-F. Chang, "Multi-modal multi-scale deep learning for large-scale image annotation," IEEE Transactions on Image Processing, vol. 28, no. 4, pp. 1720–1731, 2018.

51. L. Windrim, R. Ramakrishnan, A. Melkumyan, and R. J. Murphy, "A physics-based deep learning approach to shadow invariant representations of hyperspectral images," IEEE Transactions on Image Processing, vol. 27, no. 2, pp. 665–677, 2017.

52. P. Liu, J.-M. Guo, C.-Y. Wu, and D. Cai, "Fusion of deep learning and compressed domain features for content-based image retrieval," IEEE Transactions on Image Processing, vol. 26, no. 12, pp. 5706–5717, 2017.

53. V. Despotovic, O. Walter, and R. Haeb-Umbach, "Machine learning techniques for semantic analysis of Dysarthric speech: An experimental study," Speech Communication, vol. 99, pp. 242–251, 2018.

54. P. Mell and T. Grance, "Draft nist working definition of cloud computing-v15," 21. Aug 2009, vol. 2, pp. 123–135, 2009.

55. T. Velte, A. Velte, and R. Elsenpeter, Cloud Computing, a Practical Approach. New York: McGraw-Hill, Inc., 2009.

56. M. A Vouk, "Cloud computing–issues, research and implementations," Journal of Computing and Information Technology, vol. 16, no. 4, pp. 235–246, 2008.

57. S. Lehrig, H. Eikerling, and S. Becker, "Scalability, elasticity, and efficiency in cloud computing: A systematic literature review of definitions and metrics," in Proceedings of the 11th International ACM SIGSOFT Conference on Quality of Software Architectures, 2015, Montréal QC Canada, pp. 83–92.

58. L. Wang, J. Tao, M. Kunze, A. C. Castellanos, D. Kramer, and W. Karl, "Scientific cloud computing: Early definition and experience," in 2008 10th IEEE International Conference on High Performance Computing and Communications, Dalian, China, 2008: IEEE, pp. 825–830.

59. I.-L. Yen, F. Bastani, Y. Huang, Y. Zhang, and X. Yao, "SaaS for automated job performance appraisals using service technologies and big data analytics" in 2017 IEEE International Conference on Web Services (ICWS), 2017, Honolulu, HI, USA: IEEE, pp. 412–419.

60. L. Li, Y. Zhang, and Y. Ding, "MT-DIPS: A new data duplication integrity protection scheme for multi-tenants sharing storage in SaaS," International Journal of Grid and Utility Computing, vol. 9, no. 1, pp. 26–36, 2018.

61. Y. Verginadis, I. Patiniotakis, G. Mentzas, S. Veloudis, and I. Paraskakis, "Data distribution and encryption modelling for PaaS-enabled cloud security" in 2016 IEEE International Conference on Cloud Computing Technology and Science (CloudCom), 2016, Luxembourg, Luxembourg: IEEE, pp. 497–502.

62. S. Bhardwaj, L. Jain, and S. Jain, "Cloud computing: A study of infrastructure as a service (IAAS)," International Journal of Engineering and Information Technology, vol. 2, no. 1, pp. 60–63, 2010.

63. K. S. Søilen, "Users' perceptions of Data as a Service (DaaS)" Journal of Intelligence Studies in Business, vol. 6, no. 2, 2016.

64. O. Terzo, P. Ruiu, E. Bucci, and F. Xhafa, "Data as a service (DaaS) for sharing and processing of large data collections in the cloud," in 2013 Seventh International Conference on Complex, Intelligent, and Software Intensive Systems, 2013, Taichung, Taiwan: IEEE, pp. 475–480.

65. S. K. Doddavula and A. W. Gawande, "Adopting cloud computing: Enterprise private clouds," Setlabs Briefing, vol. 7, no. 7, pp. 11–18, 2009.

66. J. Li, J. Peng, Z. Lei, and W. Zhang, "An energy-efficient scheduling approach based on private clouds," Journal of Information & Computational Science, vol. 8, no. 4, pp. 716–724, 2011.

67. P. Hofmann and D. Woods, "Cloud computing: The limits of public clouds for business applications," IEEE Internet Computing, vol. 14, no. 6, pp. 90–93, 2010.

68. B. Sotomayor, R. S. Montero, I. M. Llorente, and I. Foster, "Virtual infrastructure management in private and hybrid clouds," IEEE Internet Computing, vol. 13, no. 5, pp. 14–22, 2009.

69. J. J. Seddon and W. L. Currie, "A model for unpacking big data analytics in high-frequency trading," Journal of Business Research, vol. 70, pp. 300–307, 2017.

70. A. Kamilaris, A. Kartakoullis, and F. X. Prenafeta-Boldú, "A review on the practice of big data analysis in agriculture," Computers and Electronics in Agriculture, vol. 143, pp. 23–37, 2017.

71. Z. Obermeyer and E. J. Emanuel, "Predicting the future: Big data, machine learning, and clinical medicine," The New England Journal of Medicine, vol. 375, no. 13, p. 1216, 2016.

72. K. Zhou, C. Fu, and S. Yang, "Big data driven smart energy management: From big data to big insights," Renewable and Sustainable Energy Reviews, vol. 56, pp. 215–225, 2016.

73. H. Li, W. Li, H. Wang, and J. Wang, "An optimization of virtual machine selection and placement by using memory content similarity for server consolidation in cloud," Future Generation Computer Systems, vol. 84, pp. 98–107, 2018.

74. P. Mell and T. Grance, "The NIST definition of cloud computing," 2011.

75. M. Armbrust, et al., "A view of cloud computing," Communications of the ACM, vol. 53, no. 4, pp. 50–58, 2010.

76. M. Arostegi, A. Torre-Bastida, M. N. Bilbao, and J. Del Ser, "A heuristic approach to the multicriteria design of IaaS cloud infrastructures for big data applications," Expert Systems, vol. 35, no. 5, p. e12259, 2018.

77. P. Trunfio and V. Vlassov, Clouds for Scalable Big Data Processing. New York: Taylor & Francis, 2019.

78. C. Ji, Y. Li, W. Qiu, U. Awada, and K. Li, "Big data processing in cloud computing environments," in 2012 12th International Symposium on Pervasive Systems, Algorithms and Networks, 2012, San Marcos, TX, USA: IEEE, pp. 17–23.

79. J. Dean and S. Ghemawat, "MapReduce: Simplified data processing on large clusters," Communications of the ACM, vol. 51, no. 1, pp. 107–113, 2008.

80. D. Bollier and C. M. Firestone, The promise and peril of big data. Aspen Institute, Communications and Society Program Washington, DC, 2010.

81. M. Sookhak, F. R. Yu, and A. Y. Zomaya, "Auditing big data storage in cloud computing using divide and conquer tables," IEEE Transactions on Parallel and Distributed Systems, vol. 29, no. 5, pp. 999–1012, 2017.

82. C. Yang, Q. Huang, Z. Li, K. Liu, and F. Hu, "Big data and cloud computing: innovation opportunities and challenges," International Journal of Digital Earth, vol. 10, no. 1, pp. 13–53, 2017.

83. R. K. Barik et al., "Fog assisted cloud computing in era of big data and Internet-of-things: Systems, architectures, and applications," In: Cloud Computing for Optimization: Foundations, Applications, and Challenges, B. S. P. Mishra, H. Das, S. Dehuri, A. K. Jagadev (Eds). New York: Springer, 2018, pp. 367–394.

84. S. P. Ahuja and B. Moore, "State of big data analysis in the cloud," Network and Communication Technologies, vol. 2, no. 1, p. 62, 2013.

85. A. Singh and K. Chatterjee, "Cloud security issues and challenges: A survey," Journal of Network and Computer Applications, vol. 79, pp. 88–115, 2017.

86. S. M. Khan and K. W. Hamlen, "AnonymousCloud: A data ownership privacy provider framework in cloud computing," in 2012 IEEE 11th International Conference on Trust, Security and Privacy in Computing and Communications, 2012, Liverpool, UK: IEEE, pp. 170–176.

87. Y. Sun, J. Zhang, Y. Xiong, and G. Zhu, "Data security and privacy in cloud computing," International Journal of Distributed Sensor Networks, vol. 10, no. 7, p. 190903, 2014.

88. V. Chang and M. Ramachandran, "Towards achieving data security with the cloud computing adoption framework," IEEE Transactions on Services Computing, vol. 9, no. 1, pp. 138–151, 2015.

89. E. Bauer, R. Adams, and D. Eustace, Beyond Redundancy: How Geographic Redundancy Can Improve Service Availability and Reliability of Computer-Based Systems. Hoboken, NJ: John Wiley & Sons, 2011.

90. M. Masdari and M. Jalali, "A survey and taxonomy of DoS attacks in cloud computing," Security and Communication Networks, vol. 9, no. 16, pp. 3724–3751, 2016.

91. E. J. Bauer, R. S. Adams, and D. W. Eustace, Method and apparatus for rapid disaster recovery preparation in a cloud network. Google Patents, 2015.

92. L. J. Sotto, B. C. Treacy, and M. L. McLellan, "Privacy and data security risks in cloud computing," World Communications Regulation Report, vol. 5, no. 2, p. 38, 2010.

93. F. S. Al-Anzi, A. A. Salman, N. K. Jacob, and J. Soni, "Towards robust, scalable and secure network storage in cloud computing," in 2014 Fourth International Conference on Digital Information and Communication Technology and its Applications (DICTAP), 2014, Bangkok, Thailand: IEEE, pp. 51–55.

94. N. McKelvey, K. Curran, B. Gordon, E. Devlin, and K. Johnston, "Cloud computing and security in the future." In: Guide to Security Assurance for Cloud Computing. S. Y. Zhu, R. Hill, and M. Trovati (Eds). New York: Springer, 2015, pp. 95–108.

95. K. Nahrstedt et al., "Security for cloud computing," A Report: Directorate for Computer and Information Science and Engineering (CISE), pp. 1–19, 2012.

96. M. R. Watson, A. K. Marnerides, A. Mauthe, and D. Hutchison, "Towards a distributed, self-organising approach to malware detection in cloud computing," in International Workshop on Self-Organizing Systems, 2013: Springer, pp. 182–185.

97. N. Praveena, S. Sofia, and D. Srinivasulu, "Anomaly detection in infrastructure service of cloud computing." Abdullah akbar, Shaik Mahobob basha, Syed Abdul basha, Syed Abdul Basha.

98. N. Sengupta and J. Holmes, "Designing of cryptography based security system for cloud computing," in 2013 International Conference on Cloud & Ubiquitous Computing & Emerging Technologies, 2013, Pune, India: IEEE, pp. 52–57.

99. V. R. Pancholi and B. P. Patel, "Enhancement of cloud computing security with secure data storage using AES," International Journal for Innovative Research in Science and Technology, vol. 2, no. 9, pp. 18–21, 2016.

100. T. Dillon, C. Wu, and E. Chang, "Cloud computing: Issues and challenges," in 2010 24th IEEE International Conference on Advanced Information Networking and Applications, 2010, Perth, WA, Australia: IEEE, pp. 27–33.

101. M. T. Sandikkaya and A. E. Harmanci, "Security problems of platform-as-a-service (PAAS) clouds and practical solutions to the problems," in 2012 IEEE 31st Symposium on Reliable Distributed Systems, 2012, Irvine, CA, USA: IEEE, pp. 463–468.

102. L. Rodero-Merino, L. M. Vaquero, E. Caron, A. Muresan, and F. Desprez, "Building safe PaaS clouds: A survey on security in multitenant software platforms," Computers & Security, vol. 31, no. 1, pp. 96–108, 2012.

103. S. Luo, Z. Lin, X. Chen, Z. Yang, and J. Chen, "Virtualization security for cloud computing service," in 2011 International Conference on Cloud and Service Computing, 2011, Hong Kong, China: IEEE, pp. 174–179.

104. M. Rosenblum and T. Garfinkel, "Virtual machine monitors: Current technology and future trends," Computer, vol. 38, no. 5, pp. 39–47, 2005.

105. S. Bahram et al., "Dksm: Subverting virtual machine introspection for fun and profit," in 2010 29th IEEE Symposium on Reliable Distributed Systems, 2010, New Delhi, India: IEEE, pp. 82–91.

106. G. Pék, A. Lanzi, A. Srivastava, D. Balzarotti, A. Francillon, and C. Neumann, "On the feasibility of software attacks on commodity virtual machine monitors via direct device assignment," in Proceedings of the 9th ACM Symposium on Information, Computer and Communications Security, 2014, Kyoto Japan, pp. 305–316.

107. T. Ristenpart, E. Tromer, H. Shacham, and S. Savage, "Hey, you, get off of my cloud: Exploring information leakage in third-party compute clouds," in Proceedings of the 16th ACM Conference on Computer and Communications Security, 2009, Chicago Illinois USA, pp. 199–212.

108. G. Wang and T. E. Ng, "The impact of virtualization on network performance of amazon ec2 data center" in 2010 Proceedings IEEE INFOCOM, 2010, San Diego, CA, USA: IEEE, pp. 1–9.
109. M. Alaluna, E. Vial, N. Neves, and F. M. Ramos, "Secure multi-cloud network virtualization," Computer Networks, vol. 161, pp. 45–60, 2019.
110. W. Luo and G. Bai, "Ensuring the data integrity in cloud data storage," in 2011 IEEE International Conference on Cloud Computing and Intelligence Systems, 2011, Beijing, China: IEEE, pp. 240–243.
111. M. McIntosh and P. Austel, "XML signature element wrapping attacks and countermeasures," in Proceedings of the 2005 Workshop on Secure Web Services, 2005, pp. 20–27.
112. R. V. Rao and K. Selvamani, "Data security challenges and its solutions in cloud computing," Procedia Computer Science, vol. 48, pp. 204–209, 2015.
113. S. M. A. Zaidi, W. A. Baig, H. Redwan, and K.-H. Kim, "DOS attack on the availability of cloud network and its avoidance mechanism," in Proceedings of the Korea Information Processing Society Conference, 2011, pp. 760–762.
114. C. Modi, D. Patel, B. Borisaniya, A. Patel, and M. Rajarajan, "A survey on security issues and solutions at different layers of cloud computing," The Journal of Supercomputing, vol. 63, no. 2, pp. 561–592, 2013.
115. K. Hamlen, M. Kantarcioglu, L. Khan, and B. Thuraisingham, "Security issues for cloud computing," International Journal of Information Security and Privacy (IJISP), vol. 4, no. 2, pp. 36–48, 2010.
116. J. Li, J. Li, D. Xie, and Z. Cai, "Secure auditing and deduplicating data in cloud," IEEE Transactions on Computers, vol. 65, no. 8, pp. 2386–2396, 2015.
117. C. Wang, S. S. Chow, Q. Wang, K. Ren, and W. Lou, "Privacy-preserving public auditing for secure cloud storage," IEEE Transactions on Computers, vol. 62, no. 2, pp. 362–375, 2011.
118. H. Chang and E. Choi, "User authentication in cloud computing" in International Conference on Ubiquitous Computing and Multimedia Applications, 2011: Springer, pp. 338–342.
119. A. J. Choudhury, P. Kumar, M. Sain, H. Lim, and H. Jae-Lee, "A strong user authentication framework for cloud computing," in 2011 IEEE Asia-Pacific Services Computing Conference, 2011, Jeju, Korea (South): IEEE, pp. 110–115.
120. J. Spring, "Monitoring cloud computing by layer, part 1," IEEE Security & Privacy, vol. 9, no. 2, pp. 66–68, 2011.
121. A. Celesti, F. Tusa, M. Villari, and A. Puliafito, "Security and cloud computing: Intercloud identity management infrastructure," in 2010 19th IEEE International Workshops on Enabling Technologies: Infrastructures for Collaborative Enterprises, 2010, Larissa, Greece: IEEE, pp. 263–265.
122. U. Habiba, R. Masood, M. A. Shibli, and M. A. Niazi, "Cloud identity management security issues & solutions: A taxonomy," Complex Adaptive Systems Modeling, vol. 2, no. 1, p. 5, 2014.
123. J. Sedayao and I. I. Enterprise Architect, "Enhancing cloud security using data anonymization," White Paper, Intel Coporation, 2012.

124. L. Malina, J. Hajny, P. Dzurenda, and V. Zeman, "Privacy-preserving security solution for cloud services," Journal of Applied Research and Technology, vol. 13, no. 1, pp. 20–31, 2015.

125. M. Alhamad, T. Dillon, and E. Chang, "Conceptual SLA framework for cloud computing," in 4th IEEE International Conference on Digital Ecosystems and Technologies, 2010, Dubai, United Arab Emirates: IEEE, pp. 606–610.

126. L. M. Austin, "Reviewing pipeda: Control, privacy and the limits of fair information practices," Canadian Business Law Journal, vol. 44, p. 21, 2006.

127. M. T. McCarthy, USA patriot act. Buffalo, NJ: HeinOnline, 2002.

128. J.-H. Morin, J. Aubert, and B. Gateau, "Towards cloud computing SLA risk management: Issues and challenges" in 2012 45th Hawaii International Conference on System Sciences, 2012: IEEE, pp. 5509–5514.

129. R. Farrell, "Securing the cloud: Governance, risk, and compliance issues reign supreme," Information Security Journal: A Global Perspective, vol. 19, no. 6, pp. 310–319, 2010.

# Chapter 3

# The ways of networks intrusion their detection and prevention

*Ali Imran and Ahsan Imtiaz*
Superior University

## CONTENTS

DOI: 10.1201/9781003107286-3

## 3.1 INTRODUCTION

In a time of pandemic, the world is advancing toward virtualization, so organizing necessities for any business continuity is rapidly increasing. As of now, clients move inside their homes to dodge contamination and stay safe as organizations request increments and their security increments too. The corporate world has moved from working environments to their homes, and information sharing on the neighborhood has increased. As coordinate and the public authority is finding a genuine way to expand their well-being and security of data. In virtualization, programmers had simple approaches to get infused with any cyberattack. To evade those means, this chapter investigates the most ideal approach to save your information from cyberattacks [1].

This chapter gives the survey on information security as a prerequisite of information sharing, which has become indispensable in the today's world, so this chapter gives information on the most proficient method to make your correspondence secure, by separating it into four sections. This chapter gives the audit on Information security as a necessity of information sharing, which had been fundamental in today's world, so this chapter gives information how to make your correspondence secure, by isolating it into four sections; the first section is about how to get to the security framework; the second section is about how to secure your correspondence; the third section is about how to secure the executives framework; and the fourth section is about how to build up the security of the board framework. Security framework, second in of secure your correspondence, third is about the security the board framework and the fourth one in how to make to build up the security of the executives framework [2].

The definition of network security is extended as a result of the vital utilization of systems and the online. There are huge number of reports, research papers, seminars moreover, workshops committed to the security parts of information security structures and implementations. Join responsibilities by systems analysts, encryptions, electrical and systems experts and information security scientists. Regardless, supporters regularly have entirely unexpected point of views on the aspects of network security-related issues and user plans. In addition, we see that information experts having a vital role in definite control, similar to coding, encoding, system hardware planner, or network security, routinely seem to have a helpless knowledge of their role made by researchers' controls. Crack in the line of network security has two ideas. First, expert in various orders may finalize endeavoring to reiterate a generally tackled issue. Second, we can see that keeping an eye on security issues exhaustively requires interdisciplinary undertakings [3–7].

While testing these issues adeptly, we comprehended that it was inconvenient, if absolutely plausible, We have to make an unremarkable overview of network security that overview all the aspect of network and its traffic. To overcome these issues, it was planned to augment the stages of reflection and provide four convincing levels of network security-related issues: permission to network, secure correspondence and improvement of secure network. Growing the level of reflection helps with making the security comprehensive. What's more physical to informative aim and the reasons of clearness as well as seeing the part of information security research in a grouping zone. The discussion turned to the responsibility of cyberattacks. Organizational network surveillances portrayed for the safety of company from not valid change, attack, or intervene, and plan of controlling to ensure that the company acts in fundamental conditions. Similarly joins plans to develop an essential PC linkage system, procedures made by the company admin to provide the linkage, and company information data from unauthenticated access [3,8].

Organization networks starts with user allowance, for the most part with a user ID and mysterious word. Organization network security includes the scenarios and methodologies developed by a company director to control and screen unapproved interferences.

Alternation in the existing system, attacked, or ignorance of system networking and links to accessible resources. Essentially, security remembers the acknowledgment of data for an origination, which the security head manages or secures. It is crucial for single system customers and related organizations. If this is affirmed, a firewall powers access, for instance, what organizations are allowed to be accessed for network customers. To thwart unapproved permission to the system, this fragment may disregard to check for potentially frightful substance, such as PC worms or Trojans, being conveyed preposterous. Intrusion detection system (IDS) recognize the malware from the network traffic to resolve and make batter security solution. Today peculiarity may similarly screen the software applications who help to monitor network live tacking of packets and data [1,9].

## 3.2 LITERATURE REVIEW

As researcher noticed, many experts are working in information security, but their knowledge is not up to mark; therefore, this chapter will benefit them by providing knowledge on these four security-related issues. Under the umbrella of IS policies and discussion with experts, this chapter provides complete knowledge on how and who will access the system, how to secure it and how to develop secure management system. To justify its research, all technical analysis was provided by mathematical way using various frameworks (analytical and technical). It outlined the basic requirements of information security (integrity, confidentiality and availability), as well as knowledge about all potential threats faced by IS experts in an organization, how they prevented its effects, and what IS Policies are and how they were developed. Researcher defines the flow of IS system in three levels (organizational, conception, and technical). IS experts were given information on the system, as well as challenges and possible threats they faced [10–13].

Possible threats and their prevention are also discussed. The researcher initiates the study by sharing the network traffic to see how network traffic flows and is managed among users, as well as and what role information security plays during user communications. Discuss the Internet protocols (Internet Protocol), researcher only emphasizes on network layer and transport layer. What types of attacks user will face, how to detect them, and what prevention had been taken to disinfect. Researchers define possible network intrusions by giving simple examples such as land attack, a more complicated attack such as surf attack and a more sophisticated attack such as teardrop attack, in which the attacker sends header fragments that are not supposed to overlap the data so it will not fit in the destination spot. Researchers define DDoS attack on various high-profile websites in the early 2000s and how it intervenes and damages the website data. Finally, what is an intrusion detected system, how it had been created, how it is updated time to time and how it is implemented in an organization as an IS policy [14–17].

As network between users had been increased, network security technology has become vital nowadays. Networks are created by using the OSI Model (Open Systems Interface) to secure the system's confidentiality and integrity. Network attacks are also discussed, with two types of attack: passive and active. Passive attacks involve intruders attacking data directly, while active attacks involve intruders using commands to attack network. Active and passive attacks are further classified into various kinds listed in paper as well. In the end, researcher concluded the paper by giving the knowledge how to protect the possible network attack and how vital to do it in our Network (MAN NET). To avoid such attack, users must use appropriate anti-virus applications [2,18,19–28].

Use proper password for authentication. Employee must be alert for physical intrusion, and proper surveillance through CCTV cameras is required. Nmap for monitoring, Nessus for vulnerability scanning, Wire Shark network protocol analyzer, Snort for intrusion detection, Net Cat for read and write data passing from TCP or UDP, and Kismet, a powerful wireless and sniffer, are some of the tools used as a recommendation by the author to make Network system secure. The author also did research on security methods including cryptography and firewall. On paper, firewall is classified into three types: application gateway, packet filtering and hybrid systems. The author also discussed what security issues any organization might face and what steps they had to take to prevent security lapse. Make the proper security policy and strictly implement it [2,18,19,29–32].

## 3.3 METHODOLOGY

This research is based on a three-phased symmetric literature review, each with its own set of activities that are calculated in different flaws. We had chosen the SLR methodology proposed by Ham and Charters. SLR consists of three major steps: planning, performing and reporting. In these three steps, we will follow many small steps to get proper outcomes of research. Every step of SLR is described below and is shown in Figure 3.1.

### 3.3.1 Plan

In this portion, we find out the main goal we want to achieve. To achieve this goal, we have to follow these steps.

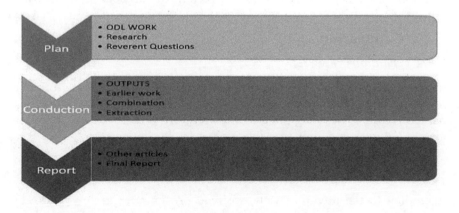

*Figure 3.1* Symmetric literature review activity.

### 3.3.1.1 Old work

When we study about the network intrusion, detection and prevention, we find out there are many vital and sensitive issues. The number of increasing articles and research provide many solutions, but the implementation is equal to 10% of total. Determining the main core solutions related to network which is useful for future research. Now we find out the need to perform SLR from the output of previous articles. In the present world, network is vital and is increasing rapidly in every sector of life.

### 3.3.1.2 Research

The objective of this chapter is to utilize the research from 2010 to 2020 to analyze network intrusion and prevention. To find out the real problem and achieve detailed information, we divided our study into these research questions.

1. What are the main types of network intrusions?
2. What are the main detection methods used by originations?
3. What are hardware and services used by origination?
4. What are the current security lacks faced by users?
5. What are the steps that are taken to literate the users from cyber-attacks?

### 3.3.1.3 Relevant question

To find out the research questions, we find out the research papers form Google Scholar, Science Direct an IEEE. The main reason to find out these papers to reach and collect the data of computer science and networking for visually challenged people. In this research, the papers are limited to journals and conferences which publish between 2010 and 2020 [25,33–35].

## 3.3.2 Conduction

### 3.3.2.1 Find out research

In this phase, we do research related to our topic. We were read out different research papers, Review papers, Survey Papers, Report Papers and article related to our topic. According to the study from these papers, approximately 314 million people worldwide are visually challenged.

### 3.3.2.2 Output work

According to the literature view, we read previous research articles and research papers. In previous work, limited articles were published for special people who face different problems during network traffic security. We collect some survey papers and review articles.

### 3.3.2.3 Extraction

Our topic is related to cyber network security. Therefore, we conducted study on network traffic using different Link-layer protocols such as Ethernet Internet protocols. We also conduct the survey to figure out the current interface problems.

### 3.3.2.4 Combine data

After searching the data from different papers, we found the data related to our topic from different papers and then we combined these data in this chapter. We sum up all the surveys and researches in this chapter and also add some technical word done by previous people.

## 3.4 RESULTS

Given the confined model size and assortment, we don't consider the agents satisfactory for making general conclusions, and we neglect a quantitative discussion of the results. In any case, the assessment uncovered a couple of charming customer mindsets that include some investigation challenges. We have a few significant revelations. The request required an answer between 1 ("not regardless") moreover, 5 ("an incredible arrangement"), and found the going with solutions: 3,3,4,2,3,4,4,5,5,3. It further permitted each subject the opportunity to offer an un-organized explanation of their response. Individuals who answered in the four to five region would overall underscore the meaning of keeping the association secure. They similarly conveyed advice (Subject #6: "How likely I use it is comparing to how correct it is"). Individuals in the arrive at one to three imparted, among various concerns, issues with progressive obstructions (Subject #4': "if I was as regularly as conceivable made mindful of IT security issues, I would fundamentally stop using the Internet."). This is unsurprising with other customer analyzes that found that solace will provide overall best security concerns. Others imparted the concern that the real system may be slanted to security issues (Subject #2: "the admonition strategy itself is slanted to security issues"). Right, when asked What do you think can be improved? Subject #10 communicated something that "looks nice" credits it a more master appearance, and thusly (Figure 3.2).

### 3.4.1 Other articles

Via looking through changed papers, we discover 1,250 article papers from the writing view. Among 750 papers, 356 papers were taken out by utilizing avoidance models. The reaming 201 papers were chosen after avoidance

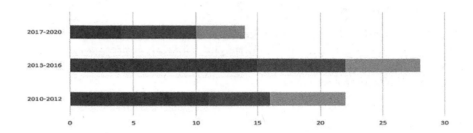

*Figure 3.2* Articles study in research.

measures. At that point, we have perused the presentations, unique, and catchphrases of 156 papers. Thus, 174 papers were not chosen after incorporation models. Forty papers were chosen as possible ID. From 35 papers 10 papers are at last chosen. That paper satisfies our paper interest. These papers are identified with our paper. In this chapter, all inquiries of our paper are satisfied (Figure 3.3).

## 3.4.2 Report

**RQ1: What are the main types of Network intrusions?**

Types of cyber attacks: In this chapter, we will discuss and study important cyber-attacks which are faced by an organization, and the sensitivities of data security. The attacks and how the infect the network of a company. Currently, the cyber-attacks are classified into two main attacks: active and dynamic attacks.

### 3.4.2.1 Dynamic assault

There are many DA which are
1. Mocking assault
2. Wormhole assault
3. Modification
4. Denial of administrations
5. Sinkhole
6. Sybil assault

### 3.4.2.2 Mocking

At the point a noxious hub which miss-present the personality, with goal that the sender changes the geography.

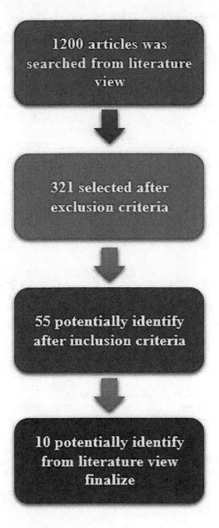

*Figure 3.3* Distribution of previous articles.

### 3.4.2.3 Wormhole

This attack, an aggressor taken information gathering at some place and passages it to alternative hazardous focus in the affiliation. Thus, an adolescent recognizes that he tracked down the most limited course in the affiliation.

### 3.4.2.4 Creation

A malicious center point makes the fake coordinating message. This infers it make mixed-up information about the course between devices.

### 3.4.2.5 Repudiation of organizations

Stubbornly uninformed of the organization's attack, the malignant CenterPoint sending a message to the center point and eat up the information transmission of the association. The guideline point of the noxious center is to be involved in the association center point. Accepting a message from an unauthenticated center will come, the beneficiary will not get that message since he is involved, and the beginner needs to keep it.

### 3.4.2.6 Sinkhole

An attack that stores the core station from acquiring total and right data. In this attack, the main attempts draw in the data to it from his all-adjoining center. Specific adjustment, deliverance and information that can be accessed through the operating in assault.

### 3.4.2.7 Sybil

Attack are identified from various replicas of pernicious centers. Because of malicious center and a mysterious key to other malevolent hubs, this attack will occur. The quantity of malicious centers increases in the organization. Assuming we can utilize the multidirectional directing, we have the chance of choosing how the malicious center will expend organization.

### 3.4.2.8 Inactive assault

The names that are not assaults are
1. Traffic examination
2. Eavesdropping
3. Monitoring

### 3.4.2.9 Traffic examination

In the busy time gridlock assessment attack, an attacker endeavors to identify the correspondence way between the sender and beneficiary. An attacker can discover the proportion of data which travels between the sender and beneficiary. There is no adjustment of data by the traffic examination.

### 3.4.2.10 Listening

This is an uninvolved attack, which occurred in the flexible unrehearsed association. The essential mark of this attack is to find some secret or private information from correspondence. Information pass from one user to another user have their own private and public keys to encrypt or decrypt information.

### 3.4.2.11 Observing

In this assault, the aggressor can peruse the classified information; however, he can't alter or change the information.

## 3.4.3 Advance assaults

### 3.4.3.1 Hustling attack

In rushing attack, the sender sends a package to the beneficiary, then pounces on a subterranean insect to change the group and forward the package to recipient. The assailant plays out a copy and sends it to the recipient over and over. Because the beneficiary recognizes that the packages come from the sender, the recipient is persistently included.

### 3.4.3.2 Replay assault

In these assaults, a malignant focus may go over the information or yield the information. This should be possible by the originator who gets the information and re-imparts it. Around that point, an assailant gets the secretive articulation.

### 3.4.3.3 Byzantine assault

A large number of broadly engaged focus works between the sender and recipient and play out explicit developments, such as making controlling circles, sending bundles through nonideal way, or expressly dropping gathering, which cause impedance or corruption of planning associations.

### 3.4.3.4 Zone divulgence assault

By getting ready and seeing the traffic, poisonous focus point collects the data about the middle and the course. So harmful focus may perform more assaults on the affiliation.

RQ2: What are the main detection methods used by originations?

## 3.4.4 Security methods

### 3.4.4.1 Cryptography

We use different types of elements to gather formal data from administrations. Cryptography works on the values, belong to the encryption method to for decoding any important information [35–37].

### 3.4.4.2 Firewalls

The firewall is used to get the parts that altogether is a handshake between one or more organizations. There are three essential firewalls:

### 3.4.4.3 Applications gateway

These are used for the workers. This application works in the top layer which is called application layer. This is the most protected and comfortable layer to work easily.

### 3.4.4.4 Packet filtering

Packet filtering is the technique in which routers have the ACLs turned on. This passes through the traffic on the gateway without any limits. Packet filtering is a technique of firewall use to monitoring the packets and characterize these packets for malware prevention. This is very difficult for an application gateway to secure the information by filtering packets form the router or switches [38,39].

### 3.4.4.5 Hybrid systems

While trying to consolidate the security feature of application layer doors with the adaptability and speed of parcel sifting, a few engineers have made a system that utilizes both standards. In a portion of these frameworks, new associations should be confirmed and endorsed at the application layer. Whenever this has been done, the rest of the association is passed down to the melting layer, where bundle channels watch the association with a guarantee that lone parcels that are important for a progressing (effectively verified and affirmed) discussion are being passed. Employments of bundle sifting and application layer intermediaries are the other potential ways. The advantages here incorporate giving a proportion of assurance against your machines that offer types of assistance to the Internet (like a public web worker), as well as providing the security of an application layer door to the inner organization. By cracking this technique, hacker can easily figure out the route to enter in and organization system. We have to secure the information in such a way that on other way left to enter in the system expect the main entrance.

RQ3: What an Organization Must Do?

The association should be set up to adjust to the improvement of the affiliation, which consequently would include new upgrades in the association both to the extent.

This could lead to the joining of various components such as inaccessible and pariah access.

Assault Assurance arrangements should ensure organization, administrations and applications as well as provide secure office association.

### 3.4.4.6 Development options

Driving security merchants provide beginning-to-end game plans that ensure that all aspects of association security are managed. Start to finish plans commonly offer a mix of gear and programming stages including security that helps an association secure their data and manage their data in well-organized form. A joined approach is one that addresses not just point-security issue (like obstruction) but also the blend of affiliation and AISC challenges. Accessible things can be mentioned in the going with streams.

### 3.4.4.7 ASIC machines

The move is from programming amassed security things that run with respect to open stages to reason fabricated, ASIC-based gadgets, truly like the way in which the switches have continued reasonably lately.

### 3.4.4.8 SSL-VPN

More critical perception of encryption on the wire are SSL and IP-VPNs. Individuals who are intelligently mindful for the security risks in sending information over the wire are clear substance. By using SSL-VPN and VPNs use to get rapid response for client and IT professionals in the same environment.

### 3.4.4.9 Obstruction DPS

IPS combines the best features for firewalls and the obstruction divulgence framework to give a contraption that changes the plans of affiliation and access-control focuses in response to changes in the risk profile of an affiliation. This presents the portion of data in network security by changing as per new assaults and obstruction attempts. Obstruction assumption has gotten an immense heap of interest in the client's area. The most association pushes in their use of impedance repudiation progression. Some will get hindering in weeks and quickly grow their discouragement as they observe the advantages of definite assault demolishing. Others will gradually expand, bit by bit. This key is used to reliably recognize and stops both known dim assaults consistent.

### 3.4.4.10 Wireless security

In the space there are many satellites to provide many services. Many organizations want maximum security for their users. These satellites play a major role in wireless signals and their security. It's really a test to work with network that spans various regions. Simply envision that should travel to that place if it helps, if not done distantly.

**RQ4:** What are security lacks that are currently faced by users?

**Information breach:** Data enters shirking requires an extent of good practices. SSL should be encoded to encrypt site traffic and trades, agreements should be carefully set for each social occasion of customers, and laborers should be separated. Laborers should be set up in how to keep away from being gotten by phishing attacks and how to practice incredible mystery express tidiness.

### 3.4.4.11 Malware infection

Most associations know here and there or one more of the security threat introduced by malware, yet various people are oblivious that email spam is at this point the principal vector of malware attack. Since malware comes from an extent of sources, a couple of one of a kind mechanical assembly are needed for thwarting defilement. A fiery email checking and isolating system are fundamental, as are malware and shortcoming assessment. Like enters, which are routinely achieved by malware pollution, laborer guidance is basic to shield associations from malware DDOS: A Distributed Denial of Service (DDoS) attack, all things considered, incorporates a social occasion of PCs being handled together by a developer to flood the target with traffic.

RQ5: What are the steps that are taken to literate the users from cyber-attacks?

A significant part of the current network protection writing bases on guarding the complex advanced frameworks having a place with enormous companies. The normal client gets significantly less consideration when it comes to getting the fundamental information and specialized abilities they ought to safeguard their PCs or independent venture systems. A digitally educated client should realize that standard work ought to be performed using a customary client account, not an overseer account. This diminishes the opportunity that an unintentional order will influence the whole framework and will forestall particular sorts of malware from accessing the framework's settings and information.

## 3.5 DISCUSSION

To get a more profound comprehension of the data commitments, particular commitments, certain data (admittance to IS, secure correspondence, security the executives, and improvement of secure IS) were advanced. Four security requirements (dependability, availability, to an examination of safety responsibilities) are identified. The issues of permission to IS and get correspondence have been the subject of much thought from information security specialists. The issues of induction to IS and correspondence have generally been moved closer at the specific level using mathematical strategies (counting rationale) as an examination approach and math (counting rationale) as the fundamental examination discipline. While authoritative-level commitments concerning the issues of admittance to IS, security the board and the board and improvement of secure IS have been advanced, the majority of the commitments stay at the specialized level. In addition, there are also studies investigating the issue of access utilizing exact theory testing and theoretical examination as exploration approaches, just as a couple of endeavors using reasoning, brain science and criminal science as reference disciplines (Figure 3.4).

From an IS perspective, the finding data research focused on specialized issues recommends a few suggestions. To begin with, the presentation of

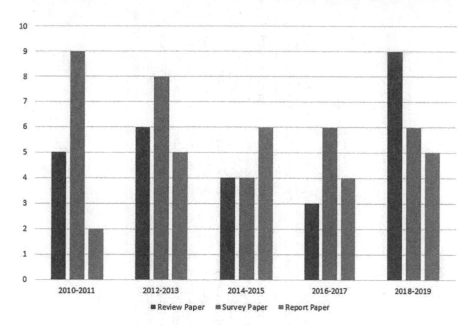

*Figure 3.4* Articles distribution per year.

mechanical arrangements consistently increases the topic of, how persuaded clients are embracing those arrangements. Second, this is cleared for writing survey that a few issues are just addressed through specialized arrangements, albeit the issues are mind boggling to such an extent that a simply specialized arrangement isn't adequate. For example, cryptography-based arrangements have been well-informed (contrasted with non-specialized security issues); however, "key administration approaches" have pulled in little interest, in spite of the reality that one of the primary issues as for symmetric or then again uneven cryptography is obviously the issue of the executives (Table 3.1).

This implies that cryptographic arrangements, regardless of where symmetric (one key frameworks) or awry (two key frameworks), rely upon fruitful key administration. Also, in close attempts, polices have pulled in incredible interest among data security analysts. Access control policies are as yet unfit to forestall spills of data; as such, access control polices try not to keep victimizers from acquiring data from approved clients (at the authoritative level) nor do they keep approved clients from having the option to spread highly confidential data. Regardless of this shortcoming, little examination has been completed to handle authoritative. A relative specific inclination is, moreover, found with regard to security systems. The assessment on security procedures has zeroed in on restricted degree formal systems, rather than more critical level just as legitimate security approaches. It gives off an impression of being that various trained

Table 3.1  Information of security and solutions

| Information security issue | Contributions | | | Reference disciplines | Research Tech |
|---|---|---|---|---|---|
| | Organizational | Conceptual | Technical | | |
| **Access information security** | Biometrical authentication, cognitive passwords, maximizing users' intent to comply with security policy (through deterrence and motivation means) | Access control matrix, modeling of access control policies | Authentication methods (passwords, token-based authentication), access control and information-flow control models, memory protection of operating systems, anti-virus techniques, watermarking, image security, audit/in-torsion detection, firewalls | Mathematicises and philosophy-call logic, biosciences, psychology, criminology, philosophy | Mathematical approaches (mathematical modelling), theory-testing re-search, conceptual analysis |
| **Secure communication** | Virtual private networks, Intranet security | Modelling security in distributed systems | Cryptographic techniques, including mess-sage encryption, digital signatures, steganography, watermarking, hash, virtual private networks, electronic cash, intranet security, anonymity techniques | Mathematic-ices (in particular cryptology), law | Mathematical approaches (mathematical modelling), conceptual analysis |

professional applicable subjects are, in the last assessment, measures. This notion about the PC-arranged nature of safety material components shows the overwhelming point of convergence of ebb and flow, particularly meta-assessments, where very few layouts are examined. We acknowledge that the negligence of informational studies, including Meta-considers, can be followed back to the otherworldly investigation premium of the security neighborhood: premium in sensible examination. Suggestion results that can be quickly brought into preparing are upheld. It has all the earmarks of being that examination that doesn't utilize mathematical methodologies, yet makes various scenarios, rules, techniques, is actually as often as possible uncritically recognized; or then again, perhaps such an investigation doesn't get sufficient premium from analysts. Our examination furthermore shows that specific game plans are made using mathematical strategies as the fundamental investigation approach. As the particular setting communities around presenting information in a construction.

## 3.6 CONCLUSION

Malware code or various attacks are currently in large number with passage of time, and they are very dangerous for data. In small time period, many companies are working and responding to these threats on emergency basis. Adopt and plan out the security mechanism and policies for their company. New hardware technologies and strategies are implementing to narrate the network more secure. As previously cyber security is Command line basis, which is now totally integrated in new way Graphical interface. In this chapter, we discussed various types of attack and their prevention. As mechanism or polices are confidential so in research the topic reality base is bit difficult and expensive to install somewhere else for home base network. Security arrangements ought not be fixed; instead, they should be adequately adaptable. As a result, information security is becoming increasingly important. Therefore, various institutes and organizations provide users with studies and lectures.

## REFERENCES

1. K. Khan, A. Mehmood, S. Khan, M. A. Khan, Z. Iqbal, and W. K. Mashwani, "A survey on intrusion detection and prevention in wireless ad-hoc networks," *Journal of Systems Architecture*, vol. 105, p. 101701, 2020. doi: 10.1016/j.sysarc.2019.101701.
2. D. Mudzingwa and R. Agrawal, "A study of methodologies used in intrusion detection and prevention systems (IDPS)," in *2012 Proceedings of IEEE Southeastcon*, March 2012, pp. 1–6. doi: 10.1109/SECon.2012.6197080.
3. B. Ge and J. Xu, "Analysis of computer network security technology and preventive measures under the information environment," in *2020 5th International Conference on Mechanical, Control and Computer Engineering (ICMCCE)*, December 2020, pp. 1978–1981. doi: 10.1109/ICMCCE51767.2020.00433.

4. E. Husni and Y. Kurniati, "Application of Mean Time-to-Compromise and VEA-bility security metrics in auditing computer network security," in *2014 8th International Conference on Telecommunication Systems Services and Applications (TSSA)*, October 2014, pp. 1–5. doi: 10.1109/TSSA.2014.7065960.

5. M. I. Tariq, "Towards information security metrics framework for cloud computing," *International Journal of Cloud Computing and Services Science*, vol. 1, no. 4, p. 209, 2012.

6. M. I. Tariq, "Agent based information security framework for hybrid cloud computing," *KSII Transactions on Internet & Information Systems*, vol. 13, no. 1, pp. 406–434, 2019.

7. M. I. Tariq, "Analysis of the effectiveness of cloud control matrix for hybrid cloud computing," *International Journal of Future Generation Communication and Networking*, vol. 11, no. 4, pp. 1–10, 2018.

8. H. Cheung, A. Hamlyn, L. Wang, C. Yang, and R. Cheung, "Computer network security strategy for coordinated distribution system operations," in *2007 Large Engineering Systems Conference on Power Engineering*, October 2007, pp. 279–283. doi: 10.1109/LESCPE.2007.4437393.

9. A. Patel, M. Taghavi, K. Bakhtiyari, and J. Celestino Júnior, "An intrusion detection and prevention system in cloud computing: A systematic review," *Journal of Network and Computer Applications*, vol. 36, no. 1, pp. 25–41, 2013. doi: 10.1016/j.jnca.2012.08.007.

10. A. Nadeem and M. P. Howarth, "A survey of MANET intrusion detection & prevention approaches for network layer attacks," *IEEE Communications Surveys Tutorials*, vol. 15, no. 4, pp. 2027–2045, 2013. doi: 10.1109/SURV.2013.030713.00201.

11. M. I. Tariq and V. Santarcangelo, "Analysis of ISO 27001: 2013 controls effectiveness for cloud computing," 2016, vol. 2, pp. 201–208.

12. M. I. Tariq, S. Tayyaba, H. Rasheed, and M. W. Ashraf, "Factors influencing the cloud computing adoption in higher education institutions of Punjab, Pakistan," 2017, pp. 179–184.

13. M. I. Tariq, D. Haq, and J. Iqbal, "SLA based information security metric for cloud computing from COBIT 4.1 framework", 2017.

14. E. A. Shams, A. Rizaner, and A. H. Ulusoy, "Trust aware support vector machine intrusion detection and prevention system in vehicular ad hoc networks," *Computers & Security*, vol. 78, pp. 245–254, 2018. doi: 10.1016/j. cose.2018.06.008.

15. A. K. Srivastava and S. Kumar, "An effective computational technique for taxonomic position of security vulnerability in software development," *Journal of Computational Science*, vol. 25, pp. 388–396, 2018. doi: 10.1016/j. jocs.2017.08.003.

16. J. González-Domínguez, C. Hundt, and B. Schmidt, "parSRA: A framework for the parallel execution of short read aligners on compute clusters," *Journal of Computational Science*, vol. 25, pp. 134–139, 2018. doi: 10.1016/j. jocs.2017.01.008.

17. S. Catalán, J. R. Herrero, F. D. Igual, R. Rodríguez-Sánchez, E. S. Quintana-Ortí, and C. Adeniyi-Jones, "Multi-threaded dense linear algebra libraries for low-power asymmetric multicore processors," *Journal of Computational Science*, vol. 25, pp. 140–151, 2018. doi: 10.1016/j.jocs.2016.10.020.

18. K. Scarfone and P. Mell, "Intrusion detection and prevention systems," in *Handbook of Information and Communication Security*, P. Stavroulakis and M. Stamp (Eds.) Berlin, Heidelberg: Springer, 2010, pp. 177–192. doi: 10.1007/978-3-642-04117-4_9.

19. Y. F. Labsiv, U. M. Ismail, A. Ahmed, and A. Asimi, "Performance method of assessment of the intrusion detection and prevention systems." 2016.

20. A. Patel, M. Taghavi, K. Bakhtiyari, and J. C. Júnior, "Taxonomy and proposed architecture of intrusion detection and prevention systems for cloud computing," in *Cyberspace Safety and Security*. Berlin, Heidelberg: Springer, 2012, pp. 441–458. doi: 10.1007/978-3-642-35362-8_33.

21. S. Gupta, P. Kumar, and A. Abraham, "A profile based network intrusion detection and prevention system for securing cloud environment," *International Journal of Distributed Sensor Networks*, vol. 9, no. 3, p. 364575, 2013, doi: 10.1155/2013/364575.

22. S. T. Zargar, H. Takabi, and J. B. D. Joshi, "DCDIDP: A distributed, collaborative, and data-driven intrusion detection and prevention framework for cloud computing environments," in *7th International Conference on Collaborative Computing: Networking, Applications and Worksharing (CollaborateCom)*, Orlando, FL, 2011, pp. 332–341. https://www.academia.edu/24297279/DCDIDP_A_Distributed_Collaborative_and_Data_driven_Intrusion_Detection_and_Prevention_Framework_for_Cloud_Computing_Environments

23. M. I. Tariq, J. Diaz-Martinez, S. A. Butt, M. Adeel, E. De-la-Hoz-Franco, and A. M. Dicu, "A learners experience with the games education in software engineering," in *Soft Computing Applications*, vol. 1222, V. E. Balas, L. C. Jain, M. M. Balas, and S. N. Shahbazova, Eds. Cham: Springer International Publishing, 2021, pp. 379–395. doi: 10.1007/978-3-030-52190-5_27.

24. M. I. Tariq et al., "Combination of AHP and TOPSIS methods for the ranking of information security controls to overcome its obstructions under fuzzy environment," *Journal of Intelligent & Fuzzy Systems*, vol. 38, no. 5, pp. 6075–6088.

25. M. I. Tariq, N. A. Mian, A. Sohail, T. Alyas, and R. Ahmad, "Evaluation of the challenges in the Internet of medical things with multicriteria decision making (AHP and TOPSIS) to overcome its obstruction under fuzzy environment," *Mobile Information Systems*, vol. 2020, p. e8815651, 2020. doi: 10.1155/2020/8815651.

26. K. Coulibaly, "An overview of intrusion detection and prevention systems," arXiv:2004.08967 cs., April 2020, Accessed: September 17, 2021. [Online] Available: http://arxiv.org/abs/2004.08967.

27. S. E. Quincozes, C. Albuquerque, D. Passos, and D. Mossé, "A survey on intrusion detection and prevention systems in digital substations," *Computer Networks*, vol. 184, p. 107679, 2021. doi: 10.1016/j.comnet.2020.107679.

28. S. Iqbal et al., "On cloud security attacks: A taxonomy and intrusion detection and prevention as a service," *Journal of Network and Computer Applications*, vol. 74, pp. 98–120, 2016. doi: 10.1016/j.jnca.2016.08.016.

29. A. Patel, Q. Qassim, and C. Wills, "A survey of intrusion detection and prevention systems," *Information Management & Computer Security*, vol. 18, no. 4, pp. 277–290, 2010. doi: 10.1108/09685221011079199.

30. M. I. Tariq, S. Tayyaba, M. U. Hashmi, M. W. Ashraf, and N. A. Mian, "Agent based information security threat management framework for hybrid cloud computing," *IJCSNS*, vol. 17, no. 12, p. 57, 2017.

31. M. I. Tariq et al., "Prioritization of information security controls through Fuzzy AHP for cloud computing networks and wireless sensor networks," *Sensors*, vol. 20, no. 5, p. 1310, 2020.

32. M. I. Tariq, S. Tayyaba, M. W. Ashraf, and V. E. Balas, "Deep learning techniques for optimizing medical big data," in *Deep Learning Techniques for Biomedical and Health Informatics*, S. Dash, B. R. Acharya, M. Mittal, A. Abraham, A. Kelemen, Eds. Amsterdam, Netherlands: Elsevier, 2020, pp. 187–211.

33. M. I. Tariq, S. Tayyaba, M. W. Ashraf, and H. Rasheed, "Risk based NIST effectiveness analysis for cloud security," *Bahria University Journal of Information & Communication Technologies (BUJICT)*, vol. 10, no. Special Is, 2017.

34. M. I. Tariq et al., "An analysis of the application of fuzzy logic in cloud computing," *Journal of Intelligent & Fuzzy Systems*, vol. 38, no. 5, pp. 5933–5947, 2020.

35. R. Janakiraman, M. Waldvogel, and Q. Zhang, "Indra: A peer-to-peer approach to network intrusion detection and prevention," in *WET ICE 2003: Proceedings. Twelfth IEEE International Workshops on Enabling Technologies: Infrastructure for Collaborative Enterprises, 2003*, June 2003, pp. 226–231. doi: 10.1109/ENABL.2003.1231412.

36. J. Peng, K.-K. R. Choo, and H. Ashman, "User profiling in intrusion detection: A review," *Journal of Network and Computer Applications*, vol. 72, pp. 14–27, 2016, doi: 10.1016/j.jnca.2016.06.012.

37. J. Feng, G. Lu, H. Wang, and X. Wang, "Supporting secure spectrum sensing data transmission against SSDH attack in cognitive radio ad hoc networks," *Journal of Network and Computer Applications*, vol. 72, pp. 140–149, 2016, doi: 10.1016/j.jnca.2016.06.007.

38. M. I. Tariq, S. Tayyaba, M. W. Ashraf, H. Rasheed, and F. Khan, "Analysis of NIST SP 800-53 rev. 3 controls effectiveness for cloud computing," *Computing*, vol. 3, p. 4, 2016.

39. S. A. Butt, M. I. Tariq, T. Jamal, A. Ali, J. L. D. Martinez, and E. De-La-Hoz-Franco, "Predictive variables for agile development merging cloud computing services," *IEEE Access*, vol. 7, pp. 99273–99282, 2019.

# Chapter 4

# Cloud-based face recognition for low resource clients

*M. Zain Abbas, Junaid Baber, Maheen Bakhtyar,*
*Azam Khan, and Adnan Saeed*

University of Balochistan

## CONTENTS

## 4.1 INTRODUCTION: BACKGROUND

Face recognition–based applications are very trendy these days. However, many solutions are desktop-based or require very high computational power. In this chapter, we propose a cloud-based framework for face recognition that provides central control for feature databases. The framework easily swaps computational processes to the client if needed or requested. The client's machines request and respond to the feature databases using APIs that are designed using FLASK. The use of feature databases makes program initialization very fast and also robust in the case of any disaster that happens to the client sites.

There are a number of applications in security, education, and daily life operations where face recognition-based systems can play a vital role. Organizations are expanding and they require more robust and reliable solutions for their operations. Let's consider the scenario of a public sector university, i.e., University of Balochistan (UOB) www.uob.edu.pk, where hundreds of employees, faculty, and students who account in thousands enter the premises on daily basis. All administrative staff, faculty, and students are registered users if there is any automation software, particularly attendance systems. However, there are more than 900 people, on average, who enter UOB daily, who are not registered but visit the campus for various reasons. Classical attendance and visitor management systems rely on database management systems (DBMSs) such as SQL Server and ORACLE which deal with structured data. The classical DBMS for attendance requires forms that are either filled by data entry operators or RFID-based

DOI: 10.1201/9781003107286-4

costly installations on the gates of entrance. There are few very peak hours where people have to queue into long lines before they can enter the premises that not only causes inconveniences to the visitors and administration but also causes security threats.

CCTV-based attendance systems require very heavy and costly installations. The main bottleneck is the computational server that loads the streaming, extracts the faces, and does necessary operations for the recognition, as shown in Figure 4.1. The computational server is responsible for streaming, face detection, face recognition, and reporting to the web server. The web server is used in case the face recognition system has web dashboards for its authorized users. In case, there is any issue with the network or the server, the whole system is at risk. Duplicating the computational server doubles the cost of the system.

In this research, we propose an infrastructure in which the client can do some computational operations at the client sites and send only the processed information to the web server, depending on the nature of the installation, as shown in Figure 4.2. There can be several possible configurations that can reduce the load from the computation server. For example, the gate which is dedicated to the administrative staff should have at least one CCTV and one normal PC that can do face detection and recognition if that PC can get only the features of permitted users of that gate. In case, there is any other user, that can be either student, faculty, or visitor, then the system sends that face to the main server for further processing.

A software programming interface characterizes connections between various programming or blended equipment software. It characterizes the kinds of calls or demands that may be made, steps to make them, the info organizes

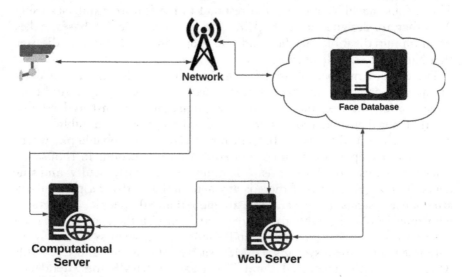

Network

Face Database

Computational
Server

Web Server

Figure 4.1 Classical implementation of face recognition systems.

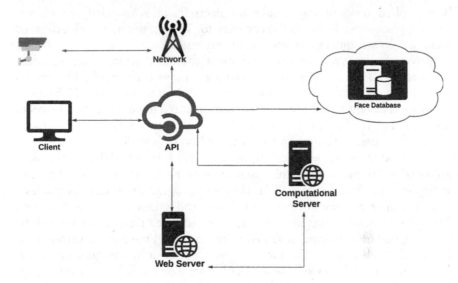

*Figure 4.2* Abstract diagram of the proposed framework.

that should really be utilized, the shows to follow along with, and so forth. Cloud-based facial acknowledgment frameworks achieve different advantages coming from natural attributes. They have the upside of continuous prepara-tion. On request, self-administration permits clients to rapidly acquire and get to the administrations they need. Also, distributed computing permits the framework to show off to be comprehensively open like in cloud adminis-trations provide the ability to snappy and dependable joining with various applications. Moreover, cloud administrations encourage high adaptability to make sure that the framework may be adjusted to an extensive client base.

Depending on the National Institute of Standards and Technology (NIST), distributed computing is a model for empowering omnipresent, helpful, on-request network admittance to a typical pool of configurable processing assets (e.g., networks, workers, stockpiling, applications, and administrations) that may be quickly provisioned and delivered with neg-ligible administration exertion or specialist organization communication. This has five attractive qualities—on-request self-administration, wide organization access, asset pooling, and fast versatility. In a facial acknowl-edgment framework actualized in cloud foundation, the facial acknowledg-ment motor is found within the cloud, not when you look at the nearby preparing unit (utilized when you look at the conventional technique).

Facial acknowledgment hinges on man-made reasoning and AI. AI includes perceiving designs from a fantastic quantity of existing informa-tion by a group calculation until it really is equipped for foreseeing new information. In AI, a Deep Convolutional Neural Network (DCNN) is a course of profound counterfeit neural organizations which has effectively been applied to examining visual symbolism. Facial acknowledgment is one of its applications. To boost the capacity for this innovation, a cloud-based facial acknowledgment framework has arisen.

Moving both the facial acknowledgment and facial acknowledgment data set onto the cloud assists with delivering a regular framework. This model is used by a couple of business applications to do security checks. The question face is caught by the client and communicated toward the cloud worker for directing verification because of the display appearances of the facial acknowledgment information base situated on the cloud.

The latest faces are selected through the User Interface (UI), or say, client application. To accomplish the assignment of Face Tagging, the UI speaks with the cloud-based web API (application programming interface) which contains the facial acknowledgment motor and a data set of countenances. The UI selects new faces and encodes the face area picture, which will be then shipped off the cloud-based API that measures the picture through the facial acknowledgment. The facial acknowledgment motor runs a precharacterized facial acknowledgment calculation. The inquiry face from the UI will be analyzed because of the facial acknowledgment motor against a display of pictures. After an indisputable match is resolved, the inquiry face should be delegated having a place with a specific individual or perhaps not. At that time, the result will likely be delivered back toward the UI.

## 4.2 RELATED WORK

In the IOT environment, the detection and resolution of the object is challenging to authenticate the identity of the object, manage the access of service, and establish loyalty between service of cloud and object. With the development of technologies related to the recognition of pattern technologies, the face has been applied as high-reliability identification procedure that has been applied in numerous fields. In the study, the face resolution method is concerned with the computing of cloud to resolve numerous issues. The study is proposed to launch the procedure of face matching and generation; however, the parallel comparison technique and cloud-based framework is proposed to efficiently solve the personal access information and receive individual's information [1]. The study proposed to investigate the chances for the use of machine learning and adaptable cloud computing environment has been implemented through the cross-platform method. The procedure authorizes multiple applications to set up with the transfer of code that can run on various OS which reduces the burden of work needed from the developers, as the similar code is compiled on mobile concerned devices and its cloud. The study makes the outcome efficiently more real. The evaluation of experiments shows its reliability and efficiency, especially in complex computations. The overall testing results showed that time of service execution and consumption of energy reduces remarkably during the execution on mobile [2].

The latest expansion in Big Data analysis, social networks, and cloud computing has fastly transformed the ordinary view of how numerous issues in the field of computer vision can be solved. The study provides the survey of these fields from the modern concept of Face Recogonition (FR) and proposed scheme that intermingled the properties of above-mentioned ideas to make an efficient partnership that can increase the FR performance in collaboration to serve widely in other fields [3]. The study goes through the accessibility of Cloud Intelligence API of Google in numerous environments. Specifically, the study explores to change video in the way so an API will replace only the opposite-wanted labels. For this, the study chose an image that varies from the content of the video and push it consistently at a minimum rate in the video. The study realized that by inserting one image after every 2 seconds, the API is swindled into interpreting the video as it consists of the inserted image. The alteration of the video is barely noticeable, for a normal rate of frame is 25, the method push only 1 image per 50 frames of video. The scheme noticed that by insertion of one image/second, overall, the label shots are returned through API are concerned with the image that is pushed. The study performed multiple experiments on numerous videos provided through the demonstration of API [4].

The study expresses the characteristics of automated gender, age, and emotion detection systems. The major part of the system comprises various DCNN that are reasonably inexpensive and allow various state-of-the-art results on numerous benchmarks. To make the proposed CNN capable, the scheme gathered huge labeled datasets by semisupervised line to eliminate the annotation time. The testing is done on multiple publicly available benchmark and describes extraordinary results [5]. The study judges the issues and problems in the establishment of numerous AI systems. A cloud platform that is known as XCloud facilitates numerous similar AI assistance in the form of RESTful APIs. The scheme is available publicly and can be retrieved for research [6]. Managing stable access to applications related to the web and its services has set off more essential with the development and usage of technologies related to the web. The reliability of services related to the web has come across challenging problems to manage the legal functions of users. The reliable protocol (Open Authorization) permits the owner of resources to give access to a third party to get access to the protected resource of the owner without releasing the authorization. Most APIs related to the web are used for conventional authentication that is unprotected from numerous attacks. To minimize such attacks, the scheme improves the OAuth security by the biometric implementation. The study introduced a verification method related to face that is managed by the server of authorization. The overall process of authentication comprises of three levels: Registration service of image, service for verification, and access to the token's service [7].

The study shows the recognition of face for purpose of education with issues and challenges of computing concerned with cloud. The usage perspective is maximum on reliable testing dependent on communications that are real-time with minimum clients and display of face embedded in the ordinary browsers but with powerful analytics of data in the cloud to authenticate and classify [8]. The scheme shows SmartRank, which is a managing scheme to handle load concerned with partitioning and also offloading for applications concerned with mobile using computing of cloud to enhance the performance in case of response time. The study has applied the method to face detection scheme dependent on cloudlet federation and ranking of a resource by metric balancing. The evaluation was done in two ways—initially, by the use of system modeling, and second, the use of overall experimental factorial design to collaborate the SmartRank with partitioning choice [9].

The study proposed a bio-metric-related detection system to preserve the privacy and also security of databases related to biometric. The system detects the cloud related on their encrypted face template. The recognition method retrieves the features of the face to privatize the privacy of the user. It also facilitates Eigenfaces features to secure the privacy of users related to the cloud and gathers biometric information that is sensitive in the form of encryption in database. The study proposed a model to evaluate the accuracy concerned with the recognition of the facial image. The system can be efficiently deployed to assess the reliability of the system and finding of the individual with no loss of information in the computation of cloud; however, the system shows limited performance with a small capacity of database [10]. The study proposed cloudlet-based mobile model to execute real-time recognition of face to execute the application in three various steps: detection of face, searching, and projection. The study analyzes that the steps are executed in numerous hardware parts: mobile, cloudlet, and cloud. The study facilitates detailed information of cloudlet utilizing to fast the three mentioned operations [11].

API is the intermediary software that is used to connect two applications for services. It sends a message to applications for connection and gets their services [12]. Mobile applications are used to connect with the world, and these applications are connected through different network resources; some of the resources are secured enough to get connected with but some of them have vulnerabilities to be connected. To resolve these security issues, face recognition system can be used with cloud computing services. The system is designed with an android face detector API that is used as a library for facial recognition and has better computational power [13]. In order to manage authentication and authorization to access the cloud application a protocol named Open Authorization is being used for securing the credentials, the author proposed a schematic approach with facial recognition for authenticating those sources that have important information [7]. The approach is developed in three phases—image registration for recognizing facial features, verification services for authentication, and token access services. Another system that uses Avatar in cloud sources to support mobile services is also proposed [14]. The challenges faced by avatar mechanism; the system needs a high-level programming model, re-build an architecture to support numeral mobile services and applications and the last challenge is privacy and security.

The author proposed a system based on android mobile devices [15] that uses an API Face.com as image data processing on cloud computing. The author utilizes augmented reality to view the information; this scheme resulted in good but computational power for this scheme is not impressive and the information fetched from augmented reality on average is 1.03. Neural networks are designed to get cognitive abilities the same as human or close to human intelligence [16] and the proposed technique is using artificial intelligence neural networks with backpropagation method to recognize face recognition [17]. A multilayer perceptron [18] architecture where multiple neural networks with hidden layers are used, are very significant. The performance of GPU is analyzed with multi-thread CPU; when small inputs are given to this architecture, the scheme performs well as compared to big input sizes.

An author proposed a scheme that utilizes mobile-cloudlet-cloud architecture to capture features and details of facial expressions [19]. The proposed system is divided into three sections to manage mobile devices, cloudlet, and Jelastic cloud. This approach is computationally faster than others, but the problem is catching other unnecessary details as well that are not even required. An android application CroudSTag [20] is used to form social groups and retrieve facial information from the groups using the social platforms. A cloud messaging framework is used to capture messaging details to push notifications to the users.

## 4.3 METHODOLOGY

Figure 4.2 shows the network diagram of the proposed framework. We additionally add client and API machines which can be commodity PC, i.e., a machine with a Core i-3 processor and 4-GB RAM. The client machine loads the streaming from the IP camera and process the frames, the processing of the frames can be made simple and smart by not processing all frames—only processing the 1–3 frames/second and sending the information to the API server/machine which then interacts with the web server or sometimes with the computational server. The API server can be a machine on cloud or even on a local area network. We configured API server on a shared cloud such as Namecheap[1] which is very economical and still solves our server problems.

The client loads the face features at the time of initialization using API server. The face features can be a small fraction of registered users, i.e., only administrative staff. In case, there is any user who is recognized, he is sent to the computational server for further verification. This trick shortens the computational load of the computational server by a very

---

[1] www.namecheap.com

large factor. So the client can send the processed information to the web server directly which makes the information ready without any delay for the dashboard.

Figure 4.3 shows the flow diagram of the recognition module. The faces are detected from the given frame video frame and represented by face landmarks. A descriptor of 128-D [21] is computed which is the final representation of any given face. The detailed implementation can be found online [22]. This is the simplest implementation of face recognition using Python. Once, the infrastructure of face recognition is set up, the recognition module can easily be replaced with new technologies. In this research, we propose the infrastructure for client/server face recognition.

The face database server contains the pre-process faces of registered users. Figure 4.4 shows the simple class diagram of face recognition system. With simple three tables, we can track the attendance of registered users and also visitors with different cameras.

The main table is Face Registration Table (FRT) where basic information of the registered employees is stored. Face Encoding Table (FET) takes the primary key and stores one or more face features of the registered person. To mark the attendance, the person's id with current picture taken from the camera, the camera number/title, and the timestamps are stored. In case there is an unregistered person enters, the system stores the person on the registration table with Unknown-UIQ, where UIQ is the unique ID. The system is capable to store registered and unregistered users that are entering the system and easily scales thousands of employees and students.

## 4.4 EXPERIMENTS AND RESULTS

We took normal off-the-shelf computers as a computational, web, and API servers. We took 1 megapixel IP camera and simulated both approaches shown in Figures 4.1 and 4.2. Figure 4.1 is a classical approach, whereas Figure 4.2 is the proposed solution. We simulated the face recognition system that captures the camera stream and process the frame one by one. For each frame, face locations are identified which is a computationally expensive task on IP cameras. Once the faces are detected, face landmarks are identified which are later represented by face encoding. The face encoding returns the 128-D descriptor vector for each given face boundary; all documentation of face recognition is online [23–25].

Face recognition is made by comparing the face encoding of a given face with all the faces in the database. The comparing of two faces is based on the Euclidean distance between the encoding. Let $a$, $b$ be the two encoding of two faces that are similar if the following condition holds:

$$\alpha_{(a \cdot b)} = \beta_{(a,b)} < \tau$$

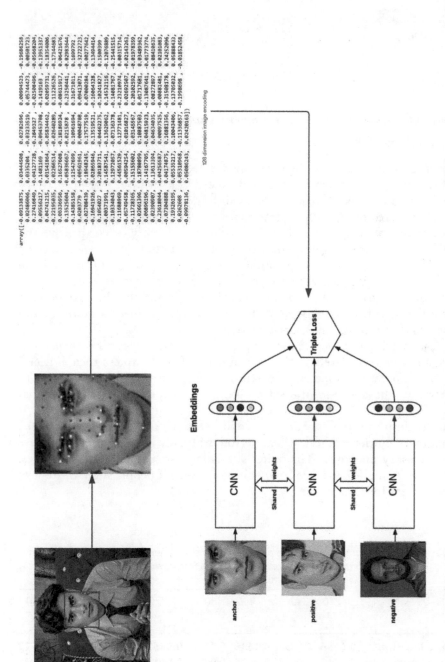

*Figure 4.3* Face recognition diagram. Initially, faces are detected and represented by face landmarks, then the descriptor of length 128-D is computed and finally matched with all template face features.

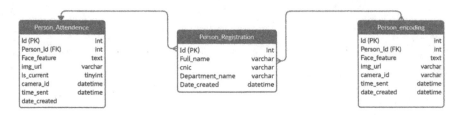

*Figure 4.4* Class diagram of the face recognition system.

where $\alpha$ turns true if $a$ and $b$ are similar, $\beta$ denotes the Frobenius norm [24] of the difference of $a$ and $b$, and $\tau$ denotes the tolerance. The lower value gives more strict comparisons. We used the default value which is 0.6.

Since there are typically 25 frames per second (FPS) in a video stream, so processing every frame for detection is computationally very expensive and also inconvenient; therefore, only three FPS are used.

Table 4.1 shows the computational time for both models: proposed and classical. The timing is the average of 100 frames processed. It can be seen that despite introducing two more machines, API and the client, the timing is still efficient. If we process all frames, our model gives a more smooth visual effect than the classical approach.

The matching of every face with the whole database is still very inconvenient as one recognized face if stays in front of sight/camera then unnecessary computation is made to search the same person again and again. To overcome the above-mentioned problem, we propose a small buffer that is initially empty. Once any face is recognized, that face with its label is pushed into that buffer. For the second iteration, the new face is matched first in the buffer to check if that person is already identified or not to save unnecessary matching. The buffer size is kept small, with only ten faces. Using this simple hack, the computation is saved if people stand in front of the camera for little time.

*Table 4.1* Timing comparison of the proposed framework with a classical approach in seconds, where P indicates the proposed framework timings and C indicates the classical framework timings

|  | 240 × 240 | | 480 × 480 | | 720 × 720 | | 1080 × 1080 | |
|---|---|---|---|---|---|---|---|---|
|  | P | C | P | C | P | C | P | C |
| **Face locations** | **0.0656** | 0.0959 | **0.2436** | 0.4061 | **0.5553** | 0.8549 | **1.2523** | 1.9722 |
| **Face landmarks** | **0.0016** | 0.0033 | **0.0016** | 0.0034 | **0.0016** | 0.34 | **0.0016** | 0.0034 |
| **Encode face** | **0.006** | 0.5865 | **0.0059** | 0.5976 | **0.006** | 0.5899 | **0.0061** | 0.5615 |
| **Total time** | **0.0732** | 0.6857 | **0.2511** | 1.0071 | **0.5629** | 1.7848 | **1.26** | 2.5371 |

## 4.5 CONCLUSION

We have proposed a client/server-based framework for face recognition. The classical implementation requires very expensive and sophisticated hardware, whereas in our case, adding light clients can save a lot of unnecessary computation. The API server even can be on cloud, VPS, with very normal configurations, i.e., 2 GB RAM and 10 GB SSD, making the face recognition system more secure and reliable. Experiments show that there is significant computational gain by using the proposed framework. The thick client adds computational contribution in the face recognition system and also saves switch traffic by not sending every single frame of the camera to the server, instead complete the necessary computation at the client side and send only textual processed information to the web server or computational server.

## REFERENCES

1. P. Hu, H. Ning, T. Qiu, Y. Xu, X. Luo, and A. K. Sangaiah, "A unified face identification and resolution scheme using cloud computing in Internet of things," *Future Generation Computer Systems*, 2018, vol. 81, pp. 582–592.
2. P. Nawrocki, B. Sniezynski, and H. Slojewski, "Adaptable mobile cloud computing environment with code transfer based on machine learning," *Pervasive and Mobile Computing*, 2019, vol. 57, pp. 49–63.
3. A. Vinay, V. S. Shekhar, J. Rituparna, T. Aggrawal, K. N. B. Murthy, and S. Natarajan, "Cloud based big data analytics framework for face recognition in social networks using machine learning," *Procedia Computer Science*, 2015, vol. 50, pp. 623–630.
4. B. Xiao, H. Radha Poovendran, et al., "Deceiving Google's cloud video intelligence API built for summarizing videos," in Proceedings of the IEEE Conference on Computer Vision and Pattern Recognition Workshops, Honolulu, HI, 2017, pp. 1–5.
5. A. Dehghan, E. G. Ortiz, G. Shu, and S. Z. Masood, "Dager: Deep age, gender and emotion recognition using convolutional neural network," 2017.
6. L. Xu and Y. Wang, "XCloud: Design and Implementation of AI Cloud Platform with RESTful API Service," 2019.
7. A. Alotaibi and A. Mahmmod, "Enhancing OAuth services security by an authentication service with face recognition," in 2015 *Long Island Systems, Applications and Technology*, 2015, pp. 1–6.
8. G.-A. Stelea, C. Gavrilua, S. Zamfir, and R. Curpen, "Intelligent Education Assistant Powered by Chatbots", *The 13th International Scientific Conference eLearning and Software for Education*, Bucharest, April 27–28, 2017.
9. S. Kumar, S. K. Singh, A. K. Singh, S. Tiwari, and R. S. Singh, "Privacy preserving security using biometrics in cloud computing," *Multimedia Tools and Applications*, 2018, vol. 77, no. 9, pp. 11017–11039.
10. N. Powers et al., "The cloudlet accelerator: Bringing mobile-cloud face recognition into real-time," in *2015 IEEE Globecom Workshops (GC Wkshps)*, 2015, pp. 1–7.

11. F. A. Silva, P. Maciel, E. Santana, R. Matos, and J. Dantas, "Mobile cloud face recognition based on smart cloud ranking," *Computing*, 2017, vol. 99, no. 3, pp. 287–311.

12. X. Chen, Z. Ji, Y. Fan, and Y. Zhan, "Restful API architecture based on laravel framework," *Journal of Physics: Conference Series*, 2017, vol. 910, no. 1, p. 12016.

13. R. F. Sari and P. Indrawan, "Cloud computing services in mobile devices using android face detector API and rest communication," in *The Third International Conference on Digital Information Processing and Communications (ICDIPC 2013)*, 2013, pp. 529–537.

14. C. Borcea, X. Ding, N. Gehani, R. Curtmola, M. A. Khan, and H. Debnath, "Avatar: Mobile distributed computing in the cloud," in *2015 3rd IEEE International Conference on Mobile Cloud Computing, Services, and Engineering*, 2015, pp. 151–156.

15. P. Indrawan, S. Budiyatno, N. M. Ridho, and R. F. Sari, "Face recognition for social media with mobile cloud computing," *International Journal on Cloud Computing: Services and Architecture*, 2013, vol. 3, no. 1, pp. 23–35.

16. J. K. Basu, D. Bhattacharyya, and T. Kim, "Use of artificial neural network in pattern recognition," *International Journal of Software Engineering and Its Applications*, 2010, vol. 4, no. 2, pp. 23–34

17. T. H. Le, "Applying artificial neural networks for face recognition," *Advances in Artificial Neural Systems*, 2011, vol. 2011, pp. 1–17.

18. A. A. Huqqani, E. Schikuta, S. Ye, and P. Chen, "Multicore and GPU parallelization of neural networks for face recognition," *Procedia Computer Science*, 2013, vol. 18, pp. 349–358.

19. P. Bhatnagar, R. Jaipur, and I. Rajasthan, "Implementation of mobile-cloudlet-cloud architecture for face recognition in cloud computing using android mobile," *International Journal of Computer Applications Technology and Research*, 2013, vol. 2, no. 6, pp. 671–675.

20. S. N. Srirama, C. Paniagua, and H. Flores, "Croudstag: Social group formation with facial recognition and mobile cloud services," *Procedia Computer Science*, 2011, vol. 5, pp. 633–640.

21. P. Viola and M. J. Jones, "Robust real-time face detection," *International Journal of Computer Vision*, 2004, vol. 57, no. 2, pp. 137–154.

22. N. Dalal and B. Triggs, "Histograms of oriented gradients for human detection," in *2005 IEEE Computer Society Conference on Computer Vision and Pattern Recognition (CVPR'05)*, 2005, vol. 1, pp. 886–893.

23. T. Baltrušaitis, P. Robinson, and L.-P. Morency, "Openface: An open source facial behavior analysis toolkit," in *2016 IEEE Winter Conference on Applications of Computer Vision (WACV)*, 2016, pp. 1–10.

24. F. Schroff, D. Kalenichenko, and J. Philbin, "Facenet: A unified embedding for face recognition *and* clustering," in *Proceedings of the IEEE Conference on Computer Vision and Pattern Recognition,* 2015, pp. 815–823.

25. V. Kazemi and J. Sullivan, "One millisecond face alignment with an ensemble of regression trees," in *Proceedings of the IEEE Conference on Computer Vision and Pattern Recognition*, 2014, pp. 1867–1874.

Chapter 5

# Data mining security for big data

*Irum Naz Sodhar*
Shaheed Benazir Bhutto University Shaheed Benazirabad

*Akhtar Hussain Jalbani, Abdul Hafeez Buller,
and Anam Naz Sodhar*
Quaid-e-Awam University of Engineering Science & Technology

## CONTENTS

DOI: 10.1201/9781003107286-5

## 5.1   DATA MINING

Data mining is the way to analyze the pattern and association from the huge amount of datasets to calculate the results. Data mining techniques are deeply used in technical research (to process a large amount of unstructured and structured data sets) as well as in organizations, institutes, businesses, social media, etc. Mostly, the dataset was used for statistics to get the information regarding the users and associations of users to increase the users and publicize the business in different areas [1]. Data mining is mostly used in big data for security solutions to determine vulnerability. The main role of data mining is in big data to provide the process of security and detect the malware [2,3]. The whole procedure of data mining such as data mining stages, data mining methods and data mining malware detection is shown in Figure 5.1.

### 5.1.1   Data mining process

Data mining is the process to analyze information, predict outcomes, making active, Knowledge based depends on huge number of datasets [4]. Data mining is also known as Knowledge Discovery Database (KDD). The main aim of the KDD is to gain valuable and previously unidentified information from huge sets of data. The data mining or KDD process has four stages (pre-processing, transformation, mining and pattern evaluation) as shown in Figure 5.2.

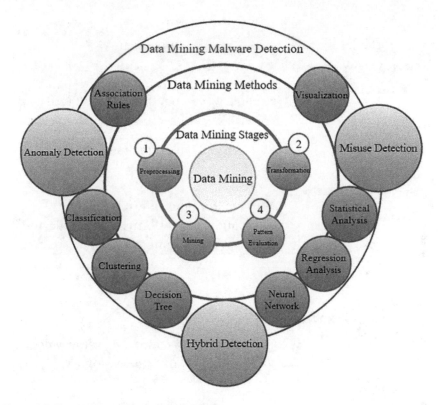

*Figure 5.1* Data mining of malware detection.

Data mining is useful to find new future trends, patterns, extract unseen valuable information and recognize the records and associations from databases [5]. To get useful information by using data mining methods such as Statistics, Machine Learning, Artificial Intelligence and so on.

## 5.1.2 Data mining methods

Lots of methods are available to use in big data mining, but most of the common methods are discussed below [6,7]:

1. Association rules
2. Classification
3. Clustering
4. Decision tree
5. Neural network
6. Regression analysis
7. Statistical analysis
8. Visualization

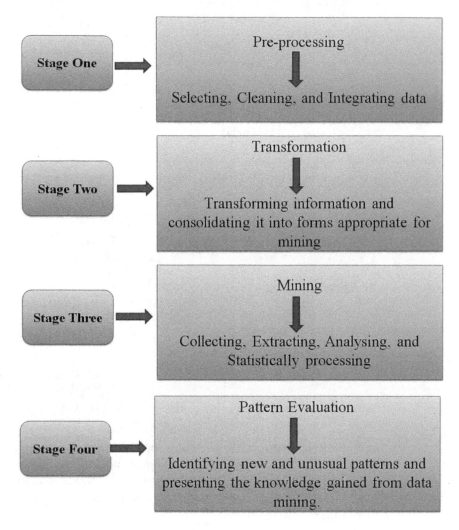

*Figure 5.2* Stage of data mining.

### 5.1.2.1 Association rules

This rule not only helps to find the connection in between inconstant in databases but also identifies the patterns of hidden data and the variables of their occurrence of frequencies.

### 5.1.2.2 Classification

Break down the huge amount of dataset into already defined groups or parts.

### 5.1.2.3 Clustering

It also provides a benefit in data items that have the same features and same understanding of large amount of data.

### 5.1.2.4 Decision tree

This rule creates the classification from data set in the form of a tree structure and also uses machine learning models that are regression and classification.

### 5.1.2.5 Neural network

This is also a method or model that is used to identify the complex association in between the input and output data sets to determine new patterns from the data set.

### 5.1.2.6 Regression analysis

This method is used to predict the value of one element that is based on the known elements of other elements in the dataset by creating a model of the association between dependent and independent elements.

### 5.1.2.7 Statistical analysis

This method helps to identify patterns and calculate the elements from a large amount of data set and provide predictive models for statistical analysis.

### 5.1.2.8 Visualization

This method is to determine new patterns by showing the outcomes in a way that is understandable for users.

Users could apply more than one data mining method to build a model that will help to detect attacks from the big data and ensure the successful detection of attacks.

## 5.1.3 Data mining for malware detection

Data mining includes four methods that can be used to detect malware and is also used for analysis, manipulation, monitoring and health checks. When developing secure applications, developers use data mining techniques to improve the speed and quality of malware detection and increase the number of attacks detected per day [8,9].

### 5.1.3.1 *Approaches of mining for malware detection*

There are three main approaches for the detection of malware is discussed below [10,11]:

1. Anomaly detection (AD)
2. Misuse detection (MD)
3. Hybrid detection.

#### 5.1.3.1.1 Anomaly detection

AD includes modeling of the system behavior in order of network to determine the pattern of normal usage. This technique can detect the attacks of previously unknown and could be used for describing the structure of misuse detectors. The main issue in ADs is any abnormality from the norm, because of appropriate behavior. AD is to produce a high ratio of false-positive [10].

#### 5.1.3.1.2 Misuse detection

MD is termed as signature or mark-based detection. To identify the already well-known attacks on the basis of the mark. This technique has low ratio of false positives.

#### 5.1.3.1.3 Hybrid detection

Hybrid detection (HD) is a combination of anomaly and MD approach to increase the number of order detected interruptions when decreasing the number of false-positives [11]. It does not create any model but is used in big data. Rule-based model used to generate by the data mining algorithm. This approach is also used in detection system searches for abnormalities from usual profile and mistreatment detection system looks after for malware mark in the code.

## 5.2 BIG DATA

Big data is a collection of records of specifically a large amount of volume, still increasing with time [12]. It is a data set that contains enormous size and complexity that could not process efficiently on the tool because no traditional tool is available for data management as shown in Figure 5.3. The features of big data contain volume (the big data is related to huge size. Size of data plays an important role to identify the output data), variety (variety refers to various sources of data that can be organized and unorganized [13]—data in the form of e-mails, images, audio, video, documented files etc.), velocity (velocity means the speed of data generation to measure how fast data is generated to fulfill the requirements), and variability (shown inconsistency of data).

Data mining is the way of determining patterns from a huge collection of datasets. The big data itself collects a large amount of data. Which can be read and write the data. It consists of a large amount of organized or unorganized data. The need to extract the knowledge from the dataset and simply storing these data is not sufficient [14].

### 5.2.1 Types of big data

There are three types of big data that are described below and shown in Figure 5.3

1. Organized data
2. Unorganized
3. Semiorganized

#### 5.2.1.1 Organized data

Any type of data that could be stored, accessed and processed in the form of static format or organized in the form of structural data. In computer science, the techniques is used on the data set.

#### 5.2.1.2 Unorganized data

Any type of data with an unidentified structure is categorized as unorganized data. Data contain a huge amount of size with unorganized data. Unorganized data is considered a different type of data with different sources containing a combination of text documents, audio, video, different format images, etc. Nowadays, huge amount of data available for organizations, institutes, social media, and so on are considered as unorganized data.

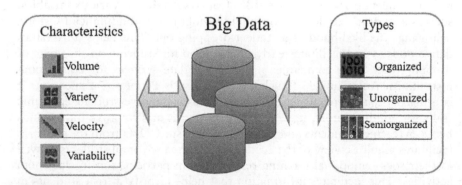

Figure 5.3 Big data management.

### 5.2.1.3 Semi-organized data

Semiorganized data contain both forms—organized and unorganized data.

## 5.2.2 Examples of big data

### 5.2.2.1 Banking system

Whether it's financing or financial management, big data has made banks more efficient for all industries. The adoption of technology has reduced customer competition, increased bank revenue and made the final information clearer and easier to understand. It starts by identifying fraud, simplifying and streamlining transaction processing, improving customer understanding, optimizing transaction execution, and facilitating the customer experience. Big data, an advanced customer service, offers a wide range of applications. An interesting example of a company using big data in this area is the Western Union. The organization facilitates an omni-channel approach to personalize the consumer experience by processing over 29 transactions per second and aggregating all data into a common platform for statistical modeling and predictive volume analysis [15].

### 5.2.2.2 Education system

For the education sector, the data collected from students, faculty, courses and achievements is enormous, and analysis can generate effective information to improve the operation and work of educational institutions. Promoting effective learning, increasing international recruitment to universities, helping students set career goals, reducing dropouts, achieving accurate student assessment, improving decision making and student success, etc., big data plays a central role in this area [15].

A good example is the University of Florida. Universities use IBM Info Sphere to extract, load, and transfer data across multiple resources and IBM SPSS Modeller for predictive analytics and data modeling to analyze and forecast student performance. Use IBM Congo's Analytics. Various variables, such as a student's grades, background, demographics and financial history, help gauge the likelihood of a student dropping out. This helps universities define policies and facilitates early intervention for students on the verge of dropping out. Some companies promote big data services for educational institutions. An example of such an enterprise is Panorama Education. It is a district management platform that aims to improve student academic skills for administrators, update student progress and improve interactions between teachers, students and families, and the staff. Data from the platform facilitates a holistic view of the academic performance of all students as well as their socio-emotional learning resulting from participation in classroom activities. This facilitates information that helps identify at-risk students in the early stages and helps educators help students in areas that need it.

### 5.2.2.3 Media system

As the latest approach to consuming online content through gadgets becomes a new trend, hype about traditional approaches to media use is fading. As a result, huge amounts of data have been generated and big data has permeated the industry. Providing information about customer status, optimizing media delivery times to customers, whether it helps predict what viewers want in terms of age group genre, music, and content. Faster product updates, cost savings and effective ad targeting. Netflix is a prime example of how big data has revolutionized media platforms. This technology affects not only the series that the platform invests in but also how those series are made available to subscribers. The user's viewing history, such as where the video for a particular show was paused, affects everything from custom thumbnails to what you see in the Spectrum on Netflix variable section. Another good example is Viacom 18. The company's big data platform is based on Microsoft Azure and will experiment with other technologies in the future. The company uses big data analytics to ensure viewers are kept in breaks between program segments by determining the appropriate time to schedule commercial breaks. This allows the platform to retain viewers during commercials, cars and advertisers [15].

### 5.2.2.4 Healthcare system

Big data plays an important role in improving modern healthcare. Reducing treatment costs; predicting epidemics; avoiding preventable diseases; improving the overall quality of life; predicting daily patient income for staff organization; using electrical health records (EHR), instantly with the application of timely alerts to drive care, medical adoption, data for more effective strategic planning and reduction of fraud and errors—technology has revolutionized the entire healthcare industry [15].

### 5.2.2.5 Agriculture system

In fields like agriculture, big data analytics drives smart farming, corrects operations, reduces costs, and opens up new business opportunities. Key areas for big data work are the smart and accurate use of pesticides to meet food needs by providing farmers with up-to-date information on changes in the factors affecting rainfall, climate and yield. Precise pesticide decision-making, agricultural equipment management, supply chain efficiency, planting and chemical application schedule, location, method planning and moisture, temperature and chemical data collection substance to test [14–16]. Bayer Digital Farming, a division of Bayer Group, has implemented an application that uses machine learning and artificial intelligence to identify weeds. Farmers share their weed catch in the app and compare their images with the full Bayer database (including about 100,000 photos) for species detection. This application is provided at the right time to protect crops and improve yields.

### 5.2.2.6 Travel system

Big data has played an important role in making transportation smoother and more efficient. Big Data has a huge impact on this industry, including managing earned revenue, managing the earned reputation, driving more strategic marketing, and performing advanced market research and targeted marketing. Big data is also used to plan routes according to user needs, effectively reduce delays and control congestion and traffic using tools such as Google Maps for low route detection traffic, even when detecting accident-prone areas to increase the level of road safety [14]. An effective example of using big data in this area is the example of Uber. The platform generates and uses large amounts of data such as driver, location, vehicle, each vehicle's route and then research to predict demand, supply, driver location and set rates of displacement. Another example is a travel booking start-up that provides search results based on airline data, customer profiles, social charts, and all buyer inquiries and reviews to expedite the flight booking process. There is Hipmunk. The platform gives customers what they need while taking care of their travel accommodation by verifying all the data provided, rather than forcing them to find out for themselves.

### 5.2.2.7 Manufacturing system

Manufacturing is no longer a meticulous manual process as it used to be. Technology and data analysis have completely revolutionized the production process. Big data has successfully played a role in improving production, customizing product design, ensuring adequate quality maintenance, managing the supply chain and assessing potential risks [15].

An interesting example of Big Data application in the industry is Rolls-Royce. Rolls-Royce uses big data analytics to improve the design process, reduce product development time, improve product performance and quality and reduce costs. The platform has also simplified the manufacturing process by removing obstacles that arise in the design process. Another example of big data being used in manufacturing is from BMW. BMW uses big data for predictive analytics to configure self-driving cars. To this end, the platform is also applying artificial intelligence by starting a partnership with Intel. With Intel's acquisition of Mobileye, BMW now has access to machine vision technology.

### 5.2.2.8 Government system

Governments, regardless of country, face vast amounts of data every day. This is mainly due to the detailed updates that must be kept on various citizen records and databases, developments, geographic surveys, energy resources and more. These data must be carefully examined and studied and become an ally in the administration of government. The government uses this data primarily in two areas: social programs and cyber security [15,16]. For welfare programs, the data are used to make quick and up-to-date decisions in the case of policy programs, identify areas of interest, monitor popular sectors of agriculture and livestock, and overcome challenges such as terrorism, unemployment, and poverty. A useful example of government adoption of big data is at the Department of Homeland Security (DHS). To protect its security, the DHS uses an intrusion detection system on sensors that can analyze Internet traffic inside and outside the federal system and identify malware attempts and unauthorized access. The National Oceanic and Atmospheric Administration (NOAA) is a platform that regularly collects data through space, land and ocean sensors. The platform uses a big data approach to collect and analyze large amounts of data to conclude accurate information.

### 5.2.2.9 Retail system

In retail, big data helps predict new trends, target the right customers at the right time, reduce marketing costs and improve customer service. Big Data keeps a big picture of every consumer, facilitates individual engagement, optimizes prices, extracts maximum value from future trends, optimizes back-office operations and improves customer service. Also, one of Canada's largest shoe and accessory retailers is leveraging big data to survive opportunities like Black Friday [15]. The platform runs on a service-oriented big data architecture that integrates multiple data sources related to billing, billing and fraud detection, facilitating the perfect electronic experience for commerce. Amazon uses big data obtained from its customers to develop a recommendation engine. The more familiar users are with the platform, the more accurately they can predict what they want to buy, simplifying the process, and encouraging users to buy, for example, by recommending specific products rather than soliciting them to pull them to buy the entire directory. The proposed technology for the platform is based on collaborative filtering. In other words, by creating an image of who the user is and showing you products offered by people with similar profiles, you decide what to expect from the user.

### 5.2.2.10 Energy and utilities system

Energy and utility platforms use a variety of big data sources such as smart meters, grid equipment, weather data, energy system measurements, storm data and GIS data. This data is used on these platforms to reduce costs, improve operational efficiency, reduce carbon emissions and meet the increased energy needs of end-users.

A useful example of big data adoption in the energy and utility sector is the Google Superstorm Sand Crisis Map. Maps not only collect, present and overlay weather data from a variety of sources but also integrate video feeds from multiple locations, evacuation routes, emergency centers, and traffic conditions.

Another successful example is the non-profit Direct Relief International. It provides medical assistance to people affected by the arrest, poverty and natural disasters of civilians in the United States and around the world. The platform identifies populations at risk of storms, assesses possible emergencies, detects clinics in flood risk areas and distributes them appropriately to those in need of assistance and medical supplies, in collaboration with Planter technologies to enable the integration [15]. Various datasets, including shelter locations and near real-time epidemiological alerts from the Red Cross and government agencies.

### 5.2.2.11 Food industry system

Are you wondering how the food industry uses big data? Big data enables food platforms to improve marketing campaigns, create innovative and popular stories, enable businesses to track customer and competitor growth, manage quality and manage purchases and prices.

This data allows owners to track factors such as product quality to determine if a product has been tampered with, such as whether raw materials have been replaced or measurements have changed for the product alternative products. It is also useful for more root causes such as seasonality and variation in storage methods.

Another example is Blue Apron, a delivery service for fresh ingredients and recipes that apply analytics through the big data analytics platform Looker to make near-real-time food delivery decisions. This reduces decision time by up to a day.

Another example is the example of Starbucks. Starbucks uses data obtained from mobile payments app users to track customer data, such as personal preferences and preferences, and uses that data for relevant marketing, including offers designed to attract customers' texting time.

## 5.3 SECURITY FOR BIG DATA

Big data security refers to measuring with a tool that is used in both data and process for analysis. The main purpose of security for big data is to provide safety against attacks, hazards and malicious activities that could harm the data [17]. Nowadays, there is a big challenge of security for big data. Due to the challenges faced by users, such as theft of stored online data, crash servers etc., security is an important component in big data these days. When compared with other fields of big data, security issues happen every second or minute. Those attacks could be on different elements of big data, like on stored data [17–20].

### 5.3.1 Component of security of big data

1. Security tools for big data
2. Authentication
3. Authorization
4. Centralized administration and audit
5. Data encryption
6. User access control
7. Physical security

#### 5.3.1.1 Security tools for big data

Huge data security should meet four basic standards: Authentication, Authorization, Centralized Administration and Audit, and Data Encryption [17–18].

#### 5.3.1.2 Authentication

Authentication is required for guarding admittance to the framework, its information and administrations. Verification ensures the client is who he professes to be. Two degrees of authentication should be set up—border and intra-bunch: Knox, Kerberos [18].

#### 5.3.1.3 Authorization

Authorization is needed to oversee access and power over information, assets and administrations. Approval can be upheld at different degrees of granularity and in consistency with existing undertaking security principles.

#### 5.3.1.4 Centralized administration and audit

It is needed to take care of and report activity on the system. Auditing is important for managing security compliance and different needs like security forensics.

#### 5.3.1.5 Data encryption

It is needed to control unauthorized access to sensitive knowledge either at rest or in motion. Knowledge protection ought to be taken into account at the sphere, and network level and applicable ways ought to be adopted for safety.

#### 5.3.1.6 User access control

It is the most basic network security tool. However, few companies apply it. This is due to the high administrative costs. This is dangerous at the network level and not suitable for large information platforms. Powerful machine-controlled user access management can be beneficial to your organization. Automated management of complex user management levels protect major information platforms from attacks [17,18].

### 5.3.1.7 Physical security

Physical security is often built after deploying a massive central information platform and is not overlooked. It can also be designed according to the security of the cloud provider's information center. These are important because they prevent strangers and suspicious visitors from accessing the information center. Security logs and CCTV work are used for certain purposes [20].

## 5.3.2 Security issues in big data

The following issues have been observed by the users [20–23].

1. Access controls
2. Nonrelational data stores
3. Storage
4. Endpoints
5. Real-time security
6. Threat in data mining

### 5.3.2.1 Access controls

It is critically vital for a corporation to own an absolutely secure system. Permission to exchange the information ought to be permissible to users [21]. Access management has to specify that it might not get hacked by attackers.

### 5.3.2.2 Non-relational data stores

Nonrelational means unorganized data

### 5.3.2.3 Storage

Big data contains massive information to tend to store information on multiple tiers. Its storage depends on business desires in terms of performance and value [24].

### 5.3.2.4 End points

Solution of security that mostly draws the log from endpoints would validate the authenticity of those endpoints.

### 5.3.2.5 Real time security

Real-time security tools generate data, the secret is to search out the way to ignore false or rough information, so human intelligence may be centered on true breaches or valuable information.

### 5.3.2.6 Threat in data mining

Data mining solutions typically notice a pattern that means business methods [25]. For this reason, there's a desire for making certain that it's secured from each internal and external threats.

## 5.4 CONCLUSION

Big data is a collection of records, specifically large amount of volume that is still increasing with time. In this surrounding having authorized access to data is important. Users would take decisions on these data, and these important decisions are a must for good. As the data is growing larger, security breaches and data are sensational to unauthorized users. An organization cannot save every type of data from unauthorized users. In data mining, this is the main concern of providing data security for information consequent and every stage from data to a decision-maker. Big data security refers to measuring with tool which was used in both data and process for analysis. Data mining uses four methods to detect malware—scanning, activity, monitoring and integrity checking. When developing a security app, developers use data mining methods to improve the speed and quality of malware detection as well as to increase the growth of the number to detect a day attack.

### 5.4.1 Future of big data

An increasing range of company's square measures adopt huge knowledge environments. The time is ripe to form certain security groups square measure enclosed in these choices and deployment, significantly since huge knowledge environments that do not embody comprehensive knowledge protection capabilities represent low-hanging fruit for hackers since they hold such a lot doubtless valuable sensitive knowledge. The future of huge information itself is most absolute to be a bright one. It is universally recognized recently that sensible analytics are often a road to business success. Therefore, this means that huge information design can each become additionally important to secure and additional oftentimes attacked. So the list of huge information security issues is still growing and that, in a very shell, is the basis of the rising field of counter intelligence that correlates security information across disparate domains to achieve conclusions.

## REFERENCES

1. Wu, X., Zhu, X., Wu, G. Q., & Ding, W. (2013). Data mining with big data. *IEEE Transactions on Knowledge and Data Engineering*, 26(1), 97–107.
2. Sowmya, R., & Suneetha, K. R. (2017, January). Data mining with big data. In *2017 11th International Conference on Intelligent Systems and Control (ISCO)* (pp. 246–250). IEEE, Coimbatore.
3. Gupta, R. (2014). Journey from data mining to Web Mining to Big Data. arXiv preprint arXiv:1404.4140.
4. Ageed, Z. S., Zeebaree, S. R., Sadeeq, M. M., Kak, S. F., Yahia, H. S., Mahmood, M. R., & Ibrahim, I. M. (2021). Comprehensive survey of big data mining approaches in cloud systems. *Qubahan Academic Journal*, 1(2), 29–38.
5. Yang, H. (2021, June). Application value of big data mining technology in the field of financial venture capital. In *International Conference on Applications and Techniques in Cyber Security and Intelligence* (pp. 333–340). Springer, Cham.
6. Wang, F., Li, M., Mei, Y., & Li, W. (2020). Time series data mining: A case study with big data analytics approach. *IEEE Access*, 8, 14322–14328.
7. Yang, J., Li, Y., Liu, Q., Li, L., Feng, A., Wang, T., & Lyu, J. (2020). Brief introduction of medical database and data mining technology in big data era. *Journal of Evidence-Based Medicine*, 13(1), 57–69.
8. Xu, L., Jiang, C., Wang, J., Yuan, J., & Ren, Y. (2014). Information security in big data: Privacy and data mining. *IEEE Access*, 2, 1149–1176.
9. Kantarcioglu, M., & Xi, B. (2016, October). Adversarial data mining: Big data meets cyber security. In *Proceedings of the 2016 ACM SIGSAC Conference on Computer and Communications Security* (pp. 1866–1867). Vienna.
10. Ageed, Z. S., Zeebaree, S. R., Sadeeq, M. M., Kak, S. F., Yahia, H. S., Mahmood, M. R., & Ibrahim, I. M. (2021). Comprehensive survey of big data mining approaches in cloud systems. *Qubahan Academic Journal*, 1(2), 29–38.
11. Dahiya, V., & Dalal, S. (2020). Parallel approaches of utility mining for big data. *Webology*, 17(2), 31–43.
12. Amanullah, M. A., Habeeb, R. A. A., Nasaruddin, F. H., Gani, A., Ahmed, E., Nainar, A. S. M., ... & Imran, M. (2020). Deep learning and big data technologies for IoT security. *Computer Communications*, 151, 495–517.
13. Chamikara, M. A. P., Bertók, P., Liu, D., Camtepe, S., & Khalil, I. (2020). Efficient privacy preservation of big data for accurate data mining. *Information Sciences*, 527, 420–443.
14. Qi, C. C. (2020). Big data management in the mining industry. *International Journal of Minerals, Metallurgy and Materials*, 27(2), 131–139.
15. Rangaiah, M. (2021). Big data application daily life, Retrieved on September, 4 2021. https://www.analyticssteps.com/blogs/11-big-data-applications-daily-life.
16. Shang, H., Lu, D., & Zhou, Q. (2021). Early warning of enterprise finance risk of big data mining in Internet of things based on fuzzy association rules. *Neural Computing and Applications*, 33(9), 3901–3909.
17. Sriramoju, S. B. (2017). Opportunities and security implications of big data mining. *International Journal of Research in Science and Engineering*, 3(6), 44–58.

18. Kim, S. H., Kim, N. U., & Chung, T. M. (2013, December). Attribute relationship evaluation methodology for big data security. In *2013 International Conference on IT Convergence and Security (ICITCS)* (pp. 1–4). IEEE, Macao.
19. Xuan, Q., Ruan, Z., & Min, Y. (2021). Graph data mining: Algorithm, security and application.
20. Wang, L., & Jones, R. (2020). Big data analytics in cyber security: Network traffic and attacks. *Journal of Computer Information Systems*, 61(5), 410–470.
21. Memon, M. S., Kumar, P., Mirani, A. A., Qabulio, M., & Sodhar, I. N. (2020). Deep learning and IoT: The enabling technologies towards smart farming. In *Industrial Internet of Things and Cyber-Physical Systems: Transforming the Conventional to Digital* (pp. 47–60). IGI Global. https://www.igi-global.com/chapter/deep-learning-and-iot/257839
22. Jaseena, K. U., & David, J. M. (2014). Issues, challenges, and solutions: Big data mining. *CS & IT-CSCP*, 4(13), 131–140.
23. Mannava, P. A study on the challenges and types of big data. *International Journal of Innovative Research in Science, Engineering and Technology*, ISSN (Online): 2319, 8753.
24. Dai, H. N., Wang, H., Xu, G., Wan, J., & Imran, M. (2020). Big data analytics for manufacturing Internet of things: Opportunities, challenges and enabling technologies. *Enterprise Information Systems*, 14(9–10), 1279–1303.
25. Xu, L., Jiang, C., Chen, Y., Wang, J., & Ren, Y. (2016). A framework for categorizing and applying privacy-preservation techniques in big data mining. *Computer*, 49(2), 54–62.

Chapter 6

# Cloud computing security challenges and their solutions

*Rimsha Khalid, Khowla Khaliq, and Muhammad Imran Tariq*
Superior University

*Shahzadi Tayyaba*
University of Lahore

*Muhammad Arfan Jaffar*
Superior University

*Muhammad Arif*
Guangzhou University

## CONTENTS

DOI: 10.1201/9781003107286-6

## 6.1 INTRODUCTION

In the past decade of computer invention, computers used to take up huge space in the room. Compared to the modern computer, parts were very costly and consumed more energy. In 1960, the computing system revolution started, named central processing units, replaced by smaller and cheaper version in modern the times so that everyone can get benefit from it [1]. Due to the capacity issue in later devices, cloud computing technology gives the ability to users to store and assess a large amount of data and information easily anytime and anywhere around the world. It also reduces cost through applications by managing and uploading files with a larger capacity to the cloud and uses an e-mail service to send. Cloud computing requires high-speed Internet that represents communication over the Internet. It provides cloud-based services including PLATFORM-AS-A-SERVICE, SOFTWARE-AS-A-SERVICE, and INFRASTRUCTURE-AS-A-SERVICE to a person or user who may not be able to purchase the required service as a whole but can access it by nominal fee to the service provider [2]. One of the biggest and important drawbacks of cloud computing is security. While adopting a solution, many companies struggle to weigh the advantages of the cloud against the cloud protection risks and obstacles they can encounter when implementing cloud technologies. Before a cloud solution is implemented by the enterprise, these cloud protection issues and threats must be handled properly. Using all the new safeguards, individual cloud storage solutions can be highly secure. In reality, cloud service providers are also able to invest more money into protecting their data centers than most organizations can, as their main business strategy is to provide connectivity to the data center networks and applications [3].

Cloud security is used to secure cloud computing systems with security policies, restrictions, and technology. It is important to secure the internal data or information of any organization that can affect its integrity and reputation. Some of the major challenges faced by the user regarding cloud security includes lack of control (maintenance of a software day to day results in having less visibility and control), cloud platforms may not comply with organization regulations (require to meet some regulatory such as HIPPA, FISMA, DSS, or PCI), data privacy issues (organization may face financial issues due to leaked data), aware users affected by data breaches (by notifying customers), user access control (users' responsibility to check the user access control come along with cloud service providers such as IaaS, PaaS, or SaaS), Vendor Lock (Security feature), and lack of personnel experienced in cloud security measures (managed security service providers tool put a team of security experts). These challenges will result in major losses in terms of computer hacking, consumer protection, and identity integrity. When we speak about some infrastructure built on an open network, i.e., the Internet, security is still the main component. The same also refers to cloud computing since it is also Internet-based. Hence, it is necessary to run a cloud security risk assessment. This risk assessment involves the identification of the biggest risks and their impacts [4].

Cloud computing security is an area of concern for scholars and practitioners in today's extremely distant world. Several research reports point out that some of these enforcement problems are data leaks, whereas others include access management. Whatever the problem, it influences decision-makers greatly when developing a software or solution alternative. C-suite managers and VPs should ensure that these issues of security are well documented. At about the same time, each provides its solution to issues discovered through the use of cloud storage to tackle operational challenges and customer demands. In short, if you take the appropriate precautions, cloud storage can be much safer and more satisfying for your business needs [5].

The present scenario shows cloud computing users who solely rely on the Cloud Service Provider for the privacy of data and security of information. Data held the top place, regardless of the infrastructure being used, when it comes to IT security issues. Cloud Infrastructure is no exception to this, and due to its hierarchical design and multitenant architecture, it focuses on additional security issues. Its generation, preservation, utilization, delivery, and degradation comprise the data life cycle. Both these steps in the data life cycle should be assisted by each CSP with sufficient protection frameworks. In addition, the data backups used to prevent data errors (scope, save intervals, storage time, etc.) should be straightforward and auditable for the customers. Both these and some other questions need to be solved by using a cloud service. This research aims to identify the challenges and issues of cloud computing security by reviewing previous data and finding new solutions for them [6].

This research paper has multiple sections. The related work of several other scholars is mentioned in Section 6.2. We made a research methodology in Section 6.3. Results and discussion are given in Section 6.4. Finally, the article is concluded in Section 6.5.

## 6.2 LITERATURE REVIEW

Farrukh Shahzad in his research work, while describing the major security issues and challenges of cloud computing, evaluated that data privacy and data security are the major areas of concern at the side of the service provider. He, in his research work, surveyed multiple papers to create a better understanding of the cloud security issues and challenges. Furthermore, he proposed approaches and solutions to overcome the security issues of the cloud including five characteristics of cloud computing, three models of cloud services, and four models of deploying cloud computing [6].

Nidal Hassan Hussein and Ahmed Khalid surveyed the existing approaches to the security of cloud computing and proposed a model for better security measurements. The proposed model consisted of three layers of security to secure the user's data at the maximum rate [7].

In this research work, P. Ravi Kumar et al. argue about the benefits of cloud computing and its security challenges for the data. They clearly described in their work the worth of data security for any organization. Customers rely on the organization for their data's security. If a cloud-based organization lacks the security of its customers' data it can collapse. In this paper, two models are discussed to get better data securities that are the deployment model and model for service delivery. In this paper, the security challenges to the customer's data and their solutions are discussed [8].

Nalini Subramanian and Andrews Jeyaraj in their paper describe threats and recent challenges associated with cloud computing. They inspected different challenges on the basis of SLA (service level agreement), communication, and computational. Various analyses related to VM's security challenges have been compared in this paper. Virtualization increases the value of cloud computing; on the other hand, its three layers such as virtualization layer, virtual layer, and physical layer face various challenges. This research can be acknowledged as a prototype for more exhaustive research via the unrevealed path in cloud computing [9].

A. Venkatesh and Marrynal S. Eastaff described in their research work the techniques that can be used to securely save the data on the cloud. They've discussed that cloud computing allows user to store their data on the cloud but the issue is data security. Furthermore, they described that the security issue can be resolved if the confidentiality, integrity, and availability of data are enclosed in the SLAs [10].

Arjun Bardhan et al. state in their research work that the cloud is considered a distributed system. Researchers claim that many surveys related to cloud computing have been made and many solutions are defined yet. Despite these solutions, a gap is still existing between the cloud security issues and their solution. In this research work, this gap is tried to be covered. In this paper, cloud computing's two working models are discussed that include the service model and the deployment model of cloud computing [5].

Iqbal Ahmed in his research work clearly explains the cloud computing services, their security challenges, and the solution for the security issues. The writer while talking about the security of cloud computing described that there can be many factors that affect its security. These factors include balancing the load, operating system management, memory management, management of database, virtualization, network management, and concurrency control. To overcome these issues, solutions include encryption of data, digital denial of service (DDoS), digital signatures, and judicial expertise [11].

Shahin Fatima and Shish Ahmad argue carefully about the security challenges of a cloud computing environment. They discussed that cloud computing is the best service provider so far. It provides services to its users on their demand. The consumers pay for the services they avail of from cloud computing. Cloud computing services are cost-effective. The user has to pay less for the services. The service consumer can store his data on the cloud and can access it anywhere and anytime. Consequently, the storage of data on the cloud can breach the security of the data. Multiple users store their data on the cloud and it can cause a high risk for the security of data. The characteristics of cloud computing include scalability of infrastructure, multiple applications, on-demand applications, access to larger networks, and multiuser framework. Cloud computing consists of two working models that are deployment model (public, private, hybrid, and community) and the service model (IaaS model of cloud, SaaS model of cloud, and PaaS model of cloud). Furthermore, cloud security issues can be categorized into three forms that are communication issues, architectural issues, and client management issues. Communication issues of security include control of access, isolation of VM, monitoring of VM, and security of communication. Architectural issues of security include privacy of data, backup of data, and integrity of data, and identity management. Client management issues include legal issues and SLA issues. In this paper, the researcher explained some measurements to the cloud security issues. This solution includes a threshold ramp scheme for cloud security, a scheme based on Boolean XOR for sharing secrets, a cryptography method based on visual format, a secret sharing scheme based on image format, a technique based on trust model, the algorithm for encryption, a method based on keys that updates dynamically, a storage system consisting on attributes, etc. Despite describing these solutions, there are still loopholes in achieving complete security in cloud computing. The future direction includes procedures involving key management that will use distributed keys on the service provider's end and help in improving the security issues of cloud computing. The text and sentence structure of this research paper are quite appealing. Simple sentence structure is easy to comprehend. This research paper appeals to the reader to go through the paper and comprehend its concepts because of its assembling structure, pictorial representation, and easy structure of text [12].

Manoj Tyagi and others in their article mainly discuss data correctness, its security, and user authentication. Manoj Tyagi and others formulated the problems and propose a framework, which is based on proposed ECIES (Elliptic curve integrated encryption scheme), TLA (two-level authentication), and AES (advanced encryption standard), AE (avalanche effect), POR (proof of retrievability), and CMA/ES (covariance matrix adaptation evolution strategies). A CMA evolution strategy with AE is implemented to detect the enhanced cipher for security betterment. POR is used for data recovery and data integrity [13].

Foram Suthar and others described challenges associated with the security of the cloud environment in their article. The writers claim that various researchers have published various papers and have conducted different surveys associated with the security of cloud-based services, but researches show a few gaps among cloud issue and their solution, few of them specify data security issue and the rest have virtualization issue. However, here an effort is made by Foram et al. to cover all factors that have concern with the security issue—proper view of cloud security as well as its challenges is provided. Many algorithms and techniques have been proposed to secure virtualization and data on the cloud platform. Hence, there is a need to understand and consider the security defects and the challenges in cloud-based systems clearly [14].

Garima Varma and Sandhiya Adhikari in their paper describe security issues concerned with cloud computing. The authors illustrate many security aspects related to cloud computing in their work and also the research of other researchers. In this paper, the authors discussed the perspective of five major stakeholders such as CSP, CU, CA, CB, and CC. Researchers have covered-up several security challenges in their research and have done a comparative survey which is based on the issues that are discussed by various researchers in this paper. This research can be helpful for researchers in choosing an area in cloud computing and starting their research [15,16].

Wahab Dashti et al., while writing their research work, clearly discuss the security challenges of cloud computing and their solution from the side of service providers. This research work describes security issues related to cloud computing and includes confidentiality, integration, and availability of data (also known as CIA). Furthermore, this paper describes the measurements that can control these cloud computing security issues. These security issues and measurements are discussed in the view of service providers. Some of the measures can be control and audit, etc. The measurements that have been developed to secure the data on the cloud are not updated frequently, which causes the risk of data security violation. In addition, the backups of the data that are kept on the cloud can also breach the security of user's data. The research work listed the current issue of data security in cloud computing and discussed some good measurements to control these data security issues [17–20].

Abrar Atif Asghar in his article argues that in previous studies between 2010 and 2020, researchers highlighted many components of cloud computing, security threats, and possible solutions. The author after discussing and analyzing the previous studies emphasized the importance of cloud computing and shows the need to enhance the scientific research in the field of cloud computing. The author argues that some studies emphasized identifying the challenges and the risk of cloud computing and the other studies offer some solutions to minimize the security threats. Lastly, the development of cloud technology challenges and security issues will minimize with many types of knowledge of their causes and how to avoid and deal with them with possible solutions [21–23].

Harsh Pratap Singh et al. described in their research work the existing security issues, security challenges, and their solution regarding cloud computing. They've discussed that the security of the cloud can be entertained if the services are provided efficiently and makes the security measures effective [24,25].

Table 6.1 Comparison of cloud security issues and challenges

| Parameters | [7] | [8] | [4] | [9] | [10] | [6] | [11] | [12] | [13] | [14] | [15] | [16] | [5] | [17] |
|---|---|---|---|---|---|---|---|---|---|---|---|---|---|---|
| CSP | | | | | | ✓ | | | | | ✓ | | | |
| Confidentiality | | ✓ | ✓ | ✓ | ✓ | | | | | | | | ✓ | ✓ | |
| Integrity | | ✓ | ✓ | ✓ | ✓ | ✓ | | ✓ | ✓ | | | ✓ | ✓ | |
| Availability | | ✓ | ✓ | | ✓ | ✓ | ✓ | | | | | ✓ | ✓ | |
| Authenticity | | | | | | ✓ | | | | | | | ✓ | ✓ |
| Security risk | | | | | | | | | | | | ✓ | | |
| Access control | | ✓ | | | | | | | | | | ✓ | | ✓ |
| Audit | | | | | | | | | | | | ✓ | | |
| Data security | ✓ | ✓ | ✓ | ✓ | | | ✓ | ✓ | ✓ | ✓ | | | | ✓ |
| Data privacy | ✓ | | | | | | ✓ | ✓ | | | | ✓ | ✓ | |
| Key management | | | | | | | | ✓ | | | | | | |
| Anomaly detection | | | | | | | | ✓ | | | | | | |
| Cloud storage | | | | ✓ | | | | ✓ | | | | | | |
| Cloud user | | | | | | | | | | | ✓ | | | |
| Data encryption | | | | ✓ | | | | | | | | ✓ | | |
| Network security | | | | | | | | | | | | ✓ | | |
| Data breach | | | | | | | | | | | | | ✓ | |
| Identity and access management | | | | | | | | | | | | | ✓ | |
| Virtualization | | | | ✓ | | | | | | ✓ | | | | |
| Cyber security | | | | | | | | | | ✓ | | | | |
| Cloud security | ✓ | | | ✓ | | | | | | ✓ | | | | |
| Crypto cloud | | | | ✓ | | | | | | | | | | |
| SLAs | | | | ✓ | | | | | | | | | | |
| Trust issues | | | | | | | | | | | | | | ✓ |
| Data reliability | | | | | | ✓ | | | | | | | | |

## 6.3 RESEARCH METHODOLOGY

We conducted a research methodology by studying past papers. This research methodology is based on three main steps:

1. Planning
2. Developing
3. Reporting

Here each step is further divided into several activities as shown in Figure 6.1.

### 6.3.1 Planning

In this, we explained the main goal of the research methodology by carrying out the following activities:

#### 6.3.1.1 Identification of needs

We identified several systematic literature reviews in the field of Cloud Computing, over time cloud computing has been spread everywhere. Their security challenges is increasing day by day though security is a key component of any network-based technology. Determining the security challenges and solutions in cloud computing will be beneficial for future research work.

#### 6.3.1.2 Identification of problem questions

The main goal of this research is to analyze and recognize the studies from 2014 to 2020 which was related to cloud computing security challenges and

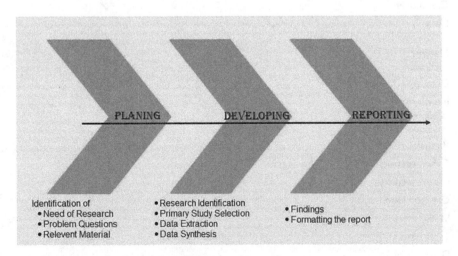

*Figure 6.1* Systematic literature review steps and activities.

their solutions. For a more comprehensive and detailed view of this topic, the goal was divided into the following research questions.

**RQ1:** What is cloud security is and why is it so important?

**RQ2:** Describe the cloud computing security issues and their recommended solution?

**RQ3:** What are the most common issues facing cloud computing today?

**RQ4:** Why users are responsible for the security of data in cloud computing?

### 6.3.1.3 Identification of relevant studies

Several digital libraries like Google scholar, IEEE, WOS, Springer, Research gat, Elsevier, PubMed, and Science Direct were searched for relevant studies. The main aim for selecting these digital libraries was to collect data related to the field of cloud computing. In this paper, searches are limited to surveys and journals that were published from 2014 to 2020.

## 6.3.2 Developing

### 6.3.2.1 Research identification

It is important to follow the research strategy. We have been taking the following steps to derive research questions.

1. Extractions of crucial terms
2. Pinpoint synonyms of crucial terms
3. Pinpoint keywords from relevant studies
4. Make use of OR for similar keywords or different keywords
5. Make use of AND to connect the crucial terms

### 6.3.2.2 Selection of papers (exclusion and inclusion)

In this step, we searched relevant papers to our research topic, reviewed them from abstract to conclusion. We selected those papers that fulfill the following inclusion and exclusion criteria.

### 6.3.2.3 Inclusion criteria

- Papers must be written in English.
- Related to our research topic
- Published from 2014 to 2020
- Should be survey or journal papers

### 6.3.2.4 Exclusion criteria

- Not written in the English language
- Not matched to our research topic
- Incomplete thesis
- Papers with a minimum of four or five pages

Inclusion and exclusion criteria are summarized in Figure 6.2.

## 6.3.3 Data extraction

We collected data from selected papers.

## 6.3.4 Data synthesis

Furthermore, to explain answers to research questions, we synthesize the collected data and apply different strategies.

## 6.3.5 Reporting

### 6.3.5.1 Finding and formatting the report

From the beginning of the research, we found 1,318 research papers on our research topic. After applying exclusion criteria, we selected 728 papers. After that, we applied inclusion criteria and filtered 50 papers. At this step,

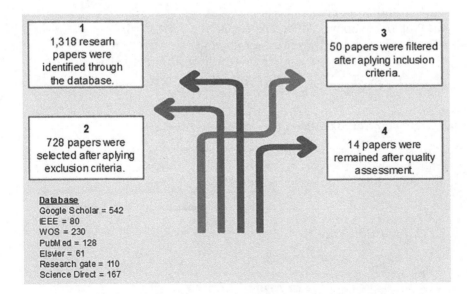

*Figure 6.2* Inclusion and exclusion of studies in the review.

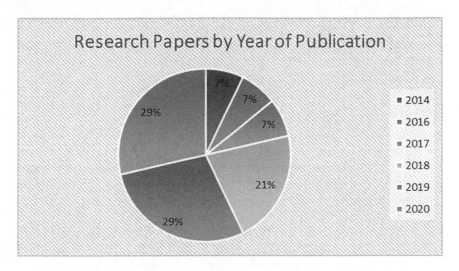

*Figure 6.3* Research work distribution by year of publication.

we read the complete article and eliminated the irrelevant papers that did not fulfill our requirements. At last, we selected 14 research papers that were most relevant to our research work and derived research queries. We showed our research in graph form as shown in Figure 6.3.

## 6.4 RESULTS AND DISCUSSION

This section indicates the results which are relevant to the research questions. Our aim of the research was to find out the cloud computing security challenges and their possible solution. All the results of each research question are discussed separately.

RQ1: What cloud security is and why it is so important?

Security of the cloud is referred to as security measures that are used to secure cloud-based information, applications, and infrastructure against cybersecurity threats, malware, DDOS attacks, hacking, and data breach. Cloud security is important for personal users as well as for businesses because everyone wants that their data or information stored on the cloud to be secure [26–29].

The cloud's popularity and security concerns are capturing thought, attention, and involvement from a wide range of industries. According to a report conducted by Gartner, a market research company, Cloud computing is one of the top ten innovations with long-term growth potential. Although cloud computing comes up with the level of security threats, because their cloud services are moving toward the third party, the third party makes it challenging to manage the security and privacy of data. It is challenging to find out the service support when we need it [29–33].

RQ2: Describe the cloud computing security issues and their recommended solution?

By reviewing the previous studies, cloud computing security issues and recommended solutions have been extracted as shown in Table 6.1. We categorized security issues as follows:

- **Key management:** In terms of cloud protection, key management is crucial. If the encryption key is breached, data stored on the device will be lost. To resist unauthorized access to data, the encryption/decryption key should be stable. The key size must be adequate to save it from cracking
- **Data security:** Data can be mismanaged or misused when there are many organizations and users in a multitenant area are working together. So, proper protection is needed to ensure the user's trust. To avoid data loss, protocols should be implemented.
- **Data privacy:** Privacy must be maintained to avoid unauthorized access to information and authentication and authorization should be ensured by the data.
- **Anomaly detection:** When it comes to data protection, anomaly detection is critical for creating a system that can detect suspicious activity in the cloud network. A variety of anomaly detection systems are used around the world to implement protection measures for cloud data.
- **Cloud data storage and sharing:** Cloud computing allows you to store a lot of data in a small amount of space. Many companies are storing their large data in the cloud due to its convenience. To avoid the loss of any individual's data, proper confidentiality, honesty, and privacy of data must be protected.
- **Vendor lock-in:** The term "vendor lock-in" refers to the period set aside by the CSP for the users using the services. Unless the user is dissatisfied with the CSP's services, he will be unable to switch until the lock-in period ends. That's why switching services in cloud computing is extremely difficult.
- Further, their issues and recommended solutions are listed in a tabular form as shown in Table 6.2.

RQ3: Which are the most common security threats facing cloud computing?

We made a comparison between previous studies and listed the most common parameters. We compared them in form of a table as shown in Table 6.2. Confidentiality, integrity, availability, data security, and data privacy are the most common security threats.

RQ4: Why users are responsible for the security of data in cloud computing?

*Table 6.2* Cloud computing security issues and recommended solutions [12]

| Category | Issues | Solutions |
|---|---|---|
| Key management | Compromised key, outsider attack, data loss | Secret sharing, Schemes, Visual cryptography, Dummy shares, Replica keys |
| Data security | Weak key management and cryptographic algorithms, confidentiality, access control, trust management | Attribute-based encryption, ant colony optimization, data classification, trust-based mechanism, Fuzzy logic, cipher text encryption, genetic algorithm |
| Data privacy | Authentication, data protection, eavesdropping | Multifactor authentication, ant colony optimization, multitenancy access control on role basis, trust-based mechanism |
| Anomaly detection | Intruder detection, compromised data, DoS attacks | Naïve bayes, decision tree, Dempster-Shafer Theory, SNORT, backpropagation neural network, and Fuzzy clustering |
| Cloud data storage & sharing | Unavailability of data, access control, storage optimization, data loss, leakage, data security, data breach | Deduplication, intelligent cryptography for big data storage, secure cloud storage, probabilistic methods for data classification, compression, attribute-based sharing |
| Vendor lock-in | Lack of interoperability, technical incompatibilities, cost, complexity, lack of portability, legal constraints | Standardization of API, fragmentation, horizontal and vertical integration |

Most people considered that CSP (cloud service provider) is responsible for cloud computing security, but it is not the same in all cases. Mostly, it is the cloud users who are responsible for any data breaches. Although with the strongest security measures in place for avoiding, tracking, and remediating breaches, the CSP won't be able to avoid a breach if the end-user doesn't configure their cloud security policy (or worse, deliberately circumvents the CSP's security tools) [13,21,34].

Table 6.3 shows the number of papers used and distributed by the year of publication. A pie chart of this table has been displayed in the methodology section.

*Table 6.3* Number of research papers distributed by year of publishing

| Year of publications | No. of publications |
|---|---|
| 2014 | 1 |
| 2016 | 1 |
| 2017 | 1 |
| 2018 | 3 |
| 2019 | 4 |
| 2020 | 4 |

## 6.5 CONCLUSION

We gave an overview of cloud computing in our paper. Cloud computing is an emerging trend in the industry of information technology. It's very beneficial for any organization and company [1]. But the security is the biggest challenge in this field. Despite all the benefits, cloud computing faces any kind of issues such as threats and challenges which we mentioned in this paper. We have also outlined the solutions to these issues that may improve cloud computing services in the future. Our whole work is based on previous studies. This survey combined the security challenges and threats in Table 6.1.

We made a comparison between different security issues and their solutions in Table 6.2. We've already discussed that cloud computing is an emerging technology; as it evolves, its challenges also increase. Although, a lot of surveys are in line that explored the challenges and threats that cloud computing is currently facing. So, we can conclude that whenever we'll talk about cloud computing security, it seems to be incomplete. As we have already mentioned that we have combined the research of other researchers in our paper. We have studied 14 papers for reviewing the used techniques to overcome the security issues and challenges of cloud computing. But our work could expose more solutions to these issues if we examine more research work.

## REFERENCES

1. M. I. Tariq, "Towards information security metrics framework for cloud computing," *International Journal of Cloud Computing and Services Science*, vol. 1, no. 4, p. 209, 2012.
2. M. I. Tariq, "Agent based information security framework for hybrid cloud computing," *KSII Transactions on Internet & Information Systems*, vol. 13, no. 1, pp. 406–434, 2019.
3. M. I. Tariq, "Analysis of the effectiveness of cloud control matrix for hybrid cloud computing," *International Journal of Future Generation Communication and Networking*, vol. 11, no. 4, pp. 1–10, 2018.
4. M. I. Tariq and V. Santarcangelo, "Analysis of ISO 27001: 2013 controls effectiveness for cloud computing," in *Proceedings of the 2nd International Conference on Information Systems Security and Privacy (ICISSP 2016)*, 2016, vol. 2, pp. 201–208. Roma.
5. S. Basu et al., "Cloud computing security challenges & solutions-A survey," in *Conference: 2018 IEEE 8th Annual Computing and Communication Workshop and Conference (CCWC)*, Las Vegas, NV, 2018, pp. 347–356.
6. F. Shahzad, "State-of-the-art survey on cloud computing security challenges, approaches and solutions," *Procedia Computer Science*, vol. 37, pp. 357–362, 2014.
7. N. H. Hussein and A. Khalid, "A survey of cloud computing security challenges and solutions," *International Journal of Computer Science and Information Security*, vol. 14, no. 1, p. 52, 2016.

8. M. I. Tariq, S. Tayyaba, H. Rasheed, and M. W. Ashraf, "Factors influencing the cloud computing adoption in higher education institutions of Punjab, Pakistan," 2017, pp. 179–184.

9. N. Subramanian and A. Jeyaraj, "Recent security challenges in cloud computing," *Computers & Electrical Engineering*, vol. 71, pp. 28–42, 2018.

10. A. Venkatesh and M. S. Eastaff, "A study of data storage security issues in cloud computing," *International Journal of Scientific Research in Computer Science, Engineering and Information Technology*, vol. 3, no. 1, pp. 1741–1745, 2018.

11. I. Ahmed, "A brief review: Security issues in cloud computing and their solutions," *Telkomnika*, vol. 17, no. 6, pp. 2812–2817, 2019.

12. S. Fatima and S. Ahmad, "An exhaustive review on security issues in cloud computing," *KSII Transactions on Internet and Information Systems (TIIS)*, vol. 13, no. 6, pp. 3219–3237, 2019.

13. M. Tyagi, M. Manoria, and B. Mishra, "A framework for data storage security with efficient computing in cloud," in *International Conference on Advanced Computing Networking and Informatics*; Springer: Singapore, 2019, pp. 109–116.

14. S. Chaudhary, F. Suthar, and N. Joshi, "Comparative study between cryptographic and hybrid techniques for implementation of security in cloud computing," in M. Pant, T. K. Sharma, S. Basterrech, and C. Banerjee (Eds), *Performance Management of Integrated Systems and Its Applications in Software Engineering*. New York: Springer, 2020, pp. 127–135.

15. M. I. Tariq, D. Haq, and J. Iqbal, "SLA based information security metric for cloud computing from COBIT 4.1 framework".

16. M. I. Tariq, S. Tayyaba, M. U. Hashmi, M. W. Ashraf, and N. A. Mian, "Agent based information security threat management framework for hybrid cloud computing," *IJCSNS*, vol. 17, no. 12, p. 57, 2017.

17. W. Dashti, A. Qureshi, A. Jahangeer, and A. Zafar, "Security challenges over cloud environment from service provider prospective," *Cloud Computing and Data Science*, vol. 1, pp. 12–20, 2020.

18. M. I. Tariq et al., "Prioritization of information security controls through Fuzzy AHP for cloud computing networks and wireless sensor networks," *Sensors*, vol. 20, no. 5, p. 1310, 2020.

19. M. I. Tariq, S. Tayyaba, M. W. Ashraf, and V. E. Balas, "Deep learning techniques for optimizing medical big data," in S. Dash, B. R. Acharya, M. Mittal, A. Abraham, and A. Kelemen (Eds), *Deep Learning Techniques for Biomedical and Health Informatics*. Amsterdam, Netherlands: Elsevier, 2020, pp. 187–211.

20. M. I. Tariq, J. Diaz-Martinez, S. A. Butt, M. Adeel, E. De-la-Hoz-Franco, and A. M. Dicu, "A learners experience with the games education in software engineering," in V. E. Balas, L. C. Jain, M. M. Balas, and S. N. Shahbazova (Eds), *Soft Computing Applications*, vol. 1222. Cham: Springer International Publishing, 2021, pp. 379–395. doi: 10.1007/978-3-030-52190-5_27.

21. A. A. Asghar, "Major security challenges of cloud computing technology," *European Journal of Molecular & Clinical Medicine*, vol. 7, no. 3, pp. 2956–2971, 2020.

22. M. I. Tariq et al., "Combination of AHP and TOPSIS methods for the ranking of information security controls to overcome its obstructions under fuzzy environment," *Journal of Intelligent & Fuzzy Systems*, vol. 38, pp. 6075–6088, 2020.

23. M. I. Tariq, N. A. Mian, A. Sohail, T. Alyas, and R. Ahmad, "Evaluation of the challenges in the Internet of medical things with multicriteria decision making (AHP and TOPSIS) to overcome its obstruction under Fuzzy environment," *Mobile Information Systems*, vol. 2020, p. e8815651, 2020. doi: 10.1155/2020/8815651.

24. H. P. Singh, R. Singh, and V. Singh, "Cloud computing security issues, challenges and solutions," EasyChair, 2516–2314, 2020.

25. Y. Pu et al., "Two secure privacy-preserving data aggregation schemes for IoT," *Wireless Communications and Mobile Computing*, vol. 2019, 11 p, 2019.

26. A.-A. O. Affia, R. Matulevičius, and A. Nolte, "Security risk management in cooperative intelligent transportation systems: A systematic literature review," in *On the Move to Meaningful Internet Systems: OTM 2019 Conferences*, Cham, 2019, pp. 282–300. doi: 10.1007/978-3-030-33246-4_18.

27. M. K. Kagita, N. Thilakarathne, T. R. Gadekallu, and P. K. R. Maddikunta, "A review on security and privacy of Internet of medical things," arXiv preprint arXiv:2009.05394, 2020.

28. A. Sohail, K. Shahzad, M. Arif Butt, M. Arif, M. Imran Tariq, and P.D.D. Dominic, "On computing the suitability of non-human resources for business process analysis," *Computers, Materials & Continua*, vol. 67, no. 1, pp. 303–319, 2021, doi: 10.32604/cmc.2021.014201.

29. M. I. Tariq, S. Tayyaba, M. W. Ashraf, H. Rasheed, and F. Khan, "Analysis of NIST SP 800-53 rev. 3 controls effectiveness for cloud computing," *Computing*, vol. 3, p. 4, 2016.

30. S. A. Butt, M. I. Tariq, T. Jamal, A. Ali, J. L. D. Martinez, and E. De-La-Hoz-Franco, "Predictive variables for agile development merging cloud computing services," *IEEE Access*, vol. 7, pp. 99273–99282, 2019.

31. S. Tayyaba, S. A. Khan, M. Tariq, and M. W. Ashraf, "Network security and Internet of things," in *Industrial Internet of Things and Cyber-Physical Systems: Transforming the Conventional to Digital*, IGI Global, 2020, pp. 198–238.

32. M. I. Tariq et al., "A review of deep learning security and privacy defensive techniques," *Mobile Information Systems*, vol. 2020, 18 p, 2020.

33. M. I. Tariq et al., "An analysis of the application of fuzzy logic in cloud computing," *Journal of Intelligent & Fuzzy Systems*, vol. 38, no. 5, pp. 5933–5947, 2020.

34. A.-A. O. Affia, R. Matulevičius, and A. Nolte, "Security risk management in cooperative intelligent transportation systems: A systematic literature review," 2019, pp. 282–300.

# Chapter 7

# Security algorithms for secure cloud environment

*Maryam Saleem, Maryam Rasheed, and Muhammad Imran Tariq*

Department of Computer Science, Superior University, Lahore, Pakistan

*Shahzadi Tayyaba*

University of Lahore, Pakistan

*Muhammad Arfan Jaffar*

Department of Computer Science, Superior University, Lahore, Pakistan

## CONTENTS

DOI: 10.1201/9781003107286-7

## 7.1 INTRODUCTION

### 7.1.1 History of cloud computing

First of all, John McCarthy used the word "computing" in 1960. In those days, mainframe computers were used, and the clients accessed the computing power through the duplicate terminals, but this method was costly because a lot of money was spent on buying resources for separate machines. Then there was the concept of shared computing for saving money. In 1970, the Virtual Machine concept was introduced by IBM. The virtual machine was the operating system that was used to run different operations on the same operating system at the same time. Then, cloud services (SaaS, PaaS and IaaS) were introduced. After this, Cloud deployment models such as Public Cloud, Private Cloud, Community Cloud and Hybrid Cloud are developed. Then the concept of a distributed data center was used in 1980 and 1990. In 2002, the Amazon Web Service was introduced that provides the features of storing like cloud. In 2009, "Google App" was invented by Google that enables the users to manufacture or produce their items and then present these items on the servers [1–3].

### 7.1.2 Cloud computing

Nowadays the most commonly used technology is Cloud computing. It has become a popular technology in a few years and spread all over the world due to its flexibility. Cloud Computing is considered the broader term used for the development of the Internet. Cloud computing is a cluster of servers that provide its services to the users on their own requirements. Its services are free of cost or at a manageable cost. In Cloud Computing, a large amount of data is stored and accessed. Information is also shared between different users day by day. Several organizations are switching to Cloud and many other wants to transfer [4].

Cloud Computing is explained by NIST as

> Cloud Computing is the technology that provides its services free of cost and on the demand of the user. There is no need to buy resources and hardware in Cloud environment because its services and resources are available as free of cost [5,6].

### 7.1.3 Cloud services and models

Cloud Computing provides its services in distributed manners. The most popular Cloud providers are Google and Amazon. A large number of people use the Google and Amazon apps at the same time to search for their desired subject. So, these are the most common and mainly used services of Cloud Computing because everyone knows about them very well and use these services at any place without any difficulty. Cloud Models are shown in Figure 7.1.

### 7.1.4 Cloud service model

Cloud Computing services are available in three types and are shown in Figure 7.2. These are as follows:

SaaS: Stands for "Software as a Service". All programs are offered to customers in accordance with their individual needs. A single service is accessed by many people simultaneously, so it is called multiusers service. It saves time by using the same service by different users at the same time. Some most common and important examples are Gmail or WhatsApp. Because many people use WhatsApp at the same time and many people use G-Mail at any time.

PaaS: Stands for "Platform as a Service". Because of having development tools and set of software, its services help to run and grow client's application on their own local computer without having tension of what's going on behind the service. It allows organization or group of organizations to access the same platform. Its most common example is Google App.

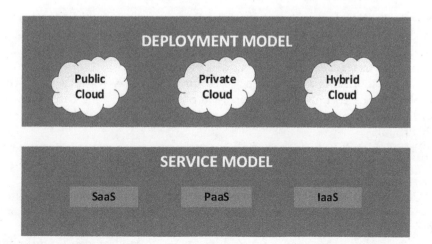

*Figure 7.1* Cloud models.

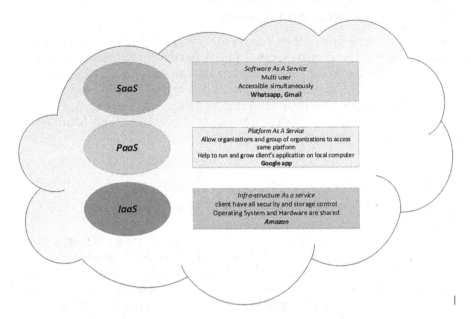

*Figure 7.2* Cloud services.

**IaaS:** Stands for "Infrastructure as a Service." Clients have all the security and storage controls in it. Operating systems and hardware are shared in it. Its most common example is Amazon. These all above of the services are provided as free of cost and are easily available with Internet facility.

### 7.1.5  Cloud deployment models

Now will discuss the models of Cloud Environment. Cloud Environment contains deployment models that are available in four categories, as shown in Figure 7.3. All models perform their tasks according to the user requirements. the explaination of these models are as follow:

**Public cloud:** It is the first type of cloud model. It is available to all the public free of cost. No restriction is applied to it. Anyone can access it without any problem. And it is the most common model that is easily available to all.

**Private cloud:** It is the second and more securable form of cloud models. It is not available to all the public. It is only accessible by one organization. Its range is limited to only one organization or one institute.

**Community cloud:** The third type is community cloud. The services of Cloud are accessible by several organizations. Groups of organizations can access it. So it has a wide range than the private cloud.

**Hybrid cloud:** It is the fourth and last type of cloud model. It works by combining the features of private, public and community cloud [7–9].

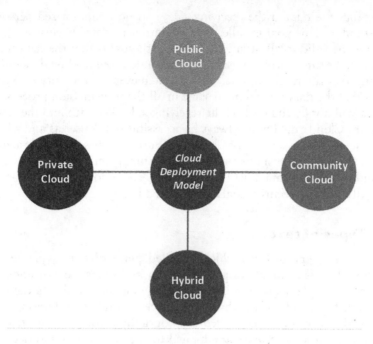

*Figure 7.3* Cloud deployment model.

## 7.1.6 Cloud security problems

Several organizations are switching to Cloud and many other wants to transfer. But those potential organizations have some concerns and obstacles while moving to cloud. One of the most common barriers is security. Security and privacy are the main problems of Cloud environment. As, nowadays, the crucial information and important files are stored in Cloud environment, if the data will not secure, the organizations will not be taking risk of transferring their data to cloud. So, it becomes essential to secure data on Cloud. Many hackers and unauthorized people are always ready to steal crucial data and important files. Important data can be leaked by an unknown person and it is also an issue of Cloud Environment. So, the security of the cloud environment must be ensured. If cloud data's security is not secure, it is obvious that the data is at a big risk and can be easily staled.

## 7.1.7 Goals of security

The first one is that the data is available to the users as and when they required according to their wish. This goal is known as the availability of Cloud to its users. The second goal is that the sender and receiver know about the data and no unauthorized person can access the data. This goal is known as the confidentiality or privacy of data. The third goal is that the receiver only understands the data at the receiving side, and no unauthorized person can understand it. This goal is called the validation of data. It ensures that the data must be valid in all situations. The fourth goal is that the data must be received in the same form as it is sent by the sender. The sending data must not be changed at the receiving side. This goal achieves the integrity of data and ensures that the data must remain same in all the transmission processes. So, the data will not be changed on the receiving side. The fifth and the last goal is that, the Cloud's data must always be accessible to the user as and when the user wants to use the services of Cloud Computing. If these goals are achieved, then the Cloud data must remain secure. It is important to achieve these goals of Cloud so that the data must be always protected and easily available to the users. All the cloud security goals are reflected in Figure 7.4.

## 7.1.8 Types of text

First, the first type of text, which is called plain text, is explained here. Plain text data is available in readable form and everyone can understand and access the plain text easily, whereas the ciphertext shows data in an unreadable form and no unauthorized person can understand the ciphertext. Security algorithms are also called cryptography algorithms or encryption algorithms. These both texts are applied to the encryption and decryption methods. Plain text is applied on the encryption method for providing security on data and the ciphertext is applied on the decryption method.

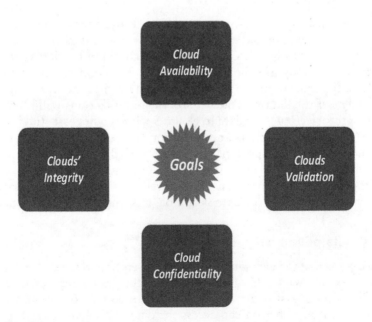

*Figure 7.4* Security goals.

### 7.1.9 Encryption and decryption method

Encryption and decryption methods are performed on two types of text, and both methods are illustrated in Figure 7.5. The first type of text is plain text and the second type is ciphertext. And these methods are opposite to each other. The encryption process is applied to actual text, which is called plain text. The decryption process is applied to encoding text, called ciphertext. Encryption is a process to change the readable text or message into an unreadable form. In this way, only an authorized person can gain access to the data and no authorized person would access it. Simple text refers to data that can be read, while ciphertext refers to data that cannot be read. The encryption process ensures data confidentiality and is a highly secure method. And decryption performs the opposite function of encryption. The decryption method changes an unread form of data into readable form. It, basically, changes the ciphertext into plain text.

### 7.1.10 Keys

Various keys are available in encryption and decryption methods to protect data. The first type of key is called a private key. Private key remains secret and is not shown by an unknown person. It is just known by both sender and receiver only. It provides more security on data because it remains secret and not available to all the public, and the security of data depends upon the private key as if the secret key is visible to an unknown person then data would be easily staled and the security of data can be easily broken by attackers. The second key is public key. This key does not remain secret. It is shown to everyone. It is available to the public. The key that is used toward the encryption side is called the encryption key. If encryption key is used on plain text, then the actual text changes into encoding text. The encryption key is used to change the readable data into an unreadable form. And the other key is used on the decryption side, so it is called the decryption key. It is applied to the ciphertext and the ciphertext is given at the end. It changes an unreadable form of data into readable form.

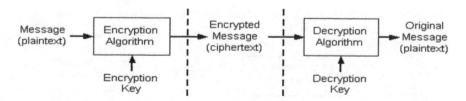

*Figure 7.5* Encryption and decryption methods.

### 7.1.11  Types of security algorithms

Security algorithms are also called cryptography algorithms or encryption algorithms. Basically, security algorithms are available in two categories as we discussed in Figure 7.6. If the Cloud's data remains protected, then it is easily available to the users, when users required it according to their requirements.

#### 7.1.11.1  Symmetric key security algorithms(SKA)

In Symmetric key security algorithms, only one unique key is used to encrypt or decrypt data and this secret key is known by both sender and receiver. An unknown person cannot access the key. These are the fast algorithms in terms of speed and time. SKA are more secured algorithms. and are mainly used in many applications nowadays. These are better algorithms because of their efficiency and performance. Security of symmetric key algorithms cannot be easily broken by attackers because they use a large number of key lengths. Symmetric algorithms use less memory for the encryption of data. Symmetric key security algorithms are available in two types of ciphers such as:

- Block cipher
- Stream cipher

Block cipher is the method that uses a block of bits of data. The block cipher takes plain text blocks of bits and transforms them into ciphertext blocks. It just works with blocks of bits and not with an individual bit.

Stream cipher takes only a single bit at a time as actual text and converts it into encoded text. It works with only one bit and not with blocks of bits. Mostly, a block cipher is used because it takes a large number of bits for the encryption and decryption method of data.

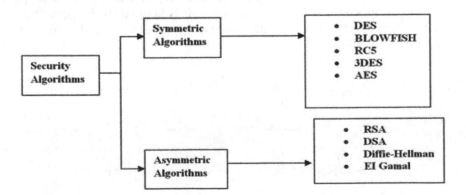

*Figure 7.6* Security algorithms.

### 7.1.11.2 Asymmetric key security algorithms (AKA)

In AKA, two separate keys are used to encrypt and decrypt the data and the third party involves in it. Usually, two keys are used in it and the one key is known to be a private key and second key is called the public key. These keys are used for protecting the data. But these are less secure algorithms and are used in small size of applications only.

The study includes only the detailed description of some important security algorithms that are explained as DES, AES, 3DES, BLOWFISH, RSA and Diffie–Hellman. These six algorithms are mainly used nowadays in many applications. So this research explains only the six most important algorithms in detail. And these algorithms are commonly used for providing security on data.

### 7.1.11.3 Types of symmetric key algorithms

Some important algorithms are discussed in symmetric algorithms and also explain the working of these algorithms. These are as follows:

- AES
- DES
- 3DES
- BLOWFISH

AES stands for "Advanced Encryption Standard." It was developed in 2001. It provides security against many attacks, and it is a very secure algorithm in the symmetric key algorithm's category. It uses different bits just like 128, 192 and 256. AES consists of some rounds. The rounds depend upon the size of bits. As the size of bits increase, rounds will also be increased according to bits. Each round further contains four keys. AES is an effective algorithm for both software and hardware. AES is a better algorithm in terms of speed and performance. It takes less time for the encryption of data and faster algorithm than others. And no nay attack is found against it. It uses less memory for the encryption of the data. Nowadays, it is commonly used in many fields just because of its security. DES is abbreviated as "Data Encryption Standard" and was developed in 1977. It provides security on data by using 64 bits. But it works with 56 bits on data and the other 8 bits applied for parity purposes. Sixteen rounds were also used on DES. DES algorithm is fast in speed as compared with 3DES. But DES algorithm is not a secured algorithm for several applications because its security can be easily cracked. It is less secure than the AES algorithm. It is only efficient for hardware but not for software. It takes more time for the execution of data. It is less reliable than the AES algorithm just because of its low performance. It uses large memory as compared to the AES algorithm. It is not too much used in many fields just because of its security. 3DES stands for

"Triple Data Encryption Standard." It is a new design of the DES algorithm and performs the same operation just like the DES algorithm. It provides more security on data because of using three-time security on data. It uses 56 bits of data as three times for providing more security on data. It is secure algorithm than DES, but it is comparatively slower. It works with 168 bits because of using 56 bits three times. Blowfish was developed in 1993. It is the strongest algorithm in symmetric key algorithm because it uses a large number of bits as 32–448 bits. Sixteen rounds are used in BLOWFISH just like the DES algorithm but Blowfish provides more security as compared to DES. It is available to the public without any cost. Its security will break down if the weak keys are used on data. No attack is found against it. So, it shows that AES and BLOWFISH algorithms are the best security algorithm in symmetric key algorithm's category. They are used in many applications just because of their outstanding security.

### 7.1.11.4  Types of asymmetric key algorithms

The second category of algorithm is described that is known as asymmetric key algorithms. Two main algorithms are discussed in asymmetric key security algorithm's category. Most important asymmetric algorithms are as follows:

- RSA
- Diffie-Hellman key Exchange

These are the most commonly used algorithms in asymmetric key algorithms. So, only two important algorithms are discussed here. RSA algorithm was developed by Rivest–Shamir–Adleman. These are the names of RSA algorithm's developers. And RSA algorithm was proposed in the name of its developers. RSA works with ten thousand twenty-four bits. It works with two different prime numbers and then numbers are multiplied. And one prime number shows the private key and the second shows the public key. Make sure that the secret key will not show to all the public because if the private key is shown by any hacker, then its security can be easily broken by attackers. It is securable for small size of applications and not suitable for large size of applications. Its security can be easily broken if small size of bits is used. It is slow because it takes maximum time for the encryption of the data. It uses large memory for the security of data. It ensures that the two prime numbers are less than by a given number "$n$." N is the total number that is used in the RSA algorithm. And the two numbers must be less than $n$. It prime numbers are greater than n then it becomes costly, and if two prime numbers are less than $n$, then its security can be easily broken. So, it is not too secure an algorithm for some applications. The second type of asymmetric key algorithm is Diffie–Hellman key exchange algorithm. It was generated in 1976. It is used to protect the data by sharing the same key between two people on an insecure medium or channel. But the two people do not know each other.

Even they have no information about each other. It provides less protection on data than the RSA algorithm. It takes more time for the encryption of data. It is not too much use in all fields. It uses more memory for the execution of data. It is not too much secure algorithm [10,11].

Section 7.1 shows the introduction to Cloud Computing in detail. Features of Cloud Computing are discussed with security issues. And the detailed introduction also explains security algorithms in this chapter. Section 7.2 includes a literature survey. The second chapter defines all the work of different researchers on security algorithms. From the literature survey, the findings are also drawn and described at the end of the chapter. Section 7.3 defines methods and materials about the security algorithms in detail. Section 7.4 draws result and the discussion about the topic was discussed above. And this chapter shows the result and finding from the literature survey and a comparison table of security algorithms is also drawn. Section 7.5 makes the summary of the above topic, and all the findings are explained in this chapter. At the end, the topic is summarized in this section.. Section 7.6 includes the references. It defines all the references of the researchers about the topic.

## 7.2 LITERATURE SURVEY

This chapter describes all the research work of different researchers in detail. From the literature survey, the conclusion and result will be drawn and stated at the end of this chapter.

Security algorithms provide security on data so that critical data may be secured and no unauthorized person can access it. Hackers and unauthorized persons are always active to steal data on cloud, so it is important to protect data by security algorithms.

The concept of the distributed data center was used in 1980 and 1990. In 2002, the Amazon Web Service was introduced that provides the features of storing like cloud in 2009, "Google App" was invented by Google, that enable the users to manufacture or produce their items and then present these items on the servers [8,12].

Prerna Mahajan and Abhishek Sachdeva [13] the encryption algorithms AES, DES, and RSA were investigated for security. The activity protecting information from unauthorized access, use, leakage, disturbance, alteration, inspection, capturing or destruction is information security. It is a generic concept that can be used irrespective of the form the knowledge can take (e.g., electronically and physically). In Cloud Computing platforms, security algorithms are used for securing cloud's data. The author discusses how to protect Cloud data using encryption algorithms. Encryption algorithms play a critical role in communication security. In this study, an overlooked is taken at current encryption techniques' effectiveness, i.e., AES, DES, and RSA algorithms. The researchers introduced three encryption techniques: AES, DES, and RSA algorithms and compared their encryption efficiency based on an analysis of stimulated encryption and decryption times at the time. The time it takes an encryption algorithm to translate plain text to cypher text is known as the encryption time. In relation to these encrypted algorithms, the AES algorithm is an excellent protected algorithm (DES, RSA). AES provides a broad block size for data encryption while consuming little power. By AES, the average number of bits needed to optimally encode a byte of encrypted data is 128 bits. AES has a quicker encryption and decryption rate than others. AES is the symmetric algorithm and uses both public and private keys for encryption and decryption of data respectively. By using these keys, the algorithm maintains the secrecy of the cloud's data between endpoints [13].

Nora Abdullah Algohany and Sultan Almotairi present a careful comparison of cloud computing security using the AES and DES encryption algorithms. The authors of this study compare previous related work. In cloud computing, security is important, particularly for the data saved in the cloud, because it has sensitive information and data imports to the too many users can access the same data. Unluckily, the growth of cloud users has been followed by an increase in cloud malicious activity and data is not entirely trustworthy. Cloud provides a virtual space for storing information and way of easiness for users that they can access their clouds data without worrying about similar space. And security is a major concerning and challenging factor for cloud database. The secrecy of the clouds is maintained by using encryption algorithms on the cloud platform. The algorithm is a step-by-step procedure or process to encrypt the data. The author studied the previous research to compare the working and efficiency of existing encryption algorithms (RSA, Blowfish, 3DES, SHA, MD5, Diffie Helman and two mainly AES and DES). In which, the author describes insight fully that in some research, algorithms are implemented by use of Net beans IDE with java and make a good comparison between encryption algorithms (AES, DES, RSA and blow fish). As a resultant, (AES uses small amount of execute time, DES uses small amount of encryption time, blow fish uses small amount of memory) and AES algorithm shows good performance on large data. The point that was highlighted by the author is that by the use of IDE, the desired requirement was achieved. The rush on computing is increasing day by day. So that cloud computing provides its services in distributed manners. This means multiple people will simultaneously use the same services. The service models are three types: IaaS, PasS and SaaS [14].

Cloud computing offers a lot of benefits, but it faces several issues and challenges about the security of data and privacy of cloud's data. For this very reason, many security-sensitive enterprises appear to stay away from cloud services, and that issue is addressed by Hibatullah Alzahrani [15] in his research study on A brief survey of cloud computing. He also goes through some of the benefits and drawbacks of cloud computing. The author's main point is that, due to security concerns, many businesses avoid the cloud environment without considering its benefits. Private clouds, social/community clouds, public clouds, and hybrid clouds are the four types of cloud computing. Cloud computing has numerous advantages, including ease of implementation, lack of maintenance and upfront costs, and fast and efficient applicability. Even though there are many issues in terms of data protection and privacy concerns and many security-sensitive enterprises prefer to stay away from cloud services for this very reason. One of the most exciting technologies is cloud computing with the potential to grow in the last decade. When Internet connectivity is becoming more and more widespread, much more quickly. It is an ideal candidate for many start-up companies in modern entrepreneurial society due to its ease of use, low maintenance and up-front costs and ease of scaling. However, private data protection remains a major concern and, in the absence of specific legislation to determine whether or not the responsibility for data leaks rests with service providers, users are bound to take preventive measures on their own and to use the cloud at their own risk. Most importantly, for the near future, cloud computing is here to stay and it would be wise for several organizations to adopt it [15].

Eghbal Ghazizadeh et al. [16] addressed the issue in regard to confidentiality of cloud's data by using the trusted computing concept to solve the identity thief in cloud computing in his research article. The authors survey different research to find issues with different protocols and weak areas. One of the modern generation technologies is cloud computing that is designed to respond to commercial needs and to drive and run appropriate software or solving IT management issues. As a helpful function for managing the users' data, federated identity and single sign-on have also been considered a critical aspect of the identity in a united league environment. Although cost and ease to operate are considered two of key advantages of cloud computing, confidence and security of data are two focal concerning areas of cloud computing for its users. Furthermore, via security and privacy guidelines, the cloud security alliance addressed and presented a broad security field for critical areas of focus in cloud computing. In a federated identity environment, there are some active issues and concerns, for example, in SPs and IDPs the misuse of information about user identity via SSO capabilities, identity theft of users, and user's trust. Such safety issues have to be taken into consideration in the actual process of implementation. Federated Identity Architecture is a form for vulnerability resolution. There are three architectures for implementing security problems in FIA, Liberty Alliance and Wfederation. The author suggested the use of trusted computing, federated identity management, and Open-ID Network Single Sign-On to combat identity theft in the cloud. The author provided an overview of the federated identity management system, cloud computing, single sign-on and SSO protocols such as Open-ID and O-Author. In addition, authors have also tried to list the security concerns of the single sign-on. While this paper also mentioned a variety of cloud authentication attacks, the key theme is to highlight the issues of identity theft, while some of the issues are partly solved already, but more consideration is needed for identity theft [16].

Sugata Sanyal and Hirohito Bhadauria addressed the various problems surrounding cloud computing and the related mitigation strategies in terms of security concerns. Cloud computing differs from other computing paradigms such as grid, and cloud computing in various aspects of on-demand services for cloud computing, such as cost, user flexibility interfaces, guaranteed Quality of Service, and autonomous structure, according to the authors. Cloud computing will allow current and new technologies' capacity and capabilities to be multiplied many times. The various types of cloud computing services can be classified into three layers. Infrastructure as a Service (IaaS) is the lowest layer, which offers all security and storage controls to clients. The PaaS layer is the middle layer that provides and enables an organization or group of organizations to access the same platform. SaaS is the top layer, which provides consumers with complete service based on their own needs and demands. The data is spread around a collection of networked resources in a cloud computing environment, allowing virtual machines to access it. Since these data centers can be located outside of the reach and control of users in every part of the world, there are many security and privacy concerns that must be addressed. Furthermore, the likelihood of a server malfunction, which has occurred often in recent times, can never be discounted. There are a variety of issues to be discussed when it comes to security and privacy in a cloud computing setting. The author's goal in writing this thorough survey paper is to expand on and discuss the numerous unresolved issues that challenge cloud computing adoption and diffusion among various stakeholders [17].

Yuhong Liu et al. [18] state the critical issues regarding computing paradigms. The author's main focus is on the limitation of the present issues of cloud computing and measures the weaknesses of present technology and draws out some future directions in the research area regarding sorting out critical issues of security and privacy of cloud computing. The rapid adoption of cloud is popular nowadays. The authors describe the main challenges which are faced by cloud computing nowadays. These main challenges are loss of control, lack of transparency, multi-Tenancy, virtualization and managerial related issues. In order to protect the cloud computing environment, numerous defense studies have been launched Reducing the probability of failure as a consequence of any adverse incident occurring is eliminated in computing such kind of previous working also under discussion by authors. The main theme of research is to also classify existing solutions (Encryption Algorithms, Third party auditing and Access control) and draw out the soft trust solutions and hard trust solutions (physical/hardware related). Some isolation handling models are also essayed by author's conclusions made from previous research. The authors, In three criteria, made classification on the current solutions according to the discussions are as:

1. Solution adopter, whose party the strategy can be used to resolve safety issues,
2. if the solution is used to help deter attacks or to respond to attacks that have already occurred, the reaction is important.
3. Hardware or software, from the firmware viewpoint, solves the security/privacy problems as an emerging and rapidly changing computing scenario. The authors highlight the future directions in a rapidly evolving computing scenario that challenges critical security and privacy issues in three directions, first challenge was based on lack transparency and management by Creation of sophisticated solutions to fix management-oriented management. The second challenge is refuted by author—to integrate several solutions from various categories shows considerable potential for solving security/privacy problems that a single, ad hoc security approach does not solve. Third, stimulating cooperation between diverse stakeholders on security is a very challenging direction in cloud computing. This paper analyzed some of the essential security and Safety issues in cloud computing, categorized various current solutions, and compared their strengths and weaknesses [18].

Muhammad Imran Tariq in his different research studies purposed a study on a framework for securing computing on the cloud. The authors addresses the most challenging topic of cloud computing protection and privacy and purposed intelligent measures in the individual and organizational environment. Cloud computing, nowadays, is a hot technology used among diverse enterprises and demands the biggest challenges in transparency, integrity, trustworthiness, confidentiality and security in all its affairs of use. So, basically the theme of the paper-based on security framework. The authors proposed an intelligent cloud computing security model that meets all the requirements of security and privacy and also compensates the others vulnerabilities. The author's main focus on to address the problem and issues regarding the security of deploying a model of cloud computing. To begin, the authors outline the security and privacy requirements (Confidentiality, Integrity, Non-desertion, Availability, Compliance and data auditing, Transparency, Governance and Accountability). The authors then summarized cloud attacks and mitigation techniques (Wrapping attack, Meta-data spoofing attacks, Denial of Service, Cloud injection attacks, Abuse and Nefarious Use of Cloud Computing, Insecure Interfaces, Malicious Insiders, Shared technology, lack of governance and compliance, data loss & leakage). Cloud risks and their counter-measures are also summarized by authors from previous research. Furthermore, a cloud computing security model was proposed that consisted four units (Verification and Validation Unit, Privilege Control Unit, Data Protection Unit, Attacks Detection and Prevention Unit). The authors concluded that designing risk estimation aids businesses in strategizing whether cloud technology is currently suitable for achieving their business goals with a reasonable level of risk. Furthermore, overseeing risk in the environment of cloud computing is going on more stimulating risks unless it meets to an acceptable level. In their conclusion, the above-discussed strategies are helpful for business utilization [10,19–26].

Muhammad Imran Tariq and others, while describing the main theme of the paper, explain the effects of vulnerabilities in Cloud and the consequent effect while focusing on security issues and solutions at different layers of cloud computing. Cloud computing offers mobile on-demand services to consumers with greater flexibility and less infrastructure investment. Because cloud services are delivered over the Internet using standard network protocols and formats, many security and privacy issues are posed by implied weaknesses in these protocols, as well as threats introduced by newer architectures. This article examined factors that influence the intent of cloud computing, weaknesses and attacks and identifies relevant solutions to enhance safety and confidentiality in the cloud environment. The above risks directly or indirectly impact the confidentiality, credibility and availability of Cloud services and resources at various levels and pose a range of Cloud security concerns. Thus, based on the various levels, we categorize security concerns: data storage level, application level, level of individualization, level of access controls, level of trust, level of network, level of compliance, level of audit and regulation. Threats at the application level have a direct impact on Cloud app security at the user layer. Threats or intrusions at the network level affect the overall security of cloud services, data and physical infrastructure. It can quickly access other clients' resources or assets by monitoring network behavior in the cloud. Attacks on data storage, including device daemons, have a direct effect on consumer data security. Individualization-level threats specifically impact the level of data storage protection and the level of application security. Authentication and access control threats affect the protection of legitimate users' services and resources. Risks at the trust level have a direct impact on the security of data-in-transit and migration applications. Audit, compliance, and policy threats directly affect a user's privacy, confidentiality, and integrity. Cloud computing will offer organizations numerous business advantages. However, there are several security and privacy-related problems. We aim to demonstrate the numerous vulnerabilities, risks and attacks that obstruct cloud computing adoption. We reviewed current strategies to resolve security concerns at various levels of the Cloud, while highlighting some open issues [6,16,18,27, p. 2013,28].

M. A. Khan [29] aims to illustrate and analyze the multiple unsolved problems threatening the acceptance and deployment of cloud computing, affecting the various stakeholders linked to it. The authors mainly focus on the comparative study of some of the current protection schemes for strengths and weaknesses. Cloud computing has the potential to destroy the facilities and solutions focused on IT used by the industries to set up a high-cost computing substructure. It argues to provide a flexible IT architecture that is accessible to lightweight mobile devices via the Internet. The entire information is stored over a set of data sources in cloud computing, enabling the data to be accessed through virtual machines. Cloud protection depends on the nature of the behavior of these artifacts and also on the relationships between them. For the most contrast, as the number of users is increasing in a public cloud allowing shared multiple environments, security risks are increasing and will become more inclusive. The attack surfaces that are susceptible to security attacks and mechanisms that enable effective defense of the client and server-side must be recognized. The providers of cloud services insist that their servers and the data stored in them are properly secure from invasion and manipulation of some kind. These companies say that the information on their servers is likely to be safer than the information on a range of personal computers and laptops. Furthermore, regardless of where the base repository of data is ultimately stored, the client data would be distributed around these individual computers as part of cloud infrastructure. The actions of these objects, as well as their relations, are crucial to cloud protection. Furthermore, as the number of users in a public cloud grows and a shared multi-tenant ecosystem is developed, security threats increase and become more common. Identifying attack surfaces that are vulnerable to security attacks, as well as mechanisms that allow successful client and server-side protection must be a priority. IT business generation architecture is a discussion of IT Enterprise's city generation architecture, which is a discussion about the city these days. Although the computer world has changed, it is still vulnerable to a range of security threats, ranging from security risks to application-level threats. These security risks need to be controlled to be able to preserve cloud security [29].

Since it belongs to the first group of encryption algorithms known as symmetric, DES encrypts and decrypts data with only one key. The main goal of this algorithm is to ensure data protection. The plain text is used first, followed by the 64 bits of data divided into two halves. Then the data of 56 bits are decreased with 48 bits. Then the output of one side is applied on the second side with XOR operation. And at the end, the ciphertext is generated. AES is also a symmetric key algorithm. First of all, for performing the encryption process, the plain text is taken, then a round key is used that contains further four keys. The keys are Substitution key, Shift Rows key, Column mixing key and add round keys. But the last cycle does not contain the Mix columns key. So, encryption is performed and for performing the decryption process the whole ciphertext is given to the next round. This round also contains four keys. In this way, the decryption process is generated and the plain text is available. 3DES performs a similar operation just like DES algorithm. But 3DES works by using DES algorithm for three times, so 3DES is considered slower than DES algorithm. It uses 168 bits because the DES is used as three times. So, it provides more security than DES algorithm. Blowfish contains 16 rounds just like DES but it is faster than DES. So, it provides more security on data. RSA is an asymmetric key algorithm that works with two different keys. Public and Private keys are used in the RSA algorithm. The public key is available to everyone and can be easily shown to the entire public, but the private key is not shown to the public. It has many faults so it is not secure for some applications. And it is a slow algorithm. Diffie-Hellman is used for the communication between two people, but its security breaks down in the middle of the communication. So, it shows that the AES algorithm is better and strong as compared to other algorithms [30,31].

## 7.3 RESEARCH METHODOLOGY

In this chapter, we discuss a systematic method of literature of taking a survey of the algorithm. It contains three phases, as given in Figure 7.7:

- Planning Phase
- Conducting Phase
- Reporting Phase

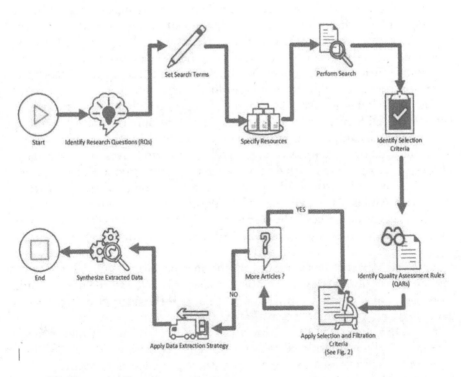

*Figure 7.7* SR protocol stages.

We established a protocol (set of rules) consisting of six levels in the first phase:

I. Specifying the issues of study
II. Developing the technique of search
III. Recognizing techniques for research collection
IV. Specifying the guidelines for quality assurance,
V. List the VI method for data extraction.
VI. Removing impurities, the data generated

Study Problem Configuration is dependent on the research purpose. At the next step, to retrieve the necessary and relevant documents, we built the search strategy that refers to the previous level. We have defined the search phrases and followed the process of selecting for the report, which is requested for an accurate search. We addressed the eligibility criteria at step three through which we define the conditions for inclusion and exclusion of survey questions. Further related links are also included from the sources we used to expand our research-related research. At level four, quality problems have been included to filter the related work. At level five, we define the retrieval method used to obtain the data needed to answer the concerns of the study. Eventually, the methodologies used to compose the collected data were established at the last point.

The following subsections give descriptions of the following protocols in this study.

### 7.3.1  Research question

RQ1: Which security algorithms were used in cloud environment?
    This query is to determine the algorithms for ensuring the data security that has been introduced for Cloud Environment.
RQ2: Which Security algorithm is best for maintaining and enhancing the security of the cloud environment?

### 7.3.2  Search strategy

i. The Question of Research concludes the key phrase.
ii. So, a new definition was adopted for search purposes by replacing main term keywords such as synonyms, jargon and alternate spellings.

### 7.3.3  Search phases

The specific search term is used to scan digital libraries while the word substitution is used to find the related article from Google scholar.

### 7.3.3.1 Survey resources

- Google Scholar
- Digital Libraries
- Researchergate.net

### 7.3.3.2 Study selection

Many articles relevant to the study purpose are supported by the search tools. It includes journals, conference proceedings and reports on studies. But none of them offer sufficient evidence for the search's intention. Paper selection phases are shown in Figure 7.8.

**Step 1:** Remove duplicated articles
**Step 2:** Apply incorporation and exclusion criteria
**Step 3:** Apply performance assurance rules to eligible articles
**Step 4:** Request references from Step 3 for certain related articles

### 7.3.3.3 Inclusion criteria

- Use Security Algorithm for Cloud environment
- Comparative studies that compare Security algorithms for Cloud's Data

### 7.3.3.4 Exclusion criteria

- Articles that include Security Algorithms but not for Cloud computing
- Articles that related to Cloud computing but not included Security algorithms

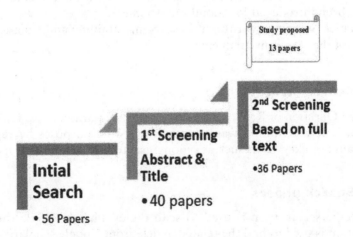

*Figure 7.8* Paper selection.

### 7.3.4  Quality assessment rules

QAR 1: Are the research priorities and objectives well-defined?
QAR 2: Is the history of cloud computing addressed?
QAR 3: Do the Security Algorithms have a simple definition?
QAR 4: Is the study suitable and acceptable?
QAR 5: Is the study performed in sufficient environment?
QAR 6: Are the experiment's results clearly established and reported?
QAR 7: Are the methods for analyzing the findings suitable?

## 7.4  RESULTS AND DISCUSSION

In this section, all results that are obtained from the literature survey are
discussed. Various security algorithms are explained and analyzed as AES,
DES and 3DES, BLOWFISH, RSA and Diffie-Hellman. A brief comparison
of security algorithms is also discussed. The Algorithms Encryption and
Decryption time charts are shown in Figures 7.9 and 7.10.

These algorithms use to increase the security of cloud data. It reveals that
all the algorithms have their own importance and benefits in term of performance and security The encryption and decryption time of these algorithms
are examined from previous studies.

And the Analysis of decryption time of these algorithms is:

As Security becomes the need of today's life. So, it's an important thing
to secure data and information from hackers. Nowadays, a large amount
of data is transferred to the cloud environment. Several organizations are
switching to Cloud and many other want to transfer. But those potential
organizations have some concerns and obstacles while moving to the cloud.
One of the often and common barriers is security. Security and privacy
of data are most important. For providing security on the cloud's data,

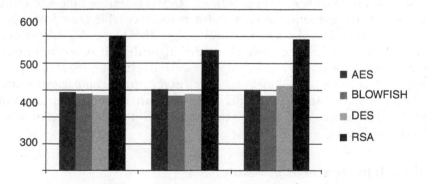

Figure 7.9 Algorithm encryption time chart.

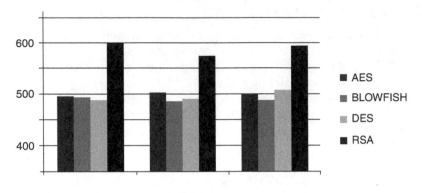

AES BLOWFISH DESAES BLOWFISH DESAES

*Figure 7.10* Algorithms decryption time chart.

different security algorithms are available. In this study, a survey on security algorithms is discussed in detail. A comparison table is also drawn which shows a comparison study between security algorithms.

Table 7.1 shows a detailed comparison between different security algorithms. And the comparison resulted that the AES algorithm is the best algorithm. AES consumes less time for the encryption process. It is too much of a secure algorithm. It is the best algorithm in terms of speed and performance. No attack is found against it. It is a very flexible algorithm, and nowadays it is commonly used in many applications just because of its outstanding security. DES is less securable than AES algorithm. And it is slower than AES algorithm. Its security can be easily broken by attackers if the weak key is used in it. 3DES algorithm provides more security on data as compared with DES but 3DES has slower speed than DES algorithm. Its security is not good as compared to AES algorithm because 3DES consumes too much time for encryption. RSA takes more time and more memory for the execution of data and it is less securable than AES algorithm. BLOWFISH is also a very securable algorithm like as AES algorithm. Diffie-Hellman is less securable than RSA algorithm. It is not too much used. Each algorithm has its own importance and is suitable for many applications. According to the brief literature survey and a comparison study, it shows that AES and BLOWFISH algorithms are the best algorithms in speed and performance. But AES is the best algorithm as compared to other algorithms [32,33].

### 7.4.1 Major features of result

From the results and discussion, it is clear that security algorithms play an important part in the protection of Cloud's data. Security algorithms become the need of today's life just because of security concern. There are many

Table 7.1 Comparison of security algorithms

| Parameters | Security algorithms | | | | | |
| --- | --- | --- | --- | --- | --- | --- |
| | DES | 3DES | AES | Blowfish | RSA | Diffie-Hellman |
| Category | Cloud computing | Cloud computing | Cloud computing | Cloud computing | Cloud computing | Cloud computing |
| Key lengths | 64 bits | 112–168 bits | 128, 192 or 256 bits according to cycle | 32 bits to 448 bits of data | 1,024 bytes | Key exchange management |
| Encryption technique | Symmetric encryption | Symmetric encryption | Symmetric encryption | Symmetric encryption | Asymmetric encryption | Used aAsymmetric technique for symmetric key exchange |
| Keys used | Same key used for both (encryption & decryption) | Same key used for encryption and decryption | Same key used for encryption and decryption | Same key used for encryption and decryption | Different (public and private) key used for encryption and decryption | Ensure secret key exchange |
| Encryption rate | High | Moderate | High | High | High | High |
| Rounds | 16 | 48 | 10, 12, 14 | 16 | 1 | 56 |
| Modification | It does not support any modification | The size of the key has been increased from 56 to 168 bits | 128, 192 or 256, its structure was flexible to multiples of 64 | Key length should be multiples of 32 | Key length can be 256, 512, 1,024, 2,048, 4,096 bits | No any modification in key length |

security algorithms like AES, DES, 3DES, BLOWFISH, RSA and Diffie-Hellman key exchange. But from results and discussion, shows that AES is a faster algorithm than all the above algorithms. It has many features such as:

- Fast speed
- Low memory usage
- Less time consumption for execution
- Better performance
- Use a large key length
- Secure algorithm
- Use the same key
- More flexible
- Includes Rounds
- Use in many fields
- It is efficient for both hardware and software.

## 7.5 CONCLUSION

Computing is a commonly used technology just because of its flexibility. Security is the main issue of Cloud's data. Security algorithms are available for security concerns. In this study, some security algorithms such as AES, DES, and 3DES, RSA, BLOWFISH and Diffie-Hellman are explained. The study enlightens those factors which play important role in maintaining security. The study helps us to determine the best security algorithm which is most efficient in its working. It is also helpful in the advance prevention of data hacking from cloud computing, so that a comparison table is also drawn which shows a comparison study between security algorithms. The table states that the AES algorithm is best in terms of speed and power consumption. The performance of the AES algorithm is better than other algorithms. Nowadays it is used in many applications just because of its security. It uses a large key length and provides more security on data. No serious attack is found against the security of the AES algorithm.

## REFERENCES

1. S. Siddiqui, M. Darbari, and D. Yagyasen, "A comprehensive study of challenges and issues in cloud computing," in *Soft Computing and Signal Processing*, J. Wang, G. R. M. Reddy, V. K. Prasad, V. S. Reddy (Eds). Singapore: Springer, 2019, pp. 325–344. doi: 10.1007/978-981-13-3600-3_31.
2. M. I. Tariq, "Towards information security metrics framework for cloud computing," *International Journal of Cloud Computing and Services Science*, vol. 1, no. 4, p. 209, 2012.

3. M. I. Tariq, D. Haq, and J. Iqbal, "SLA based information security metric for cloud computing from COBIT 4.1 framework," *International Journal of Computer Networks and Communications Security*, vol. 1, no. 3, pp. 95–101.

4. M. Khari, M. Kumar, and Vaishali, "Comprehensive study of cloud computing and related security issues," in *Big Data Analytics*, V. B. Aggarwal, Vasudha Bhatnagar, Durgesh Kumar Mishra (Eds). Singapore, 2018, pp. 699–707. doi: 10.1007/978-981-10-6620-7_68.

5. M. I. Tariq, S. Tayyaba, M. W. Ashraf, and H. Rasheed, "Risk based NIST effectiveness analysis for cloud security," *Bahria University Journal of Information & Communication Technologies (BUJICT)*, vol. 10, no. Special Is, pp. 23–31, 2017.

6. M. I. Tariq, S. Tayyaba, M. W. Ashraf, H. Rasheed, and F. Khan, "Analysis of NIST SP 800-53 rev. 3 controls effectiveness for cloud computing," *Computing*, vol. 3, p. 4, 2016.

7. I. Ahmed, "A brief review: Security issues in cloud computing and their solutions," *Telkomnika*, vol. 17, no. 6, pp. 2812–2817, 2019.

8. M. I. Tariq, S. Tayyaba, M. U. Hashmi, M. W. Ashraf, and N. A. Mian, "Agent based information security threat management framework for hybrid cloud computing," *IJCSNS*, vol. 17, no. 12, p. 57, 2017.

9. M. I. Tariq, "Analysis of the effectiveness of cloud control matrix for hybrid cloud computing," *International Journal of Future Generation Communication and Networking*, vol. 11, no. 4, pp. 1–10, 2018.

10. A. Bhardwaj, G. V. B. Subrahmanyam, V. Avasthi, and H. Sastry, "Security algorithms for cloud computing," *Procedia Computer Science*, vol. 85, pp. 535–542, 2016. doi: 10.1016/j.procs.2016.05.215.

11. S. Behal and K. Kumar, "Trends in validation of DDoS research," *Procedia Computer Science*, vol. 85, pp. 7–15, 2016. doi: 10.1016/j.procs.2016.05.170.

12. M. I. Tariq, "Agent based information security framework for hybrid cloud computing," *KSII Transactions on Internet & Information Systems*, vol. 13, no. 1, pp. 406–434, 2019.

13. D. P. Mahajan and A. Sachdeva, "A study of encryption algorithms AES, DES and RSA for security," *Global Journal of Computer Science and Technology*, 2013. Accessed: September 10, 2021. [Online] Available: https://computer-research.org/index.php/computer/article/view/272.

14. N. A. Al-gohany and S. Almotairi, "Comparative study of database security in cloud computing using AES and DES encryption algorithms," *JISCR*, vol. 2, no. 1, 2019. doi: 10.26735/16587790.2019.004.

15. H. Alzahrani, "A brief survey of cloud computing," *Global Journal of Computer Science and Technology*, December 2016, Accessed: September 10, 2021. [Online] Available: https://computerresearch.org/index.php/computer/article/view/1454.

16. E. Ghazizadeh, M. Zamani, J. Ab Manan, and A. Pashang, "A survey on security issues of federated identity in the cloud computing," in *4th IEEE International Conference on Cloud Computing Technology and Science Proceedings*, 2012, pp. 532–565. doi: 10.1109/CloudCom.2012.6427513.

17. S. Sanyal and P. P. Iyer, "Cloud computing: An approach with modern cryptography," March 2013, Accessed: September 10, 2021. [Online] Available: https://arxiv.org/abs/1303.1048v1.

18. Y. Liu, Y. L. Sun, J. Ryoo, S. Rizvi, and A. V. Vasilakos, "A survey of security and privacy challenges in cloud computing: Solutions and future directions," *Journal of Computing Science and Engineering*, vol. 9, no. 3, pp. 119–133, 2015, doi: 10.5626/JCSE.2015.9.3.119.

19. S. A. Butt, M. I. Tariq, T. Jamal, A. Ali, J. L. D. Martinez, and E. De-La-Hoz-Franco, "Predictive variables for agile development merging cloud computing services," *IEEE Access*, vol. 7, pp. 99273–99282, 2019.

20. M. I. Tariq et al., "Combination of AHP and TOPSIS methods for the ranking of information security controls to overcome its obstructions under fuzzy environment," *Journal of Intelligent & Fuzzy Systems*, vol. 38, pp. 6075–6088, 2020.

21. M. I. Tariq et al., "An analysis of the application of fuzzy logic in cloud computing," *Journal of Intelligent & Fuzzy Systems*, vol. 38, no. 5, pp. 5933–5947, 2020.

22. M. I. Tariq et al., "A review of deep learning security and privacy defensive techniques," *Mobile Information Systems*, vol. 2020, 18 p, 2020.

23. M. I. Tariq et al., "Prioritization of information security controls through fuzzy AHP for cloud computing networks and wireless sensor networks," *Sensors*, vol. 20, no. 5, p. 1310, 2020.

24. M. Almorsy, J. Grundy, and A. S. Ibrahim, "Collaboration-based cloud computing security management framework," in *2011 IEEE 4th International Conference on Cloud Computing*, July 2011, pp. 364–371. doi: 10.1109/CLOUD.2011.9.

25. M. Almorsy, J. Grundy, and A. S. Ibrahim, "Collaboration-based cloud computing security management framework," in *2011 IEEE 4th International Conference on Cloud Computing*, Washington, DC, July 2011, pp. 364–371. doi: 10.1109/CLOUD.2011.9.

26. M. Tyagi, M. Manoria, and B. Mishra, "A framework for data storage security with efficient computing in cloud," 2019, pp. 109–116.

27. M. I. Tariq and V. Santarcangelo, "Analysis of ISO 27001: 2013 controls effectiveness for cloud computing," vol. 2, pp. 201–208, 2016.

28. M. I. Tariq, S. Tayyaba, H. Rasheed, and M. W. Ashraf, "Factors influencing the cloud computing adoption in higher education institutions of Punjab, Pakistan," 2017, pp. 179–184.

29. M. A. Khan, "A survey of security issues for cloud computing," *Journal of Network and Computer Applications*, vol. 71, pp. 11–29, 2016. doi: 10.1016/j.jnca.2016.05.010.

30. S. Tayyaba, S. A. Khan, M. Tariq, and M. W. Ashraf, "Network security and Internet of things," in *Industrial Internet of Things and Cyber-Physical Systems: Transforming the Conventional to Digital*, P. Kumar, V. Ponnusamy, and V. Jain (Eds). Hershey, PA: IGI Global, 2020, pp. 198–238.

31. M. I. Tariq, S. Tayyaba, M. W. Ashraf, and V. E. Balas, "Deep learning techniques for optimizing medical big data," in *Deep Learning Techniques for Biomedical and Health Informatics*, A. Kelemen, A. Abraham, M. Mittal, S. Dash, and B. R. Acharya (Eds). Amsterdam, Netherlands: Elsevier, 2020, pp. 187–211.

32. A. Sohail, K. Shahzad, M. Arif Butt, M. Arif, M. Imran Tariq, and P. D. D. Dominic, "On computing the suitability of non-human resources for business process analysis," *Computers, Materials & Continua*, vol. 67, no. 1, pp. 303–319, 2021. doi: 10.32604/cmc.2021.014201.

33. M. I. Tariq, N. A. Mian, A. Sohail, T. Alyas, and R. Ahmad, "Evaluation of the challenges in the Internet of medical things with multicriteria decision making (AHP and TOPSIS) to overcome its obstruction under fuzzy environment," *Mobile Information Systems*, vol. 2020, p. e8815651, 2020. doi: 10.1155/2020/8815651.

# Chapter 8

# Cloud computing security challenges, analysis of security problems and cloud computing forensics issues

*Muhammad Tahir Zaman and Maryam Rani*

Superior University Lahore

## CONTENTS

## 8.1 INTRODUCTION

Cloud technology is the next phase of interties, realistically distributed databases that deliver computing power "as a service." NIST proposes the most frequently used description of the cloud services concept as "a paradigm for providing on-demand networking provisioning of customizable computational power (e.g., networking, computers, memory, programs, and activities) that may be swiftly provided and dispersed with minimum administrative labor or network operator ability to interact." The cloud

DOI: 10.1201/9781003107286-8

model has two main elements: multitenancy and elasticity. Multitenancy allows several tenants to share the same service instance. Elasticity allows a service's resources to be scaled up and down in response to current service needs. Both features are aimed at maximizing resource usage, lowering costs, and increasing accessibility. Industry and academics have embraced cloud services to serve a broad range of applications, from cognitively complex queries to lighter services, thanks to the virtual machine. Small and medium enterprises will benefit from the approach since it allows them to embrace IT without having to spend on infrastructure, software licensing, or other necessary items upfront. Furthermore, governments are becoming increasingly crucial of cloud computing to decrease IT expenses while also increasing the abilities and mobility of their offered services.

Data processing has evolved into numerical computation, edge computing, and, most frequently, cloud computing over the network. Cloud computing is now one of the most contentious problems in the telecommunication sector, prompting many businesses to move their information to the server since it offers several technological and economic advantages. Competitive servers include Google, Microsoft's Cloud Data Capabilities, and Amazon Web Services. In addition, several open-source web platforms, such as Solar Common Cloud Infrastructure and Phoenix, have persuaded consumers to use the Internet than in the past. When telecommunications companies began selling virtual private networks, the term "cloud" was coined. McCarthy proposed the fundamental notion of cloud computing in the 1960s, stating "calculation may ultimately be structured as a public service." Prior to VPN, telecommunications providers offered specialized step data connections, which squandered capacity. As a result, VPN connections are often used to transfer traffic in order to manage networking use, and information technology expands this to include servers and network architecture.

As per a Gartner report on cloud computing sales, the cloud segment was valued USD 58.6 billion in 2009, USD 68 billion in 2010, and USD 148 billion by 2014. Cloud computing appears to be a viable platform based on these figures. On the other side, it piques hackers' attention in exploiting any known flaws in the design.

In this article, we look at the current problems and issues surrounding security and efficiency. These concerns are divided into four categories: architectural design concerns, process improvement design concerns, cloud particular type concerns, and cloud decision maker concerns. Our goal is to figure out where the cloud model's flaws are. To emphasize the fundamental reasons of each shortcoming, we provide a comprehensive study. This will aid cloud providers and security suppliers in better comprehending the issue. It also aids investigators in recognizing the proportions and holes in the current problem.

The following is a breakdown of our paper's structure. In part two, we look back at prior attempts to define cloud security issues and concerns. Parts III through VII analyze the security issue from several angles. The major security enablers in the cloud paradigm are discussed in Section

VIII. Section IX summarizes our findings and identifies the essential characteristics that any cloud security solution should address. Furthermore, in part X, we talk about future work focused on one of the privacy factors we talked about before.

## 8.2 LITERATURE REVIEW

Numerous authors address the problems related to cloud computing security. The Cloud Services Use Factors division delves into the many use case scenarios and related needs that may be found in the cloud computing platform. Users, designers, and system administrators all contribute to their analysis of use cases. ENISA looked into the many security concerns related to cyber adoption, as well as the assets involved, as well as the hazards' probability, effects, and weaknesses in cloud computing that might lead to such hazards. CSA discusses similar attempts in "Top Risks to Cloud Services." Balachandra et al. go over the privacy service level agreement (SLA)'s requirements and goals for data storage, separation, and rescue. High-level security problems in the cloud computing model, such as data quality, invoicing, and confidential information protection, are discussed by Kresimir et al. Kresimir talked on ITIL, ISO/IEC 27001, and the Open Virtualization Format, among other incident response standards (OVF). XML-attacks, Browser-related assaults, and flooding attacks are among the technological security concerns raised by implementing the cloud computing architecture, according to Meiko et al. Bernd and his colleagues examine the cloud network's security flaws. The system divides the critical threats into three categories: innovation, cloud-related, and security controls-related. Subashini et al., concentrating on the SaaS model, examine the security problems of cloud service delivery models. The CSA addresses the most important aspects of cloud computing. In each category, they propose a set of best practices for cloud providers, customers, and campaign featured to follow. For several of these topics, the CSA produced a set of thorough reports. In our study, we looked at the cloud model in depth to determine the fundamental causes and major contributing aspects in the privacy problems addressed in earlier studies. It will aid in a greater understanding of the issue and the delivery of remedies.

## 8.3 DATA ANALYSIS

To support this research, we gathered 47 relevant articles on forensic investigation and subjected them to a study quality evaluation, keyword research, and research framework, which served as a data-collecting technique. This is critical to research since it gives a clear picture of the research topic in the subject. As shown in Figure 8.1, recent research advances in cyber forensic

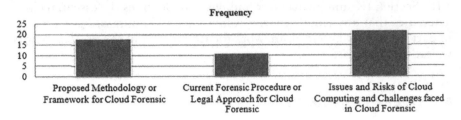

Figure 8.1 Research nature.

are mostly focused on concerns and dangers in cloud computing, as well as the obstacles that cloud forensic poses. In this sense, several publications are either two or three types of study. There's a whole total of 22 articles that discuss these concerns, indicating that knowledge of cloud security vulnerabilities has grown over time as computing has evolved.

The lowest number of study attention is on articles that illustrate existing forensic processes and legislative strategy toward the web platform; it may imply that the present forensic strategy has failed to address cloud computing. Scientists, on either side, are suggesting new regulations, techniques, and frameworks to improve the capacity to do cloud forensics, as seen by the 18 papers we examined in this area. Moreover, phrases convey to users the overall theme of a document. Strong relevance was carried out in this study to determine the pattern of presence of specific terms in the cyber science industry among the evaluated articles, as shown in Figure 8.2.

Information technology is mentioned 21 times out of 47 times in all of the articles. Computer evidence and data encryption are both close behind, with 15 and 14 times, accordingly. Specific keywords like digital

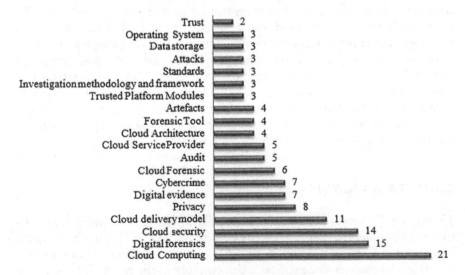

Figure 8.2 Analysis of keyword frequency.

attribution, incident generation, and 16 additional phrases, on either side, have only been mentioned once. The importance of the findings reveals that the majority of studies focused on the overall field of cloud forensics rather than a specialized one.

## 8.4  CLOUD COMPUTING ARCHITECTURE AND SECURITY IMPLICATIONS

There are three performance management methods and three major technology architecture in the Cloud Computing paradigm. The three existing solutions are (1) private cloud: a database server specific to a given organization, (2) public cloud: a cloud platform publicly accessible for registration and use of basic facilities, and (3) hybrid cloud: a hybrid cloud that can broaden to use funds in public clouds. Since cloud services are open for customers to serve their operations, including malevolent users, they are the most susceptible main contributions. The following are examples of cloud initiatives, as shown in Figure 8.3.

### 8.4.1  Infrastructure-as-a-service (IaaS)

Cloud services offer computational power, memory, and networking as web operations. The network virtualization underpins this service architecture. The most well-known IaaS supplier is Amazon EC2.

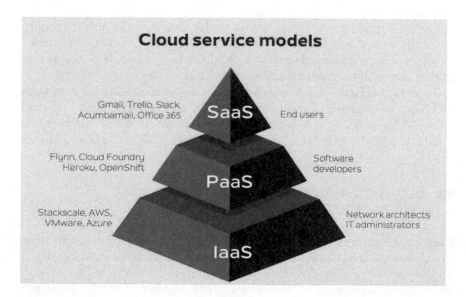

*Figure 8.3* Cloud service delivery models.

### 8.4.2 Platform-as-a-service (PaaS)

Wherein cloud services give systems, resources, and some other profes-sional services that let clients to create, publish, and maintain their own apps while configuring some of these systems or supplementary services through their own computers, the PaaS paradigm can be built on top of an IaaS model or immediately on front of data centers. The most well-known PaaS are Google App Engine and Windows Server Azure.

### 8.4.3 Software-as-a-service (SaaS)

Cloud providers deliver programs housed on network infrastructure as a web resource to end customers, rather than asking the consumers to down-load the apps on their PCs. This approach may be served in front of PaaS, IaaS, or network infrastructure directly. Sales Force CRM is an instance of a SaaS application.

## 8.5 TRUST AND SECURITY MODELS IN CLOUD COMPUTING

The capacity to interact with AR displays is perhaps one of the most impor-tant features. A partnership of five Japanese institutions, comprising JAIST, launched the enPiT-Security training plan (also known as SecCap) in April 2013. Tohoku University, Nara University of Science and Technology, Keio University, and the University of Management Safety are all the other coopera-tion participants.

The SecCap program is intended for undergraduates and aims to acquire the skills needed by IT security professionals through lectures and hands-on actions on protection elements of web browsers, programs, networking, as well as malicious software defenses and techniques.

As shown in Figure 8.3, every care model contains a variety of alternative solutions, complicating the creation of common security architecture for every service delivery model. Furthermore, various service provision methods may cohabit in a single virtual machine, complicating the risk management further.

## 8.6 CLOUD COMPUTING CHARACTERISTICS AND SECURITY IMPLICATIONS

Cloud services must enhance resource usage yet lowering costs in order to achieve effective resource use. At the same time, users must be able to acquire assets only as far as they are required, with the ability to raise or reduce energy usage in response to real demand. The cloud comput-ing model provides a win-win solution by including two essential features:

integrin and mobility. All traits have major consequences for the privacy of the cloud paradigm.

Multitenancy implies sharing of computational resources, storage, services, and applications with other tenants. Multitenancy has different realization approaches, as shown in Figure 8.2. In Method 1, each tenant has their own dedicated instance with their own customizations (customization may include special development to meet customer needs).

In method 2, every tenant has their own specialized server, similar to strategy 1; however, all versions have distinct settings. All tenants utilize the same example with real-time customization in method 3 (the program is separated into main network elements and additional components that are launched given current tenant requests—similar to Amazon web services.

In method 4, tenants are routed to a cloud infrastructure, which routes their requests to the most appropriate example depending on the load on the current context. The most dangerous approaches are 3 and 4 because tenants share the same storage and equipment. This information sharing compromises the anonymity of tenants' IT property, necessitating the use of protected virtualization. To prevent coordinated attacks that tries to founder with the accuser funds, there must be segregation between tenants' information (at remainder, storing, and transformation) and destination accountability, during which tenants have really no expertise or regulate from over particular location of their assets (could have a high ranking influence on data preservation like nation or continent extent).

Separation in IaaS must take into account VM capacity, processor, cognition, cached storage, and networking. Segregation in PaaS should include isolating between operating services and API calls. Separation in SaaS must be used to separate telecommunications service in on the same example by various tenants, as well as tenant information.

Flexibility refers to the ability to adjust the number of resources given to a system based on demand. The ability to scale up and down a tenant's contributions to the development of other tenants to utilize the tenant's given threshold value assets. This might cause problems with security. For instance, tenant is used to free up resources, which are now given to tenant B, who uses them to determine tenant A's former contents (similar to lag problem between DNS and DNS cache). Flexibility also contains a provider allocation mechanism that keeps track of the existing resources from supplier's number of eligible assets.

## 8.7 CLOUD COMPUTING STAKEHOLDERS AND SECURITY IMPLICATIONS

Various people are engaged in the cloud computing platform: private cloud (an entity that schedule to cloud users), Internet provider (an entity that utilizes network infrastructure to deliver systems to end-users), and trade consumer. Every participant has its own current security technologies, as well as obligations (specifications) and abilities (provided) from many other participants. As a result, (1) a collection of protection criteria is defined on a system by several tenants that may be incompatible, so that every provider's protection specifications must be preserved and implemented at the provider-recommended intervals and at execution time, taking into consideration the potential of new conditions given current users' requirement to ameliorate potential risk. (2) User and provider must try to negotiate and cooperate on the imposed system security. However, there are no basic security specification expressions that cloud participants may use to describe and argue about the security features they offer/require. (3) Every participant can have their own safety new strategies for defining resources, anticipated risks, and their consequences, as well as how to avoid problems. Both cloud service providers (who are unaware of the elements and safety needs of services housed on their networks) and cloud users (who are unaware of the materials and security measures of activities based on their technologies) lose control when they embrace the public cloud. Security SLA made critical an element of the strategy for defining, enforcing, and analyzing security characteristics. SLAs, on the other hand, still leave security characteristics out of their requirements [14]. Furthermore, SLAs are greater contracts that do not include the specifics of security rules and controls, as well as how to alter them in real time.

Data centers, on either hand, are unable to implement efficient and safe security measures since they are unaware of the designs of managed services. Moreover, computing resources are confronted with a slew of new safety regulations, even while maintaining a diverse set of security controls that must be maintained. The protection controllers' jobs are made much more difficult by this. Between cloud producers and recipients, there must be information about what safety is implemented, what dangers present, and what breakdowns happen on the cloud infrastructure and its components. This is referred to as "trust but verify," in which cloud users should have faith in their suppliers but cloud services should give tools to assist users in verifying and monitoring privacy compliance.

## 8.8 SECURITY AND TRUST MODEL IN CLOUD

Aside from a basic inspection, numerous related recent studies have generated many approaches for forensic investigation, particularly in the security and trust areas. Some Internet users are not necessarily specialists in the area of computers. Traditional firms handle all sensitive information inside and have total control over their personnel, which is one of the most noticeable issues found.

According to Dimitrios et al., cloud migration has reduced the development of effective security procedures. Since the cloud's characteristics vary from architectural design, this is being re-evaluated. So, in order to secure the secrecy and integrity of data, it is advised that you use a suggested trustworthy third party; it can be regarded as a protection system in the cloud that forms a network of confidence.

In this context, it is argued that even if the cloud model is not completely open, suppliers can exercise some openness to outline what is really being performed in a certain region also discusses the necessity of cloud providers proposing security rules and the many types of security problems. In terms of privacy, corporations are accountable for all of their sensitive data; moreover, there is a fundamental weakness in organizations that are unfamiliar with data storage and control. The major barrier for adopting cloud services, as shown in Figure 8.4, is data protection safety problems around the cloud, which span seven phases of the information life cycle, including data production, transmission, usage, sharing, storage, archive, and elimination.

They do, however, give a few information securities that are now available. Standard process techniques are not designed for companies and data in the cloud since organizational borders have been stretched to the cloud. They also bring up the question of computer security.

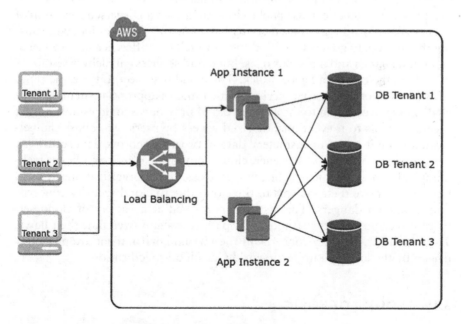

*Figure 8.4* Cloud computing characteristics and security.

## 8.9 CLOUD FORENSIC ISSUES AND CHALLENGES

Scientists have attempted to develop conceptualizations to solve these challenges; nevertheless, only a few of these are accepted standards for data gathering and proper work on the Internet. They suggest an iteration platform based on the currently utilized McCamish and NIST frameworks, which have common similarities but different methods. They propose that forensic experts produce evidence using a methodology in addition to current forensic methods. Regarding trust in a cloud context, the need for a security-based certification is emphasized that includes technology in order to improve cloud service confidence. It also demonstrates that the present use of SAS 70 (II) certification as an industry standard is merely the start and that it is currently unable to offer consumers the safety features that they want. According to Stephens and Stylianos, in addition to targeting consumers who profit from cloud platform providers' offerings, criminals will look at cloud computing to exploit any potential vulnerability in this new architecture and operating model. They argued that in order to prevent cybercrime, service providers (SLAs) should be strong. They also stress that safety must be a type of cloud solution, with designers focusing on management, hazard, and management as part of the design. There appears to be a tendency in existing Standards to a better knowledge of the cloud environment and tailoring business standards to it. Stated that while cloud service providers can be used for a variety of purposes, they can also be misused by customers with bad intentions; for instance, a consumer can use public cloud to launch a Dispersed Rejection of Service (DDoS) offensive on other customers or the cloud on its own, causing the services to go inactive. It's difficult to tell the difference between legal content demands and malicious ones, but cloud services can deliver resources quickly in the case of a DDoS attack. The cloud is subject to the same types of assaults as other Internet services, which makes appropriate management challenging. According to the authors, cloud providers should establish tight access controls to prevent unauthorized access by users who abuse the network and limit access to customers' data in order to improve data security.

According to Birk and Wegener, cloud computing offers significant technological and economic benefits; nevertheless, many organizations are still hesitant to move their systems to the cloud due to cloud security concerns and unknown dangers. The researchers looked at a variety of cloud settings and came up with methods to help these systems overcome their flaws. To summarize, security concerns in the virtual environment are primarily driven by the lack of a uniform worldwide cloud specification.

## 8.10 CLOUD FORENSIC

Currently, digital gadgets are growing at a breakneck pace, and analyzing the data created by these devices necessitates a massive amount of processing power. The notion of a 'Forensic Cloud' has been presented, with the goal of allowing a researcher to concentrate entirely on the investigative process. Although cloud computing has a clear definition, Svantesson and Clarke assess and disclose the dangers of cloud technology from the user and privacy perspectives.

In terms of cloud computing, according to Biggs and Vidalia, criminal users represent significant difficulties and dangers to end customers who use the cloud service supplier's products. The hackers will also investigate big data to see if there are any flaws in this new idea, architecture, or business strategy in cloud forensics. They argued that in order to prevent cybercrime, SLAs must be strong. They also mention bridge laws as a key concern. Because of the numerous locations of cloud data centers, as well as the ability for information to be kept across various nations, digital investigators and their capacity to perform successful investigations may be harmed. They also looked at the influence of cloud technology on criminal examination and discovered that, despite its efforts to be safe, cloud technology is still not suited for forensic science. ChengYan addressed the present cloud system's dangers, which include big data, individual rights, and provider (CSP) trust issues. He claimed that the cloud ecosystem is more vulnerable to cybercrime than in the past, necessitating the use of digital forensics. In terms of the CSP, he claims that end-users' data is kept and housed in the data center of the cloud provider, which saves business money on equipment and operations. Some organizations are unsure about the legal consequences of how CSP manages data passed over by consumers, which is one of the primary reasons to designate data centers to maintain the benefits of cloud computing. He also mentioned that the cloud ecosystem had issues with cybercrime forensics and proof retention.

In the article, he also suggested architecture for the cloud process that involves a dynamic allocation management system and an information gathering and analysis engine to address these challenges. Mason and George discuss the data flow of electronic data and the use of cloud computing for forensic investigation as a trend. That it has gotten greater attention in recent years and, as a result, generates uncertainty in the present judicial system, which isn't equipped to deal with cloud technology. The scientists clearly illustrate how to conduct an inquiry using the UK legal system, as well as how to collect evidence from foreign countries, in their article.

## 8.11 PRIVACY AND PERTAINING RISK IN CLOUD COMPUTING

Cloud technology is a technical system in which users entrust their data to third parties who store it on a web computer. As stated, virtualization has received only a small level of publicity from a private and legal standpoint. As Hou et al. point out, cloud computing comes with clear privacy and user hazards that must be addressed. Remote forensics, also known as cloud forensics, allowed researchers to gather evidence without physically visiting the place and examining the storage devices.

Parts of the cloud's fragmented data may belong to numerous data owners, while other parts are useless to a computer crime investigation. Evidence may disperse, resulting in the cloning of data exposing unnecessary features to investigators without the authorization of cloud providers. If a search is obtained, the server administrator can obtain the necessary data and pass it over to the investigator, but this contradicts the objective of the legal case's secrecy. To address these concerns, he offers a system that uses numerous relevant keywords for evidentiary material across stored files, preserving the inquiry's secrecy while only harvesting the data required for the inquiry.

Yan Zhu et al. developed the concepts of proof of retrievability (POR) and proven data presence (PDP) in this respect, arguing that audit services are essential for ensuring data integrity and availability. They suggested that audit services may be implemented using cryptographic techniques such as PDP. They also talked about the present challenges of checking the accuracy of data in a cloud context. Key encryption solutions for data integrity, depending on neural networks and sign systems, they claim, cannot operate on data owners without a local memory of the information.

They claim that most current systems cannot provide security properties versus untrustworthy CSP's deceit and forgery, but that POR/PDP methods provide a publicly available remote interface to verify and manage data in order to achieve public auditability. As a result, they argued that a new framework is needed in cloud inspection services that enable the safety of the traditional authentication method. They suggested an analytical review exporting infrastructure for validating the security of contracted online storage using cryptography evaluation method. They also construct a sample of an inspection system to assess the suggested technique. The efficiency of the aforementioned techniques and algorithms has been confirmed by their experimental findings. Their solution also has a reduced computationally and requires less additional storage for validation, according to the results. To assess the suggested method, they designed an architecture for audit service outsourced and built a prototype of an audit system. The efficacy of the mentioned methods and algorithms has been confirmed by their experimental findings. By understanding the prevalent digital forensic investigation methods that are linked with security, they are confident that the cloud computing model is in direct contradiction with a digital forensic investigation.

## 8.12 CLOUD FORENSIC INVESTIGATIONS

In the case of cybercriminals or other illegal activity, various police authorities frequently conduct digital forensics inquiries. They follow processes and standards that must be obeyed when dealing with evidence collected, which are outlined in standards. This is required to guarantee that the information found during the procedure meets legal standards and may be presented in court. Because of its fleeting nature, cloud inquiries provide a unique set of challenges for these forensic experts.

## 8.13 ISSUES DURING FORENSIC INVESTIGATIONS INVOLVING THE CLOUD

We explored the many types of difficulties that detectives face when working with the Internet and discovered that examining cloud services using current methodologies was inefficient. The most important difficulties appeared to be the researchers' physical, personal, and legal restrictions. When it comes to cloud investigations, this can be much more difficult since it involves thousands of virtual machines, many systems, and a huge number of cloud users, just one of which is relevant to the matter. It would cause service interruptions for people who aren't participating in the lawsuit. The machines are connected to the data center and communicate with each other without the participant's awareness. Furthermore, because of the accessible nature of the cloud, the only way to maintain identification when there is no physical connection is to utilize user IDs and passwords, which may be captured and misused by unauthorized users. As a result, there is a significant gap in the technologies able to help detectives in working with cloud data centers. It's tough to build these technologies for forensic information gathering since there's a lot of bridge creation and a lack of resources standardization.

## 8.14 SUMMARY OF SOLUTIONS PRESENTED

After some thought, we've included some of the answers given in the selected articles in this section. First, we looked for cloud-based digital forensics options. Cloud suppliers offer software as a service, which includes a specialized investigative system for researchers to use. Because the researchers would have to deal with huge disk disks, they also offer investigations as a service. This platform may offer investigators terabytes of data of memory to handle numerous pictures and can also assist them in cracking cryptography keys. Another of the suggested frameworks integrated the conservation and recognition stages to aid data protection; the framework's distinctiveness resides in the iteratively necessary for evaluating consumer equipment as evidence. Other frameworks presented include the use of a different data tracking system, which is relevant to the continuously changing cloud environment, as well as a data collecting and processing system to address cloud-related concerns. We have discovered solutions for specific stages of standard sensitivity analysis. For difficulties with the identification phase, it was proposed that a capability to monitor the status of client usage and logging be added to the

Software as Service architecture. Some innovative approaches, such as the usage of a threshold level in a monitoring system, were also presented. Next, there are approaches to safety, trust, and privacy problems in the cloud, with a secure informed cloud that uses a cloud authentication scheme being offered as a solution. It has an inner confidence element, which is performed using the physical system's hardware security module. In summary, the majority of cloud security issues are caused by the lack of a single standard paradigm, this can increase scientific researchers' capacity to conduct examinations by ensuring that worldwide standards are followed.

## 8.15 CONCLUSION

After some thought, we've included some of the answers given in the selected articles in this section. First, we looked for cloud-based digital forensics options. Cloud suppliers offer software as a service, which includes a specialized scientific server for researchers to use. Because the researchers would have to deal with huge hard drives, they also offer investigations as a solution. This service may offer investigators terabytes of data of memory to handle numerous pictures and can also assist them in cracking security keys. One of the suggested systems integrated the conservation and recognition stages to aid data protection; the program's distinctiveness resides in the iterative process necessary for evaluating a client's equipment as proof. Another framework presented included the use of a different data management system, which is important to the continuously changing cloud environment, as well as a data collecting and processing system to address cloud-related concerns. We have discovered solutions for specific stages of standard forensics frameworks. For difficulties with the analysis phase, it was proposed that a capability to monitor the condition of customer consumption and reporting be added to the Software as Service architecture. Some innovative approaches, such as the usage of a minimum value in remote monitoring, were also presented. Next, there are remedies to secure, trust, and privacy problems in the cloud, with a safe aware cloud that uses a cloud trust model being offered as a solution. It has an inner trust component, which is performed using the physical system's trusted platform component

In summary, the majority of cloud security issues are caused by a lack of a uniform general framework, which can increase forensic analysts' capacity to conduct examinations through the correct application of world standards.

Even though governments can strive to establish agreements to protect privacy for the sake of bridge inquiry, choosing which court or judicial system to present the subject remains problematic. However, the tools that are ready to facilitate a thorough audit cannot be used to conduct a forensic examination on the Internet. As a result, appropriate application of worldwide standards aids detectives in improving cloud performance.

For telecom operators, virtual servers, and cloud customers, the big data paradigm is one of the most promising computing models. However, in order to get the most out of the model, we need to plug in the current security flaws. Based on the information presented above, the Internet security issue may be summarized as follows:

- Many security issues are passed down from the technology employed, like virtualization and SOA.
- Multitenancy and isolation are significant aspects of the data protection challenges that necessitate a vertically approach from the SaaS level to physical infrastructure.
- To oversee and monitor such a large number of needs and procedures, risk management is necessary.
- The hybrid cloud should have a comprehensive security layer, as shown in Figure 8.3 so that any interaction to any cloud platform asset must first travel by security features. We suggest that cloud computing security remedies:
  - Focus on issue abstract, utilizing model-based techniques to capture diverse security viewpoints and link them in a cohesive cloud security model.
  - A feature of data center. Flexible regulatory interface should be provided through delivery mechanisms (such as flexibility motors) and APIs.
- Project Integration for multitenancy, in which each user may only view his or her own provided based, and flexibility, which allows you to scale up or down depending on the situation.
- Assist with the integration and coordination of other security measures at various tiers in order to provide integrated security.
- Adapt to environmental changes and the demands of users.

## 8.16 FUTURE WORK

We're looking at the cloud's current security issue. Our goal is to close the security gap that has emerged in cloud users' and cloud providers' system security procedures as a result of the cloud designer's adoption. To solve this problem, we must (1) describe various investors' regulatory standards from varied angles and level of care; (2) chart security standards to surface structure, safety shapes, and protection criminal laws; and (3) give information to cloud suppliers and customers on existing security condition. In order to address the challenge of cloud system security, we suggest using an adaptive model-based method. Patterns will aid in the abstraction of problems and the capture of different stakeholders' security needs at various degrees of detail. Adaptability will aid in the delivery of a cloud security paradigm that is interconnected, flexible, and enforced. The vicious circle will track system security in order to improve the present cloud security paradigm and keep cloud users informed about the protection of their property.

## FURTHER READING

1. P. Mell, and T. Grance, "The NIST definition of cloud computing," 2009, http://www.wheresmyserver.co.nz/storage/media/faq-files/cloud-def-v15.pdf, Accessed April 2010.
2. F. Gens, R. P Mahowald, and R. L. Villars, "IDC cloud computing 2010", 2009.
3. IDC, "IDC ranking of issues of cloud computing model," 2009, http://blogs. idc.com/ie/?p=210, Accessed on July 2010.
4. Cloud Computing Use Case Discussion Group, "Cloud computing use cases version 3.0," 2010.
5. ENISA, "Cloud computing: Benefits, risks and recommendations for information security," 2009, http://www.enisa.europa.eu/act/rm/files/deliverables/ cloudcomputing- risk-assessment, Accessed On July 2010.
6. Cloud Security Alliance (CSA), 2010. Available: http://www.cloudsecurity-alliance.org/.
7. B. Reddy Kandukuri, R. Paturi, and A. Rakshit, "Cloud security issues," in *Proceedings of the 2009 IEEE International Conference on Services Computing*, India, 2009, pp. 517–520.
8. K. Popovic and Z. Hocenski, "Cloud computing security issues and challenges," in *The Third International Conference on Advances in Humanoriented and Personalized Mechanisms, Technologies, and Services*, France, 2010, pp. 344–349.
9. M. Jensen, J. Schwenk, N. Gruschka, and L. L. Iacono, "On technical security issues in cloud computing," in *IEEE ICCC*, Bangalore, 2009, pp. 109–116.
10. B. Grobauer, T. Walloschek, and E. Stöcker, "Understanding cloudcomputing vulnerabilities," *IEEE Security and Privacy*, vol. 99, pp. 50–57, 2010.
11. S. Subashini, and V. Kavitha, "A survey on security issues in service delivery models of cloud computing," *Journal of Network and Computer Applications*, vol. 34, no. 1, pp. 1–13, 2011In Press.
12. T. Ristenpart, E. Tromer, H. Shacham, and S. Savage, "Hey, you, get off of my cloud: Exploring information leakage in third-party compute clouds," in *Presented at the Proceedings of the 16th ACM Conference on Computer and Communications Security*, Chicago, IL, 2009.
13. Microsoft. (2006, October, 2010). "Multi-tenant data architecture." Available: http://msdn.microsoft.com/en-us/library/aa479086.aspx.
14. Amazon. Amazon EC2 SLA, October 2010. Available: http://aws.amazon. com/ec2-sla/.
15. D. K. Holstein and K. Stouffer, "Trust but verify critical infrastructure cyber security solutions," in *2010 43rd Hawaii International Conference on System Sciences (HICSS)*, Hawaii, 2010, pp. 1–8.
16. Z. Wenjun, "Integrated security framework for secure web services," in *IITSI*, China, 2010, pp. 178–183.

17. W. Bin, H. H. Yuan, L. X. Xi, and J. M. Xu, "Open identity management framework for SaaS ecosystem," in *2009 IEEE International Conference on e-Business Engineering, ICEBE 2009*, Macau, China, 21–23 October 2009. pp. 512–517.

18. F. Elizabeth and O. Vadim, "Web application scanners: Definitions and functions," in *HICSS, USA*, 2007, pp. 280b–280b.

19. NIST. National Vulnerability Database (NVD), October 2010. Available: http://nvd.nist.gov/home.cfm20.OWASP; The ten most critical web application security vulnerabilities. Available: http://www.owasp.org/index.php/OWASP_Top_Ten_Projec.

20. H. Guo, T. Shang, and B. Jin, "Forensic investigations in cloud environments." in *Computer Science and Information Processing (CSIP)*, China, pp. 248–251, 2012.

21. J. Lee and D. Hong, "Pervasive forensic analysis based on mobile cloud computing," in *International Conference on Multimedia Information Networking and Security*, United States, pp. 572–576, 2011.

22. S. Hou, T. Uehara, S. M. Yiu, L. C. K. Hui, and K. P. Chow, "Privacy preserving multiple keyword search for confidential investigation of remote forensics," in *International Conference on Multimedia Information Networking and Security*, United States, pp. 595–599, 2011.

23. Y. Zhu, H. Hu, G. Ahn, and M. Yu, "Cooperative provable data possession for integrity verification in multi-cloud storage," 2012.

24. C. Kessler. "Anti-forensics and the digital investigator," in *Proceedings of the 5th Australian Digital Forensics Conference*, Australia, 2007.

25. D. Liu, J. Lee, J. Jang, S. Nepal, and J. Zic, "A cloud architecture of virtual trusted platform modules," in *IEEE/IFIP International Conference on Embedded and Ubiquitous Computing*, China, pp. 804–811, 2010.

26. M. Damshenas, A. Dehghantanha, R. Mahmoud, and S. Bin Shamsuddin, "Forensics investigation challenges in cloud computing environments," in *Cyber Warfare and Digital Forensics (CyberSec)*, Malaysia, pp. 190–194, 2012.

27. F. Daryabar, A. Dehghantanha, F. Norouzi, and F. Mahmoodi, "Analysis of virtual honeynet and VLAN-based virtual networks," in *Science & Engineering Research (SHUSER)*, Malaysia, pp. 73–70, 2011.

28. S. H. Mohtasebi and A. Dehghantanha, "Defusing the hazards of social network services," International Journal of Digital Information, vol. 2, no. 2, pp. 504–515, 2012.

29. A. Dehghantanha, R. Mahmoud, and N. I. Udzir, "Towards green frameworks for digital forensics investigation," *Journal of Convergence Information Technology (JCIT)*, vol. 8, no. 2, pp. 669–678, 2013.

30. M. Sidheeq, A. Dehghantanha, and G. Kananparan, "Utilizing trusted platform module to mitigate botnet attacks", *International Journal of Advancements in Computing Technology(IJACT)*, vol. 2, no. 5, pp. 111–117, 2010.

31. A. Aminnezhad, A. Dehghantanha, and M. T. Abdullah, "A survey on privacy issues in digital forensics," International Journal of Cyber-Security and Digital Forensics (IJCSDF), vol. 1, no. 4, pp. 311-323, 2013.

32. H. Salehi, R. Boostani, and A. Aminnezhad, "A new hybrid algorithm to solve the task scheduling problem in grid computing," International Journal of Computer Applications, vol. 62, no. 4, pp. 37-40, 2013.

33. A. Dehghantanha, R. Mahmod, N. I. Udzir, and Z. A. Zulkarnain, "User-centered privacy and trust model in cloud computing systems," in *Computer and Network Technology*, India, pp. 326–332, 2009.
34. A. Dehghantanha, "Xml-based privacy model in pervasive computing," Diss. University Putra Malaysia, 2008.
35. C. Sagaran, A. Dehghantanha, and R. Ramli, "A user-centered context-sensitive privacy model in pervasive systems," in *Communication Software and Networks*, Singapore, pp. 78–82, 2010.
36. A. Dehghantanha, N. Udzir, and R. Mahmod, "Evaluating user-centered privacy model (UPM) in pervasive computing systems," in *Computational Intelligence in Security for Information Systems*, Spain, pp. 272–284, 2011.
37. A. Dehghantanha and R. Mahmod, "UPM: User-centered privacy model in pervasive computing systems," in *2009 International Conference on Future Computer and Communication*, Malaysia, pp. 65–70, 2009.
38. S. Parvez, A. Dehghantanha, and H. G. Broujerdi, "Framework of digital forensics for the Samsung Star Series phone," *Electronics Computer Technology (ICECT)*, vol. 2, pp. 264–267, 2011.
39. S. H. Mohtasebi, A. Dehghantanha, and H. G. Broujerdi, "Smartphone forensics: A case study with Nokia E5-00 mobile phone," *International Journal of Digital Information and Wireless Communications (IJDIWC)*, vol. 1, no. 3, pp. 651–655, 2012.
40. F. N. Dezfouli, A. Dehghantanha, and R. Mahmoud, "Volatile memory acquisition using backup for forensic investigation," in *Cyber Warfare and Digital Foresnsic*, Malaysia, pp. 186–189, 2012.
41. M. Ibrahim, M. T. Abdullah, and A. Dehghantanha, "VoIP evidence model: A new forensic method for investigating VoIP malicious attacks," in *Cyber Security, Cyber Warfare and Digital Forensic*, Malaysia, pp. 201–206, 2012.
42. F. Daryabar, A. Dehghantanha, and H. G. Broujerdi, "Investigation of malware defence and detection techniques," *International Journal of Digital Information and Wireless Communications (IJDIWC)*, vol. 1, no. 3, pp. 645–650, 2012.
43. F. Daryabar, A. Dehghantanha, and N. I. Udzir, "Investigation of bypassing malware defences and malware detections," in *Conference on Information Assurance and Security (IAS)*, Malaysia, pp. 173–178, 2011.
44. N. Borhan, R. Mahmod, and A. Dehghantanha, "A framework of TPM, SVM and boot control for securing forensic logs," International Journal of Computer Application, vol. 50, no. 13, pp. 15–19, 2012.
45. A. Dehghantanha, N. I. Udzir, and R. Mahmod, "Towards a pervasive formal privacy language," in *Advanced Information Networking and Applications Workshops (WAINA)*, Australia, pp. 1085–1091, 2010.
46. A. Dehghantanha, R. Mahmod, and N. I. Udzir, "A XML based, user-centered privacy model in pervasive computing systems," *International Journal of Computer Science and Networking Security*, vol.9, no, 2, pp. 167–173, 2009.
47. A. Dehghantanha, R. Mahmod, N. I. Udzir, and Z. A. Zulkarnain, "User-centered privacy and trust model in cloud computing systems," in *Computer and Network Technology*, India, pp. 326–332, 2009.

# Chapter 9

# Impact of big data in healthcare and management analysis

*Shahra Asif Haafza, Muhammad Subhan Dar,*
*Muhammad Imran Tariq, and*
*Muhammad Arfan Jaffar*
Superior University

*Shariq Aziz Butt*
The University of Lahore

## CONTENTS

DOI: 10.1201/9781003107286-9

## 9.1 INTRODUCTION

The term Big Data is used to promote technological development trends. It opens up new perspectives for understanding the world and making decisions. This number is increasing at a rate of 50% every year, or more than doubling every 2 years. Official statistics, job statistics, and other information are constantly being transmitted to the Internet. Not only has data become more accessible, but computers have also become easier to understand [1]. Big Data, defined as a large data set, has a high degree of disorganization [2]. In current years, various organizations around the world have produced a large amount of Formulated, half-structured and unorganized information, this heterogeneous data is called Big Data [3]. Big Data is used for larger data, more diverse, and complex structures that are difficult to store, analyze, and view for further processing or obtaining results. Big Data, produced by more and more resources, are based on the collected Internet clicks, account details, content created by users and social media, and also some online or commercial censorship contracts such as sales investigations and transactions of purchase. Big Data was also generated, for example, in the areas of genomics, health, engineering, operational management, industry, and the Internet. Until 2003, 5 Terabytes of human data have already been established in this volume of data in 2 days [4,5].

The public believes "Big Data" to be a revolutionary technology that drives a broad spectrum of technological advances, production processes, and opinions for knowledge management [6]. The specific characteristics of Big Data (capacity, diversity, accuracy, and dynamics) make it challenging to collect data from different scattered locations, store, share, and process data in real-time. Big Data has shown great potential in real-world industries and research communities [7,8]. Furthermore, to the aforementioned Big Data functions, by the wide range of applications offered, many present studies add new functions. The initiative of early 3Vs was extended to 4Vs of 5Vs of 7Vs [9]. The amount and demand for Big Data in healthcare are gradually increasing [10]. In current years, healthcare information systems built on Big Data quickly adopted different approaches to medical information to evoke current points in health and to inspire timely preventive healthcare [11].

The healthcare industry is a combination and supplement of various departments in the business system. These departments provide various facilities to provide patients with preventive medical care, social, and rest assured care. The healthcare organization includes nursing homes, telemedicine, medical trials, medical insurance, outsourcing, charitable organizations, and medical equipment [12]. The data gathered in the form of electronic health records, registration forms, patient medical records, and the outcomes of physical examinations and wearable sensors has grown exponentially. Lots of information and benefits are extracted from this data, for example, increased quality of work, diagnosis of a sickness, treatment, and delivery of medical services. In healthcare, Big Data has many traits, vast numbers, heterogeneity, and velocity [2].

Nowadays, researchers are working to connect Big Data and cloud computing but due to several security constraints, still security issues arise. The authors studied several security frameworks regarding the security of cloud computing and also check their feasibility with Big Data and concluded that still cloud security is a big challenge to handle Big Data [13–18].

This data needs proper managing and analysis to derive meaningful information [19,20]. Compared with other industries, the accessibility of Big Data in a healthcare organization is huge, and it is expected to increase exponentially in the near future [2,21]. Healthcare service providers usually involve doctors, hospitals, medical labs, clinics, pharmacies, imaging, and other specialists [2]. The rise of Big Data provides new opportunities for understanding and predicting the background or problems in the healthcare field [22–25]. As shown in a 2012 poll, the health data racked up almost 550 PB, accumulating almost 26,000 PB by 2020 [3]. The Organization of Health Technology broadcasts that the US medical Big Data has reached the scale of Zettabyte and may soon reach the scale of yottabyte [9].

To imagine this size, we would have to allocate ~5,200 GB of data for all individuals [19]. As per a McKinsey Global Institute investigation, if American healthcare providers use Big Data aggressively and strategically, they may yield over $300 billion a year. Due to declining healthcare expenditure, two-thirds of these savings will be accomplished. Thus, Big Data is more and more prominent in the medical field due to its various aesthetics and reliability [8]. Big Data is an EHR brain, as it is qualified to implement science information systems into social, administrative, and clinical analysis. Evidence-based medicine makes it much easier to explore past clinical data that notify decision-makers [26]. In aggregate, authors predicted the digital revolution to improve medical quality, minimize waste, and also provide physicians and researchers with specialized tools and resources from the extensive media [20,27–30].

Big Data's dream offers great potential for new medicinal research findings such as pharmaceutical discoveries, advancements in treatment, personalized medicine, the highest capital expenditure, and strengthened prognosis of patients. The massive amount of data presented in grand plans are generally alienated by trillions of dollars [31]. The use of Big Data in healthcare by Google Flux and HealthMap was officially publicized, and no general classification has been detected to date [15]. The emerging field of Big Data introduces many difficulties for medical institutions with the surge in data and information on health [16].

The medical Big Data-related concerns include contradictory data, fantastic numerous variables, and the need for data analysis in legitimate. A modern trend has also been initiated by Big Data projects to explore services and solve health problems [2]. The interpretation of Big Data is really a very difficult task, because of its special properties. Because Big Data itself will not have any complications, analysis is a very complex job [27]. Insights on the possible pitfalls of using Big Data concepts internally in the healthcare sector include:

- Medication error
- Threats to patient safety
- Protection of privacy [32].

The hurdles for its use have included a deficit of getting things done as quickly as possible, joint data interfaces, conflicting designation of biological entities, and poor supervision for data exchange frameworks. In a short period, one or more machinery cannot gather and process large data sets. All these limitations and obstacles have led to Big Data problems. As data becomes a more crucial part of our daily lives, Big Data problems become more significant. In addition to the difficulty of managing this data, failure to handle Big Data may represent a major

- Loss of economic share
- Negative impact on the organization's reputation
- Several ethical issues

Some Big Data instances violate fundamental political, social, political, and social rights. The data security of personal information is also addressed [15,27,33]. Although the healthcare sector uses Big Data, security and privacy of data are still the vulnerabilities that continue to grow [34]. The role of health Big Data has become a challenging job, a healthcare system built on early decision-making has huge potential to reduce the care cost, boost care importance, and eliminate costs and mistakes. Scientific programming has a major role to play in overcoming contemporary challenges in sizeable health care data management. The key steps of Big Data management in the healthcare sector are

- Data collection
- Data storage
- Manage data
- Data analysis
- Data visualization [10].

A huge proportion of health data needs to be checked and investigated in order to provide true medication administration. Antiquated data management tools are not appropriate to evaluate Big Data, also because the variety and number of data suppliers have improved over the last two decades. Need innovative Big Data tools and technologies to meet and manage healthcare data. Big Data is used to forecast diseases based on medical records [10]. As the volume of data in the medical industry continues to grow, it is inevitable to adopt Big Data technology to increase the quality of medical services. Although Big Data processing methods and platforms are integrated into the existing data management architecture of the healthcare system, these architectures still face difficulties in avoiding emergencies [35]. In health research, Big Data management is a major challenge in bio-medical computer technology for intelligence intensity and incorporation. It's not tough. and important optimized solutions that can provide high-quality and cheaply accessible information resources [36].

The process of studying a large volume of data to disclose hidden patterns and secret relations is called Big Data analysis [37]. Although data preparation and organization are essential to facilitate the record of raw data into the information process, it is necessary to study the newest infrastructure and technologies of health research to improve the worth of Big Data. The quantity, speed, biodiversity, and fairness of Big Data face numerous previously discussed data-management representations. The absence of analyzable data, the hindrances of data access, and the lateness of obtaining information hinder the progress of science and increase the working complexity of technical management [36].

Although part of Big Data analysis platforms technologies and tools has been understood in various fields, their impact on the execution and delivery of new use cases for potential medical applications by medical organizations demonstrate promising research directions [38]. Due to the extensive use of mobile and wearable sensor technologies, the number of data sources in the healthcare organization has grown quickly, which has filled the healthcare sector with a large volume of data.

**Generally, are four types of analytics in the healthcare field.**
- Analysis descriptive
- Assessment of diagnosis
- Analysis linear
- Recommended analytics [35].

BDA are the technology, techniques, method, and application that analyzes a large magnitude of data to comfort an organization, to better understand its business, and market and mark timely decisions. In particular, healthcare is very data-intensive and requires interactive and dynamic Big Data platforms and innovative technologies to advance patient care and services [39].

Our study focuses on the impact of Big Data in healthcare, we will discuss the positive as well as negative impacts of Big Data, how the use of Big Data helped in the healthcare field, and the evaluation of Big Data in healthcare. We also analyze healthcare management; in this paper, we review different tools and techniques used to manage health data. The importance of Big Data in healthcare has also been analyzed.

## 9.2  LITERATURE REVIEW

Big Data can also be used to predict illness based on clinical data. Big Data holds the potential so that doctors and researchers and leaders in health policy can reasonably think and eventually enhance the care of patients. The author uses Google Trends to analyze the big Healthcare data from 2010 to 2015. The results indicate that the term "big data healthcare" began to spread around the start of 2013. The authors highlighted a McKinsey & Company report showing that the cost of the public health system amounts to only about 17.6% of GDP [10].

The author, Patricia A H Williams, will participate in the vast assessment of knowledge in the space in which the potential for a beneficial view of both the aid is significant but have some problems in its utilization and choice like handling the degree, speed, veracity, and worth, uprightness, and therefore the linguistics translation is of the additional outstanding space of worries in clinical application and more explains that these kinds of difficulties haven't stopped the employment and investigation of giant data as a symbol supply in medical services [26].

The corresponding author, SAFA BAHRI, of this article, shows the effect of Big Data on health workers, patients, pharmaceuticals, and medical firms, etc., and investigates complex difficulties. In this article, the author also stated different areas, many of which are widely used by researchers to support their conclusions and findings. However, the researchers' main theme is to focus on the positive impact of Big Data in healthcare. Authors describe the concept of Big Data and its different definitions discussed in different papers and its evolution—how it evolves, from three Vs.: Volume, Velocity, and Variety to ten Vs. The article explains in the second sentence the mechanism whereby large data generate profit. For each step, the relevant emerging technologies are outlined and elaborated in detail. This section represents a great opportunity for technological analysis and processing of massive amounts and genres of data from various sources [9].

Author Michael A. Talias explains clearly that information and data related to healthcare increases rapidly. Furthermore, in the Arena of Healthcare, the Author Michael A. Talias spotlights their advantages, difficulties, and morals giving an expansive review to healthcare analysts, specialists, and wellbeing strategy producers. In Introduction, Author

Michael A. Talias concentrates on a myriad of problems relevant to ethics and problems that emerged in the healthcare era through the use of Big Data [27]. This Big Data framework has demonstrated potential for making changes and improvements in consideration conveyance and revelation of medicines, for example, diminishing medical cost, decreasing in clinic reconfirmations, emergency of patients in ED, and some more. Further in Data Section, the researcher complains strongly that Big Data is not as big as it seems as he proved this by giving some authenticable examples [31].

Mowafa S. Househ and others in this article review the current Big Data trends and pay special attention to the unintentional negative impact of Big Data especially medical care involving patients and clinical care. However, the author also discussed how knowledge management may also have damaging impacts on employee care, which many hospitals examined—medical expenses, patient mortality, and wrong decisions by healthcare policymakers. The authors also discussed that when it comes to healthcare, Big Data can create more problems than solutions, so we cannot say that the size is everything especially when it is related to healthcare [32]. The author proves that a tiny low range of the investigator is talking regarding security and privacy within the care discipline. This shows that there was a shortage of massive information analytics regarding privacy. More author describes some positive impacts of massive information in care. Some positive impacts like improved health delivery, reduction in crime, and terrorist act. What is more, the Author describes insightfully some advantages that area unit documented like finding the sickness at the sooner stage, inventory insufficiency in pharmaceutical, and higher pursuit of viruses through location-enriched social media massive information [40].

The authors state that Big Data doesn't just refer to instances of Big Data. It is made up of three attributes: volume, speed, and variety, named 3 V. In a few years, this definition has added two more Vs value and veracity. Also discussed is that biomedical data is not just very Big Data compared with other fields. The authors also suggested that to convert biomedical Big Data into sources of knowledge, the implementation of infrastructure and algorithms for continuous data storage, implementation, and monitoring can fill the unsatisfied gap in healthcare [41].

Uddin and Gupta share some studies that tell that every day we have generated 500 petabytes of healthcare data and say that more likely is expected to grow to 25,000 petabytes by the year 2020. It does not have an outstanding level if you accept it in the ground; however, once we notice ways to ingest, curate, and analyze the info in alternative ways, like in Watson, huge knowledge becomes fascinating. The author shares that his motivation for inscribing this article comes from the fact that huge knowledge has become a neighborhood of our lives and massive knowledge hides in it the solutions to several issues in any trade [7].

## 9.3 RESEARCH METHODOLOGY

The aim of the Systematic Literature Review (SLR) analysis methodology, based on supporting paperwork and publications in science articles, is to investigate the opposing perspectives of the theory of the big datasets of healthcare and to discover the history of Big Data in healthcare. Kamble et al. advocate bringing out a comprehensive review to find research discrepancies in a given research region and plan additional studies to be sought out to validate the limitations detected. Management theories used SLR techniques to analyze Big Data applications [2]. A thorough search of articles has been conducted on different documents such as Scopus, Springer, Science Direct, and Science Web.

We will follow the SLR steps in this manner in our research paper:

Each of them has been searched for, as shown. All search was undertaken between 2012 and January 2020. The search results are shown in Figure 9.1. We also discuss the number of articles which we refused as duplicates and because of a title not intertwined with our subject. Finally, after 150 articles and consulting their abstracts, we selected 35 to see whether the articles were of relevance. Although we discussed earlier Big Data in health in other articles, we rejected to mention Big Data without going into a study and simply outlining areas of health. Correspondingly, we opposed them because they

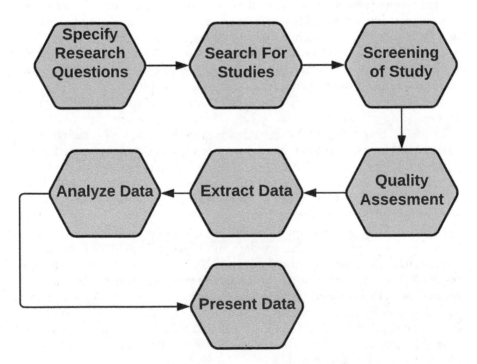

*Figure 9.1* SLR steps to be carried out.

did not have any information [42, p. 2]. We feared to propose mass amounts without coming through a concise summary and outline only the portion of healthcare so that those other statements could historically discuss vast numbers on health issues [43].

Because clarification was not provided, we left the information. Authors who work on a specific instance approachwe have investigated articles in the English and Spanish languages and when required to answer their abstracts and thesis papers were sorted. All these modules collect information from the web, namely cookies tracking, search history, buying history, and social networking. The site provides a Google Grippe Dynamics tool to monitor disease clusters in actual environments in the health sector [43].

The title and abstract and also the entire article are read when requested, to achieve a conflation of the articles. In this point, we can prove that the process of this project in this study poses some constraints. There was even a great risk of uncertainty when the data were retrieved. In many cases, it is just not easy to have a paper in the work, since the text is incomprehensible and can be slightly altered. We improved the review process by free verification to avoid this fool [42].

The present SLR protocol as shown in Figure 9.2 is based on three identical items: review planning, conduct review, and report review [43]. To pick the winner, this tool can assume the proportion of people living with influenza associated with Internet searches [44]. This is an inspection method. In terms of choosing the articles, the numerous different titles and scholarly articles of the knowledge gained were read. In reading the inclusion and exclusion criteria of the results of a few of the papers, the selection process of publications was solved.

## 9.3.1 Planning the review

In order to check for the actual database study results, proper words and phrases were only detected. Scopus, this year's web of science, Scihub and Springer seem to be the biggest databases in this SLR. These databases would be the largest determinants of research related to technological for medical health. Qualification was reviewed for reference lists of studies that seem valid. Next, efficiency and solidity were measured in studies meeting the minimum standards (inclusion and exclusion criteria). Finally, backward tariff searches and further quote searches were decided to carry out before the specimens of the selected studies were made official on the going SLR.

### 9.3.1.1 Performing the review

A search on Google Scholar, with the expression "big data analytics in healthcare," was devised to determine the key keywords. From the inaugural 100 search discoveries, the most excessive quantity was identified. From keyword professional and non, we characterized the term "trend

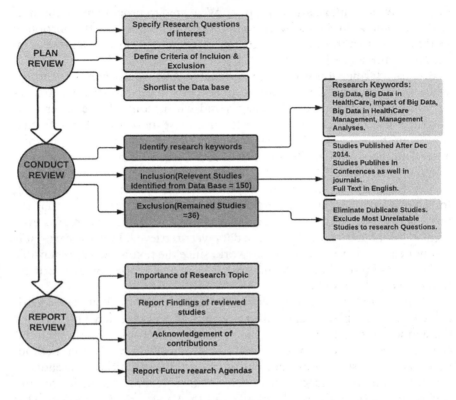

*Figure 9.2* Protocol for systematic literature review.

maintenance" as always being in use for "Big Data." The authors have identified Big Data Analytics applications in the area of health, including the statistical treatment of patient profiles with accurate modeling, prediction of the results of different treatments, and appraisal of the customers' most scientifically and financially beneficial treatments.

### 9.3.1.2 Presenting the review

The earliest known paper commissioned in the sample was in 2013, and as such, the character under discussion is presumably a rather novel concept for literature. The annual dissemination of findings indicates that the subject in recent years has gradually grown in importance. In turn, an improvement in average quotes collected through interviews in the experiment shows that the current topic of the SLR quickly will become more widespread in universities [43]. The objective is to identify the potential downsides including opportunities of healthcare analytics.

The comprehensive examination aims to enhance the understanding the reliable information problems around the world of healthcare. A full research report of the document mentioned the "Big Data" investigation. A critical evaluation was used between 2013 and 2020 to evaluate the papers on Big Data in healthcare [10].

The allocation of the 36 picked papers by year is shown in Figure 9.3. According to the same graph, the frequency of massive data publications in the health sector wasn't really consistent in the very first 4 years approximately (there were some articles identified in these years). Therefore, from the table below it is disclosed that the majority of reports is progressively escalating by 2018.

## 9.3.2 Research questions

For the energy transfer including its SLR of these strategies, those are the major research troubles:

RQ1. What are the strengths of big research in the world of universal health care?
RQ2. What are the impacts of Big Data in Healthcare?
RQ3. What are the healthcare Big Data's hurdles and prospects?
RQ4. What are the traits of healthcare of predictive analytics?
RQ5. How are Big Techniques and tools used throughout healthcare?

### 9.3.2.1 SLR protocol

This literature review comprises the general recommendations, based on whether the SLR handles the issue in Ref. [32].

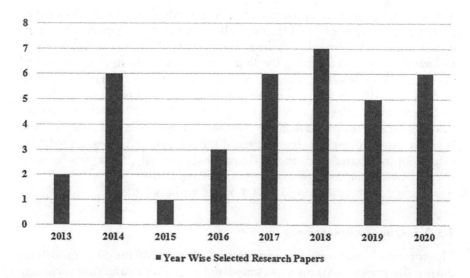

■ Year Wise Selected Research Papers

Figure 9.3 Year-wise selection research criteria.

### 9.3.2.2 Search strategy

Web of Science and Springer were two key automated information databases for digging for the compilation of related journal articles. Nevertheless, several strong and pertinent works have indeed been written. In this research, they should be included.

### 9.3.2.3 Search string

"Big Data," "Big Data in HealthCare" "Impacts of Big Data" and "Big Data in Healthcare Management" for the general and application were just the keywords mentioned by the search developers. In fact, necessary to ultrasound imaging an SLR, the analysis technique found the important keywords for the research questions using a different algorithm based on defined keywords.

### 9.3.2.4 Selection criteria

Reports depending on the relevant inclusion-exclusion criteria were chosen also by authors:

- Criterion for inclusion (e-publications leaning to the study of Big-Data healthcare and the analytics of Big-Data (e-documents posted from 2015 to 2019)
- The exclusion standards (reviews not targeting the timeframe from 2015 to 2019)

### 9.3.2.5 Study selection process

The knowledge appraisal procedure has been studied in various phases. The convergence of all Big Data, Healthcare Big Data and Big Data Analytic articles, is evaluated thoroughly in the automated application process according to keywords censored during the first process and therefore not dispersed between 2015 based on awareness and funds. In the very first stage, these articles were already found to have significant effects on the sampling frame, and irrelevant articles not published between 2015 and 2019 have been withheld. The relevant articles would be further screened on a title, excerpt, and keyword basis during the second stage of the screening. Also exempted were pieces not associated with the study proposed. Finally, these articles were selected based on countries. After completing all due process, 35 papers were picked for further consideration by the authors [45].

### 9.3.2.6 Quality assessment

The top-notch assessment is an essential element of the SLR guidelines during the review. (All findings supported a quality evaluation including its article after monitoring and feedback of abstracts of the PubMed database (the articles were selected based on the inclusion–exclusion criteria for each described major research matter [45]. The review strategy is given in Figure 9.4.

## 9.4 RESULTS AND DISCUSSION

Developed and preserved data types (e.g., imagery and textual descriptions) differ dramatically among different sectors. In the past, medical practitioners generated vast amounts of data in so many ways, such as record-keeping and situational demands. Predominantly, these large data can be stored on paper, but the current trend is to decode them quickly. A few of those in the healthcare field were included.is defined as a "set" <of electronically wellbeing data so big and convoluted that the integration of business approaches and/or machinery is difficult and costly.

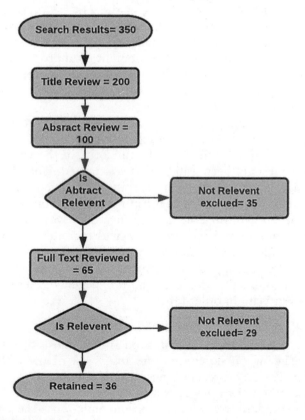

*Figure 9.4* Review strategy.

Health partners now and for the upcoming have but will have access to new valuable evidence stored as large data, only with scope, ambiguity, and heterogeneity of that knowledge.

Healthcare is very high in comparison with other areas and has been estimated to grow considerably in subsequent years. This information relates primarily to care providers and is designed and processed by healthcare providers in the remainder of developed countries. Health service providers comprise doctors, public and private hospitals and clinics, service providers (for example X-ray specialists), and healthcare professionals [27]. As with EHR, the standard medical and clinical data obtained from patients are kept through an electronic medical record (EMR).

The opportunities for improvements in performance, service efficiency, and insurance premiums together with minimal health errors can be garnered from EHRs, EMR's, PHR, MPM, and several other healthcare information components. The major insurance data contains the methodology of the healthcare payer (e.g. EMRs, medical prescription, and insurance records), genome studies (e.g., genotyping, energy metabolism), and some other evidence collected from the smart Internet of Things (IoT) site. At the beginning of the 21st century, the adoption of EHRs was slow, but after 2009, it improved exponentially. The implementation and use of such health data are dependent on information technology more and more. The development of appropriate technology that can elicit alerts and share patient data between patients, specifically by implementing a biomedical and health management system in real time, has gained momentum [19].

Healthcare has been one of the companies that create a massive amount of high-speed data including laboratory testing, prescribing medications, and appointments. Unfortunately, in the United States in 2011, there have only been 150 exabytes attained. The clinical trends are expected to rapidly overwhelm zettabytes or even yottabytes. The authors estimate the unfocused prescription notes, laboratory data, and ECG data for 90% of all clinical evidence The way to obtain, store, manage, and analyze high quantities of health content in many forms, and often provide sensitive information for users to promptly locate value proposed and insight, is recognized as Big Data capacities in the medical sector and according to the authors. Hence, there is a need to analyze this Big Data in order to:

- Lead to greater customer satisfaction and diagnosis quality
- Start reducing public expenditure to 17.9% of the 2010 domestic product. The report recommends the clinical collection
- To tackle the normal improvement opportunities, data should represent the standard strategies and recommendations. These features are obtained from many electronic sources [9] (Table 9.1).

*Table 9.1* Comparison table of different studies carried out for utilization of Big Data in healthcare

| Sr# | Authors and references | Subject studied | Results and description |
|---|---|---|---|
| 1 | Kamble et al. [2] | Advanced analytics applications in community health | All databases were compiled: general healthcare, diagnostic criteria, and research, operational efficiency, disease transmission, prevention, and treatment as well as provident fund. The conclusion is the recommended BDA capacity framework and its impact on the firm performance of healthcare organizations |
| 2 | Bahri et al. [9] | Big Data for healthcare | The present review identifies the profound impacts of Big Data on medical stakeholders, patients, doctors, pharmaceutical and health insurers and looks at tough activities to be properly considered to make the finest of all these Big Data and the applications available |
| 3 | Stylianou and Talias [27] | Big Data, massive issues in healthcare | This chapter investigates the growing era of sizeable data in healthcare and its benefits, challenges, and ethics, providing health researchers, practitioners, and health policy experts with a broad overview. In fact, a three-dimensional model was proposed for the medical evaluation of Big Data problems. This section addresses the aspects faced or faced in the near future by experts in healthcare |
| 4 | Dash et al. [19] | Management, analysis, and future prospects | Focus on providing details on the research on the influence on our everyday lives of Big Data on the revolution and national health sector |
| 5 | Adibuzzaman et al. [31] | The promises, challenges, and opportunities | Serve the same purpose to overcome the issue in three categories: data, equality, and interpretation. The institutional use of an existing list of an ICU considers these issues |
| 6 | Househ et al. [32] | Big data, big problems | In several cases, small quantitative tests are more exact and can contribute to improvements in health outcomes than Big Data methods. In short, Big Data for the health care industry can lead to more problems than remedies and, in brief, the "size is not always in healthcare when it applies to the use of data" |
| 7 | Senthilkumar et al. [10] | Big Data in healthcare management | Researchers compared the effective techniques for knowledge discovery and introduced new tools for the visualization of Big Data management. This document is useful to understand Big Data processes that can be used in health management |

*(Continued)*

Table 9.1 (Continued) Comparison table of different studies carried out for utilization of Big Data in healthcare

| Sr# | Authors and references | Subject studied | Results and description |
|---|---|---|---|
| 8 | Aishwarya et al. [46] | Big Data awareness in healthcare | In order to illustrate how it's used for creating public awareness, an attempt is required to investigate all Big Data technology used throughout multiple stages of cancer therapy |
| 9 | Nanayakkara et al. [41] | Big Data influence on dental health results | The following discussion highlights the recent progress, constraints, and challenges of biomedical Big Data in oral health care and investigates the alternative research use of oral big information to raise the efficiency |
| 10 | Nazir et al. [31] | Management, assessment, and academic programming of Big Data in health care | The ongoing published research paper is organized and evaluated based on the following research question and described criteria for the search process. This evaluation of the research processes would help doctors and practitioners to decide more quintessentially, hoping to be able to use the study as evidence to help patients and thus to formulate medications |
| 11 | Alonso et al. [44] | Big Data technologies and resources in the health sector | Monitoring of examined scientific articles demonstrates that data stores and procedures used in the health sector are a key element in accomplishment as they enhance the sensor for the diagnosis of propulsion patients or indeed the healed of hospital diseases or medical problems, the model parameters acquired |
| 12 | Wang et al. [36] | Challenges of Big Data processing of health research | To confirm the booking up for revisions, legislature research and business principles, tools, and processes of data management. Recognize the feasibility and relevance of biomedical information technology of these advances. Alternatively, discuss various problems which have massive consequences for technological solutions that will enable raw information to the customer value in health research in ways to construct the very next generation of digital devices |
| 13 | Asare-Frempong and Jayabalan [47] | Impact of Big Data on the enforcement of patient privacy in healthcare and education | This researcher looked at technologies for protecting the integrity of patients in the health sector with attention to information displayed in electronic health registries (EHRs). The use of a data management framework essentially incorporates the differences were found in the traditional designs, thereby providing more credible policies to protect privacy and safety |

(Continued)

*Table 9.1 (Continued)* Comparison table of different studies carried out for utilization of Big Data in healthcare

| Sr# | Authors and references | Subject studied | Results and description |
|---|---|---|---|
| 14 | Raja et al. [45] | Healthcare Big Data systemic review | The goal of this review was to evaluate the progress of Big Data healthcare analysis, in connection with applications and health adoption difficulties. The paper also mentions large databases of information, Big Data features, and intricate experiences when processing large data, as well as how large data analysts contribute to useful insights into these data packages. In brief, it explains the retrospective chart growth in healthcare and supports scholars to lay down the platform for effective health studies |
| 15 | Costa [33] | Big Data in biomedicine | This research highlights the main developments when incorporating omics and clinical health data in synthetic biology. The difficulties to nothing but the use of large data were thoughts of in biomedicine and translation science |

## 9.4.1 Big Data applications in healthcare sector

### 9.4.1.1 Healthcare prediction

Implementing Predictive AlgorithmsThe purpose of this section is to create a model which can predict new observations based on historical data. Accurate calculation of the quality of a predictive model. These predictions are based on fulfils by the proposed system in the statistics and predictive analytics store. Batch-oriented results are assembled into a model store [35].

### 9.4.1.2 Performance enhancement

Big Data and its analyses in the hospital industry help lower demand when clinical studies are managed on medical electronic records. These will give doctors down patient information in real-time, empowering them with just a solid foundation for a final diagnosis. Big Data's main objective is to reduce exploration expenses and enhance healthcare quality. The aim is to identify a method to inform of patients' medical trials, quicker discussion of results extracted from trials as well as to help nursing professionals to have even more medical knowledge. The achievement of real-time results enhances the personalization and results of working with various groups, involving chemists, doctors, and social services [42].

### 9.4.1.3  Determining risk factors

The appraisal of risk factors is amongst the most interesting outcomes to be used in larger datasets. The controlled research on the use of medicines used data to more rapidly and efficiently assess the allergic reactions of the drugs. Many parties are engaged in these clinical trials and it can also reveal new factors with the connections in very many centers. All information can be blended with risk factors. In comparison, much requires heavy involvement in the field of Big Data in healthcare [42].

### 9.4.1.4  Healthcare knowledge system

Cellphones and wearable technology remain part of normal life and have resulted in a large number of behavioral and psychological data generated. Moreover, machine learning has enhanced its scope significantly and has boosted data analysis speed. The IoT has designed the new concept "Smart health" in the Healthcare industry, encouraging systems to connect with the Internet and cloud computing. Smart Health guarantees therapist and correct healthcare for the prevention, diagnosis, and acceptance of all information on the Internet in real-time. The communication permits for innovative behavior of technology platforms includes the assessment of the experience of a patient who could really participate to a happier life and encourages users to screen their unilateral health care more intimately and deliberately [41].

### 9.4.1.5  Healthcare management system

For almost every healthcare sector management, research information can be applied. The theoretical fields of application include fraudulent activities, the prediction of disease outbreaks, omics, clinical results, pharmaceutical drug design, the insurance industry, personal care, and production of patients.

### 9.4.1.6  Big data in oncology

The data gathering on the tumor Genome, transcriptome, and medical evidence is indeed very widespread in oncology. There are also many authoritative documents. The possibility of handling features collected from these research findings in a detrimental calm treatment. Researchers and physicians acknowledge that improving the prevention of illness hinges on a profound knowledge of malignancy. The age of information accumulation in the disease primarily comes from the heavy improvements in the sciences of "Omics." A brain-boggling mystery was created by the NIH in 2006 [46].

### 9.4.1.7 Pharmaceuticals

Big Data, particularly in drug discovery, are being used in all phase of pharmaceutical development. Pfizer finally began Precision Medicine Analytics Environment, which blends electronic records data, clinical trials, and genomics to identify innovative drugs for specific patient populations [10].

### 9.4.1.8 Personalized patient care healthcare

Big information will enable the best and modified nursing experience to be delivered. New, massive impacts will prompt accurate therapeutic assisting updates, clinical guidelines, and patient emergency medicine in the immediate future to encourage specific and amended treatment to advanced patient medical interventions [10].

## 9.4.2 Big data: challenges and perspectives

Hurdles include interoperability and unstructured data, affordability, real-time analysis, load balancing, and many more, but obstacles to the users include a lack of and/or collaborative, common data interfaces, poor supervision to information delivery frames, and minimal visibility in the attribution of biological entities. The ability of Big Data may not only create considerable financial or market share losses but also have a negative effect on organizational reputations, as well as difficult system integration. In addition, the use of data glaciers introduces many moral concerns. The cybersecurity of personal data is, however, a matter of concern. While massive data management could have been a valuable tool in disciplines such as cancer research and climate change, it also could disrupt personal privacy and decrease civil liberties [27].

### 9.4.2.1 Data collection

In massive data administration, data collection is a massive issue even though it is difficult to handle from multiple studies. With its developments and countless avenues in data collection and transportation in the health industry, scientific advancement in the use of phones has led to. Like most other warehouses, most medical records dependencies receive data from a wide variety of sources, including EHR and social networks [47].

### 9.4.2.2 Data processing/analysis of Big Data

The concept of data processing is just not a new task in healthcare. There's always a very straightforward need to encrypt health records and keep them confidential, but to make them available if they are important for individual physicians, insurance firms, and registered agents. Due to the unique traits of larger datasets, their analysis is quite nuanced. Business information may also interpret the so-called 4 BVs, volume, speed, volatility, and forthrightness. But, while information technology is itself perfect, its assessment is a very tough challenge. The biggest issues emerging from the Big Data era are mainly exclusive to Big Data analysis [27].

### 9.4.2.3 Economic challenges

The amounts incurred depend on the bonuses paid to patients and clinicians during all clinical trips in the medical profession. Then momentum in this stage of manufacturing would impose taxes on the pharmaceutical sector and would negatively damage the workforce on those services without paperwork [45].

### 9.4.2.4 Data security and privacy

Given that insurance coverage leaders in the era of information technology are associated with important disturbed, the authenticity of healthcare information needs to be handled. Health data are particularly dangerous data, which must never be accompanied by unlawful activity to the public, and attacks can sometimes minimize potential fraud. Data security has become one of the largest health issues [45].

### 9.4.2.5 Data quality (bad data)

In the case of large-scale data frames, stored data is amongst the most difficult challenges, particularly in healthcare monitoring systems incorporating large quantities of data. Professional analysis of data also considers these systems unacceptable for supervision. This can be HDFS, NoSQL, or a combo of them, like MongoDB and SQL. It is, therefore, scalable and promises higher durability [35].

### 9.4.2.6 Healthcare data quality and interoperability

The concerns related to data quality and interoperability are a greater huge impediment for Big Data. In relation to other companies which might threaten the use of large data in the healthcare sector, the validity of the research is doubtful. The need to comprehend every moment of connection between some of the patients and the healthcare system would be another serious factor, often ignored whilst exploring Big Data [32].

### 9.4.2.7 Economic

Both of the above issues would also impact the global economy and insurance companies substantially. Additionally, the success of the health care industry to access and use available technology to assess large numbers of data would lead to substantial revenue and profits losses. As expectations are increasing, health agencies are pushing for new approaches in terms of managing scarce healthcare resources [27].

### 9.4.3 Management and analysis of Big Data

Due to technological advancements and digital transformation of hospital data, the medical industry produces a significant volume of health records. In recent years, HIT has enhanced the capacity to achieve, store, and send information globally securely in seconds and can enhance tremendously enhanced service performance and efficiency. It requires all applications of information to do their patient record database in digital form Ref. [45].

Big Data are the biggest challenge in treating this large amount of data. The data must be recorded in a structured document thatt is widely available and readable for accurate management in needed to create it available and for the science community. Can see the need for great quality access to technologies, protocols, and high-end hardware to be incorporated in a clinical environment as part of health data. Biology, IT, statistics, and mathematics specialists from diverse nationalities are expected to work together to accomplish this milestone on a huffed with preinstalled acoustic tools developed by estimation techniques developers, the extracted information can be found available but by sensors. Although maintenance and restoration are vital can be software and moment, a storage architecture that provides rapid information recovered and responsibilities based on the analyzed requirements important crucial. The information, which encompasses Hadoop, is still current. With its capacity to process and quantify large volumes of data, MapReduce and MongoDB are ideal candidates.[32–34] (Table 9.2).

### 9.5 CONCLUSION

In the present era, people are stronger and expected to donate substantial revenues to health care in order to achieve high infrastructure for health. As the world itself is a business world and everything is seen from a business perspective, the medical companies also move to realize higher values and advantages, the customer would lead to improved medical services.

Our analysis gave some insight into the "evil side" of the healthcare use of Big Data. And while we do not necessarily help to minimize the health benefits of Big Data, we believe that physical care cannot be implemented because of a variety of reasons, such as a loss of desire on the part of doctors, an inexperienced healthcare culture, dangers to patients' safety, health data quality problems, data privacy worries, and Big Data failures.

This research evaluated Big Data literature in healthcare. The substantive gap is identified and referred to in the empirical research. Some limitations were discovered, first, limited writings on Big Data in the health

*Table 9.2* Tools and technologies used to analyze and manage Big Data in healthcare

| Sr# | Tools and technologies | Description |
| --- | --- | --- |
| 1 | **Hadoop** [35] | Hadoop is a parallel processing framework that stocks and registers very modern computing clusters in its core architecture |
| 2 | **MapReduce** [3] | MapReduce data are commonly associated with Hadoop. An effective force used in many application areas, the MapReduce matters specified is more common than many other users realize. There are two stages in MapReduce: a mapping stage and a regression phase |
| 3 | **YARN** [36] | YARN is a framework for web-based planning and the tracking of cluster resources. It came with the introduction as a processes tab by Apache. YARN is usually classified as a large-scale number of different products for Big Data applications |
| 4 | **Spark** [19] | The spark has been seen as a confident attitude in preference to other techniques, including Hadoop or storm, also for batch and stream processing. It can connect a variety of methods such as HDFS, Cassandra, and HBase |
| 5 | **MongoDB** [36] | MongoDB is an open-source storage tool for visualizing the data. It has key features, such as good development and deployment, robust security |
| 6 | **Apache Pig** [29] | Apache Pig is an Apache Hadoop interface distributed processing framework. Pig Latin is the vocabulary for that platform used along with its centralized network to analyze big amounts of information |
| 7 | **Apache Spark** [11] | The open-source alternative to Hadoop is Apache Spark. The SparkSQL, streaming data (spark streaming), Machine Learn (MLib), and Web processing consisted of a coherent engine for optimum protection which involves higher degree libraries for SQL queries supports (GraphX) |
| 8 | **Apache Flink.** [19] | This is an open-source approach for asynchronous and real-time analysis of data. The Flink and MapReduce programming models share many characteristics. It allows recursive processing of pool information recorded through technologies such as flume and KAFKA in real-time. Apache Flink has several functions such as FlinkML |
| 9 | **STORM** [35] | For Hadoop MapReduce, Apache Storm is indeed an alternate if we really need heavy real-time treatment. Therefore, Apache Storm seems to be the standout keeper to develop such solutions whenever our mathematical formulation is expected to process an enormous amount of data at a quick rate |
| 10 | **Hive** [28] | Hive is an open data large volume of data summary, query, and interpretation. It allows large data sets maintained in HDFS analysis and incompatible shared folders like Amazon S3. Translates all requirements and refers them to Hadoop for assessment |

management system are available. This article comprises the news comments scattered year after year from 2015 to 2019. This paper describes the essential considerations and influences of conventional medical data submitted by plenty of researchers.

While evaluating the quality of journal articles, the other databases are neglected and can be tackled in future research. The research proposed integrates an SLR protocol and regulations to challenge existing systematic studies and the splitting of papers of massive healthcare data. This information will guide organizations to discover the current state of affairs of Big Data and its applications on a reasonable framework for formulating work.

## REFERENCES

1. S. Lohr, "The age of big data," *New York Times*, vol. 11, 2012.
2. S. S. Kamble, A. Gunasekaran, M. Goswami, and J. Manda, "A systematic perspective on the applications of big data analytics in healthcare management," *International Journal of Healthcare Management*, vol. 12, no. 13, pp. 226–240, 2018.
3. S. Kumar and M. Singh, "Big data analytics for healthcare industry: impact, applications, and tools," *Big Data Mining and Analytics*, vol. 2, no. 1, pp. 48–57, 2018.
4. S. Sagiroglu and D. Sinanc, "Big data: A review," in 2013 International Conference on Collaboration Technologies and Systems (CTS), San Diego, CA, 2013, pp. 42–47.
5. M. I. Tariq, S. Tayyaba, M. W. Ashraf, and V. E. Balas, "Deep learning techniques for optimizing medical big data," in *Deep Learning Techniques for Biomedical and Health Informatics*, A. Kelemen, A. Abraham, M. Mittal, S. Dash, and B. R. Acharya (Eds). Amsterdam, Netherlands: Elsevier, 2020, pp. 187–211.
6. A. Lugmayr, B. Stockleben, C. Scheib, and M. A. Mailaparampil, "Cognitive big data: survey and review on big data research and its implications. What is really 'new' in big data?" *Journal of Knowledge Management*, 2017.
7. M. F. Uddin and N. Gupta, "Seven V's of Big Data understanding Big Data to extract value," 2014, pp. 1–5.
8. S. Tayyaba, S. A. Khan, M. Tariq, and M. W. Ashraf, "Network security and Internet of things," in *Industrial Internet of Things and Cyber-Physical Systems: Transforming the Conventional to Digital*, P. Kumar, V. Ponnusamy, and V. Jain (Eds). Hershey, PA: IGI Global, 2020, pp. 198–238.
9. S. Bahri, N. Zoghlami, M. Abed, and J. M. R. Tavares, "Big data for healthcare: a survey," *IEEE Access*, vol. 7, pp. 7397–7408, 2018.
10. S. Senthilkumar, B. K. Rai, A. A. Meshram, A. Gunasekaran, and S. Chandrakumarmangalam, "Big data in healthcare management: A review of literature," *American Journal of Theoretical and Applied Business*, vol. 4, no. 2, pp. 57–69, 2018.
11. P.-T. Chen, C.-L. Lin, and W.-N. Wu, "Big data management in healthcare: Adoption challenges and implications," *International Journal of Information Management*, vol. 53, p. 102078, 2020.

12. D. Thara, B. Premasudha, V. R. Ram, and R. Suma, "Impact of big data in healthcare: A survey," pp. 729–735, 2016.

13. M. I. Tariq, "Towards information security metrics framework for cloud computing," *International Journal of Cloud Computing and Services Science*, vol. 1, no. 4, p. 209, 2012.

14. M. I. Tariq, D. Haq, and J. Iqbal, "SLA based information security metric for cloud computing from COBIT 4.1 framework", 2015.

15. M. I. Tariq, S. Tayyaba, M. W. Ashraf, and H. Rasheed, "Risk based NIST effectiveness analysis for cloud security," *Bahria University Journal of Information & Communication Technologies (BUJICT)*, vol. 10, no. Special Is, 2017.

16. M. I. Tariq, S. Tayyaba, M. U. Hashmi, M. W. Ashraf, and N. A. Mian, "Agent based information security threat management framework for hybrid cloud computing," *IJCSNS*, vol. 17, no. 12, p. 57, 2017.

17. M. I. Tariq, "Analysis of the effectiveness of cloud control matrix for hybrid cloud computing," *International Journal of Future Generation Communication and Networking*, vol. 11, no. 4, pp. 1–10, 2018.

18. M. I. Tariq, "Agent based information security framework for hybrid cloud computing," *KSII Transactions on Internet & Information Systems*, vol. 13, no. 1, pp. 406–434, 2019.

19. S. Dash, S. K. Shakyawar, M. Sharma, and S. Kaushik, "Big data in healthcare: management, analysis and future prospects," *Journal of Big Data*, vol. 6, no. 1, pp. 1–25, 2019.

20. M. I. Tariq et al., "A review of deep learning security and privacy defensive techniques," *Mobile Information Systems*, vol. 2020, 2020.

21. H. Chang and M. Choi, "Big data and healthcare: building an augmented world," *Healthcare Informatics Research*, vol. 22, no. 3, p. 153, 2016.

22. S. Ryu and T.-M. Song, "Big data analysis in healthcare," *Healthcare Informatics Research*, vol. 20, no. 4, pp. 247–248, 2014.

23. S. A. Butt, M. I. Tariq, T. Jamal, A. Ali, J. L. D. Martinez, and E. De-La-Hoz-Franco, "Predictive variables for agile development merging cloud computing services," *IEEE Access*, vol. 7, pp. 99273–99282, 2019.

24. M. I. Tariq et al., "Combination of AHP and TOPSIS methods for the ranking of information security controls to overcome its obstructions under fuzzy environment," *Journal of Intelligent & Fuzzy Systems*, vol. 38, pp. 6075–6088, 2020.

25. M. I. Tariq et al., "An analysis of the application of fuzzy logic in cloud computing," *Journal of Intelligent & Fuzzy Systems*, vol. 38, no. 5, pp. 5933–5947, 2020.

26. R. Hermon and P. A. Williams, "Big data in healthcare: What is it used for?" 2014.

27. A. Stylianou and M. A. Talias, "Big data in healthcare: A discussion on the big challenges," *Health and Technology*, vol. 7, no. 1, pp. 97–107, 2017.

28. M. I. Tariq, N. A. Mian, A. Sohail, T. Alyas, and R. Ahmad, "Evaluation of the challenges in the Internet of medical things with multicriteria decision making (AHP and TOPSIS) to overcome its obstruction under fuzzy environment," *Mobile Information Systems*, vol. 2020, p. e8815651, 2020. doi: 10.1155/2020/8815651.

29. M. I. Tariq et al., "Prioritization of information security controls through fuzzy AHP for cloud computing networks and wireless sensor networks," *Sensors*, vol. 20, no. 5, p. 1310, 2020.

30. M. I. Tariq and V. Santarcangelo, "Analysis of ISO 27001: 2013 controls effectiveness for cloud computing," vol. 2, pp. 201–208, 2016.
31. S. Nazir et al., "A comprehensive analysis of healthcare big data management, analytics and scientific programming," IEEE Access, vol. 8, pp. 95714–95733, 2020.
32. M. S. Househ, B. Aldosari, A. Alanazi, A. W. Kushniruk, and E. M. Borycki, "Big data, big problems: A healthcare perspective.," ICIMTH, pp. 36–39, 2017.
33. F. F. Costa, "Big data in biomedicine," Drug discovery today, vol. 19, no. 4, pp. 433–440, 2014.
34. H. K. Patil and R. Seshadri, "Big data security and privacy issues in healthcare," pp. 762–765, 2014.
35. L. Benhlima, "Big data management for healthcare systems: Architecture, requirements, and implementation," Advances in Bioinformatics, vol. 2018, 2018.
36. X. Wang, C. Williams, Z. H. Liu, and J. Croghan, "Big data management challenges in health research: A literature review," Briefings in Bioinformatics, vol. 20, no. 1, pp. 156–167, 2019.
37. G. George, M. R. Haas, and A. Pentland, "Big data and management," 2014.
38. V. Palanisamy and R. Thirunavukarasu, "Implications of big data analytics in developing healthcare frameworks: A review," Journal of King Saud University-Computer and Information Sciences, vol. 31, no. 4, pp. 415–425, 2019.
39. P. Galetsi, K. Katsaliaki, and S. Kumar, "Values, challenges and future directions of big data analytics in healthcare: A systematic review," Social Science and Medicine, vol. 241, p. 112533, 2019.
40. K. D. Strang and Z. Sun, "Hidden big data analytics issues in the healthcare industry," Health Informatics Journal, vol. 26, no. 2, pp. 981–998, 2020.
41. S. Nanayakkara, X. Zhou, and H. Spallek, "Impact of big data on oral health outcomes," Oral Diseases, vol. 25, no. 5, pp. 1245–1252, 2019.
42. I. de la Torre Díez, H. M. Cosgaya, B. Garcia-Zapirain, and M. López-Coronado, "Big data in health: A literature review from the year 2005," Journal of Medical Systems, vol. 40, no. 9, pp. 1–6, 2016.
43. S. Khanra, A. Dhir, A. N. Islam, and M. Mäntymäki, "Big data analytics in healthcare: A systematic literature review," Enterprise Information Systems, vol. 14, no. 7, pp. 878–912, 2020.
44. S. G. Alonso, I. de la Torre Diez, J. J. Rodrigues, S. Hamrioui, and M. Lopez-Coronado, "A systematic review of techniques and sources of big data in the healthcare sector," Journal of Medical Systems, vol. 41, no. 11, pp. 1–9, 2017.
45. R. Raja, I. Mukherjee, and B. K. Sarkar, "A systematic review of healthcare big data," Scientific Programming, vol. 2020, 2020.
46. H. Aishwarya, P. Pooja, K. Sowmya, and C. Manjunath, "Big data-awareness in healthcare", 2018.
47. J. Asare-Frempong and M. Jayabalan, "Exploring the impact of big data in healthcare and techniques in preserving patients' privacy," IJCSNS, vol. 17, no. 8, p. 143, 2017.
48. A. Belle, R. Thiagarajan, S. Soroushmehr, F. Navidi, D. A. Beard, and K. Najarian, "Big data analytics in healthcare," BioMed research international, vol. 2015, 2015.

# Chapter 10

# Privacy and security issues of big data

*Muhammad Arslan Yousaf and Muhammad Imran Tariq*
Superior University of Lahore

*Shahzadi Tayyaba*
University of Lahore

*Shariq Aziz Butt*
The University of Lahore

## CONTENTS

## 10.1 INTRODUCTION

A field that consumes conventional data processing applications software to deal with those data packets which are hard to deal and methodically withdrawing of information and examining techniques is called big data [1].

Tremendous data suggests huge and tangled datasets that normal creating Personal Computer (PC) programs are deficient for controlling. Big data can be explained in numerous ways through V's. 5V's are usually used to distinguish big data. velocity, volume, value, variety, and veracity (Figure 10.1)

DOI: 10.1201/9781003107286-10

*Figure 10.1* Five V's of big data.

Capacity content is a part of information. It travels rapidly. It contains different kinds of data and shows mixed data categories. It supports veracity, consistency and reliability of data. In this age of information, it offers illuminating records from colossal and assembles it quickly. It also cuts off the center in today's robotized world [2]. The data has been replicating ordinarily since 2015. Ordinarily, the data will develop on different occasions from 140 exabytes in 2007 to 42,000 exabytes in 2021. By the goodness of this imaginative amazement, the titanic data is ending up being logically a fundamental issue. Big data is an illuminating wide chamber for storing data, which is difficult to store on any other station and there sharing of data can lead to destruction of data. In-spite of such troubles, you can adjust enormous data. It also offers you better association and many other new features which are totally covered in data science. Furthermore, what does data science thinks about the same and streamed managing resemblance, graphs, stream planning, demanded directions and Artificial Intelligence

(AI) estimations[3]. For any situation in this rash appraisal environment traditional security and assurance parts are missing to investigate massive data. These troubles in monster data recall computation for spread and non-social conditions cryptography evaluations data source guaranteeing and separating safe data amassing granular framework control and consistent checking. Distinguishing the clarifications behind issues will achieve more capable usage of huge data. Thus this paper dissects and depicts bases on security and affirmation breaks and plans in massive data. This perspective would prompt an excitement for epic assessment areas and the advancement of new strategies. Likewise, the use of monstrous data in evaluation would make the plans safer. Section 10.2 presents a negligible rundown of huge data. Section 10.3 contains a depiction of huge data concerning the protection and attestation moves recorded as a printed adaptation. The results procured with security and security issues in immense data are discussed in Section 10.4, and Section 10.5 uncovers how to use gigantic data to stay aware of prosperity finally the end joins the importance and necessities to get colossal data correspondence [1,4].

## 10.1.1 Background of big data

The essential critical data design is developed in 1937. And it was mentioned by Franklin D Roosevelt's association in the United States and the common security act form into the rule in 1937 and the public authority expected to screen responsibilities from 26 million Americans and numerous million supervisors International Business Machines Corporation (IBM) got the consent to encourage a punch card scrutinizing machine for the tremendous bookkeeping project [5].

The essential data planning mechanism was displayed in 1942 and it was made by the British people to decode Nazi codes at the hour of the Second World War. Colossus was a device which was use to find the figures in seized messages at a rate of 5000 digits per seconds. Then task shrunk from weeks to days and days to hours. In 1964, the United States decided to build the fundamental worker ranch to store more than 742 million cost structures and 175 million courses of action of fingerprints by moving that load of information onto alluring PC tape that should be taken care of in a lone region, The endeavor was therefore left fear for 'Senior kin' anyway it is generally recognized that this was the beginning of the automated data amassing period [6].

In 2005, Roger Mogale's since O'Reilly Broadcasting created the tenure of big data curiously a time after the fact they completed the term Web 2.1. It recommends a huge game strategy of data that is hard to direct and deal with using regular business knowledge mechanical assemblies. In year 2004 new open source Hadoop was created by yahoo for recording purpose of whole world wide web. The goal was to record the entire World Wide Web (www) and nowadays the open source. Hadoop is used by a huge load of relationships to work through gigantic proportions of data. Relational association started to take shape which was regularly enlarging. Continuously spreading of data was removed fairly by Web 2.0. Imaginative new organizations progressively start to dive into this colossal proportion of data and governments start working on big data drives. In 2008, the Indian administration decides to take an iris yield special imprint and photograph of the total of 1.3 billion out of 2009. Eric Schmidt talks at the Taphonomy gathering in Lake Tahoe in California and he communicates that there were five exabytes of information made by the entire world between the start of advancement and 2003 Since a similar aggregate is made as expected [7].

McKinsey is reported on big data in 2010 that *"The next frontier for innovation, competition, and productivity"* and it was said that in 2019 united stat will face the shortage of 150,000 – 190,000 data experts as well as 1.5 million data supervisors. In the past several years, there has remained a huge development in big data. New organizations will be endeavoring to oversee big data and helping relationships with seeing big data, and more associations are steadily embracing and shifting toward big data. Nonetheless, big data is around for a surprisingly long time successfully to be sure. Big data is the degree that the web was in 1993. The colossal big data change is still before us everything going to change in the coming one year from now and the big data time starts [8].

## 10.2 LITERATURE REVIEW

The quantity of data is growing day by day due to smarts phone and social networks. The data set of big data has a large and complex structure or sorting analyzing and visualizing for more processes and results. The new type of data gives new challenges. The first thing the author discusses in this paper is the concept of big data such as volume, variety, the velocity of data, and a large number of data sources, and second, he reviewed the security and privacy of big data. In the privacy section, they said that to ensure confidentiality of the information is for the privilege of having some control over how to personal data will only be collected and used [9].

In the last, he also discusses the current challenges and further research perspectives such as privacy (conserving social network removal), safety problems of a vast outsourced database, security aspect during big data exchange, preserving big data analytics, preservative big chart breakdown, and mining, and interrogating the cloud-enabled database [10–13].

The importance of big data and the role of big data in different applications has no doubt but privacy and security problems in the big data have the highest priority among all other challenges. Due to lack of security or privacy, the data of organization and personal data is stored in cloud storage, and hackers' attacks on data and misused. The main objective of the article is privacy and security challenges in big data through Indian perspectives. They collect existing solutions and give a comprehensive overview including their advantages or disadvantages and also discuss cyberattacks and they are also interested in knowing criminals behind cyberattacks [14–18].

The author describes the importance of big data in different sectors and also describes the challenges of security and privacy in the second section. They write about the characteristics and value of big data. Some of the challenges of privacy and security are given as follows:

1. A person's personal information, in combination with outside huge data sets, leading to the conclusion of new truth approximately that somebody, and it is thinkable that these are realities about you in on a secret, and someone strength did not need the Data to the owner or to any other person, to distinguish all about them [19].
2. Material about our users will be together and used to add worth to the administration's activities. This is completed through the creation of ideas in their life that they don't have to know about.
3. Another important result of the uprising, the social stratification, in which the right person, you will have to use predictive big data analytics; and, on the further side, fewer people will be simply able to be recognized and preserved far inferior.
4. Big data is being used by police to grow the chance to get some highlighted of people who have been suffering negative impacts due to the not-to-do, or even know that they are being discriminated against [20].

They provide some privacy techniques and conclude that the association of huge data is the key which is the root of the use of big data [21].

Dr Bhavani Thuraisingham is to fabricate a local area in large information security and protection to investigate the difficult exploration issues. Likewise, he recorded the challenges of security in information the executives and the whole space of safety protection uprightness information characteristics and trust approaches must be analyzed inside the setting of enormous information protection. Which is the fitting strategy for enormous information? How could these approaches be taken care of without influencing execution [4]?

Julio Moreno says that data is presently one of the most valuable properties for corporations in all sectors. The continued development in value and size of data has created a new trick: it can't be managed by old-style analytical strategies. This tricky was then resolved with the formation of a new model [22].

Mosavi describes that big data analysis has become an important tool in various industries. The flexibility allows for the continuous development of several applications. Among other things, the benefits of this approach are efficiency, decision-making, modeling, and forecasting. With them, it has become easier to find the most accurate and possible solutions to current engineering problems. In addition, there are many data applications in the industry [23,24].

The author describes the issues of big data security in this book. They describe the encryption-related challenges of big data also provide some solutions to those problems. The publisher says that security is not only encryption of data but also depends on security policies that are you to access data. In our industry sectors such as marketing advertising retail and financial services, big data privacy has become cruel. Big data security challenges make a very difficult scenario and make life difficult for many organizations.

The researcher focuses on the security issues of cloud computing, big data, and cut cards. It mainly focuses on key security issues in cloud computing [21,25–28,29, p. 2013,30]. Data big data applications have brought tremendous value to organizations, businesses, enterprises, and many industries large and small. We also discuss various options to solve the problems such as cloud computing and security on Hadoop. Cloud computing security has developed rapidly, including computer security, network security, information security, and data privacy [31–34].

The amount of data in the world increases every day. Due to the size of the data, traditional systems cannot capture, store, or analyze it. The amount of data is large. On the website, the amount of big data continues to increase. The data, that is, the data, is not managed or used. Some applications are in the fields of health, life, and education management. The organization is more flexible and practical [5,35–38].

In this paper, the author describes that big data has become China's national strategy for meeting social and economic needs and developing information technology. Massive big data not only brings suitability to people's everyday life and empowers creativity but also additional tasks to material safety. In this article, we explore new types and structures of material security problems in the era of big data and propose solutions such as building a major data security management platform, creating and implementing an information security system [39,40].

## 10.3 RESEARCH METHODOLOGY

Based on a specification by Kitchenham and Charters [42], Figure 10.2 explains the three steps of the systematic literature review (SLR) as professional in our research specifically planning, manage the analysis, reporting the review and result. After observing the need for an SLR and identifying the research questions, the following phases will explain the upcoming two steps of the planning phase, explicitly creating and afterward assessing the survey convention then proceed with summarizing the consequences of the directing stage and the revealing stage independently.

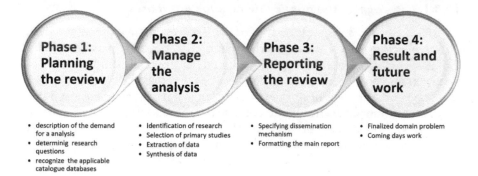

*Figure 10.2* Systematic literature review and their phases.

### 10.3.1 Planning phase

All through this, still up in the air the fundamental point of the survey and completed the accompanying exercises that clarified each progression exhaustively.

#### 10.3.1.1 Description of the demand for an analysis

In Phase 1, there is no SLR (systematic literature review) in the sector of big data. Based on the expanding number of researches on big data applications, applying this technique in an alternate setting had problems such as the major application range of privacy and security for future research. Not set in stone is the need to play out an SLR as indicated by the consequences of the past investigations [41].

#### 10.3.1.2 Determining research questions

The general aim of SLR is to acknowledge and survey published researches between 2000 and 2021 that correlated to privacy and security issues of big data. To accomplish more point-by-point and exhaustive perspectives on this subject, the principal aim is partitioned into the following research questions:

1. What are the previous and current problems and future research interpretation of privacy and security of big data?
2. What are the current challenges of big data in privacy and security?
3. What are the main security dimensions on which researchers are focusing their efforts?
4. What techniques, methodologies, and models with which to achieve security in big data exist?

### 10.3.1.3 Recognize the applicable catalog databases

As indicated by the exploration questions, the accompanying computerized book collection was a focus for the mandatory research papers: Scopus, Google Scholar, Science Direct, PubMed, and Springer. The fundamental justification for choosing these advanced libraries was that they gather research identified with the fields of software engineering and clinical science and that they list research papers from different distribution stations like diaries, meetings, books, and studios. In this research, the quests were restricted to diary and gathering procedures research that were distributed inside 2001–2021.

## 10.3.2 Manage the analysis

The searching thread will design extensive coverage but logical scope. Accordingly, for the determination of the searching thread. The catchword relating to the research question draws out the synonyms similar to the major expression were observed. Usually we do not use the terms like as, or, another, etc .

Privacy and security issues in big data have many challenges benefits and future scope in that work we also explain in point section wise.

### 10.3.2.1 Instruction choice

We studied the paper of their abstract, summary, procedure, and decision. Among all the papers, we have carefully chosen those types of papers which are written in English and follow some techniques.

In upcoming era, studies are launching some novels related to privacy and security issues of big data. This content consists of security features and explain the conventional big data privacy and security issues and way to fix them so that one can tackle with future challenges.

Moreover, many other applications are also introduced related to Big Data's security and privacy issues. All those studies are going to be published after year 2000 and before year 2021.

## 10.3.3 Quality assessment

Basically, Quality assessment is based on qualitative and quantative research. This also explains designing and experimenting in detail. The accuracy of the method is measurable in paper report. This also shows some benefits of different methods.

## 10.3.4 Data mining and synthesize

In that type of directive to get answers to the Research Questions (RQ), we analyzed the data and also synthesize the data as follows:

1. **RQ 1**: What are the previous and current problems and future research interpretation of privacy and safety of big data?
2. **RQ 2**: What are the current problems of big data in privacy and security?
3. **RQ 3**: What are the main security dimensions on which researchers are focusing their efforts?
4. **RQ 4**: What strategies, systems, and models with which to accomplish security in big data exist?

To analyze the data and synthesize the data in the research studies to get some type of research questions. These question answers are got by analyzing data and synthesizing the data.

We identified the data through the database and get the 15 articles then we select the 7 papers after the applications of the exclusion criteria. Then, five papers have remained after the application of inclusion criteria and three papers have remained after the application of the quality assessment indicator. The complete steps of the systematic literature review are shown in Figure 10.3.

### 10.3.5 Reporting the review

**RQ 1**: What are the previous and current problems and future research interpretation of privacy and security of big data?

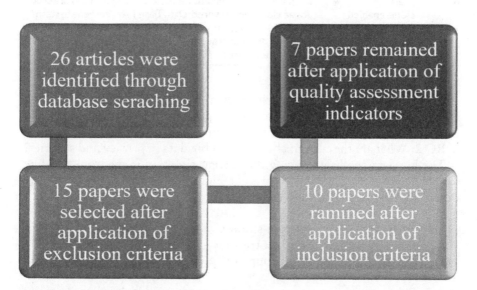

*Figure 10.3* Flow diagram of the systematic review.

*Table 10.1* Problems and explanation

| Sr No. | Problems | Explanation |
|---|---|---|
| 1 | Privacy-preserving social network mining | Public network data remain the most reliable source of real-life big data, thanks to well-known social network sites like Facebook, Twitter, and Instagram. Here mining such information is of essential interest, however, the requirement for protection and security regularly restricts the genuine effect of these errands. |
| 2 | Protection issues of big outsourced database | In cloud frameworks, information bases are frequently reevaluated dependent on the Desktop as a Service paradigm. This proposal caused some critical security issues like important informational collections became easy target to be tempered and this broke safety and security features. [24]. |
| 3 | Security aspects during big data Exchange | Information trade procedures will turn out to be increasingly more significant later on because of the notable attributes of cloud frameworks. Here applications are probably going to trade enormous scope heft of big data being this an unmistakable wellspring of safety infringement chances. |
| 4 | Privacy-preserving big data analytics | Big data are vital and significant since they are preserved as a wellspring of data that goes to be useful for dynamic and assumption goals. |
| 5 | Protection-preserving big chart breakdown and mining | Enormous graph examination and mining are among the new wildernesses for logical figuring. On account of the comparable idea of consistent tests, these diagrams are oftentimes dispersed over fogs. |
| 6 | Querying cloud-enabled DBMS | In an average examination motor, information is scattered over cloud-empowered Data Base Management System (DBMS). Here to thwart insurance and security breaks, a despise drive pursues the possibility of exploiting the encryption part to get data. |

Stephen Kaisler et al. [20] describe several numbers of open problems and future research perspectives related to the privacy and security of big data. Some of the expected challenges are shown in Table 10.1.

**RQ 2:** What are the current challenges of big data in privacy and security?

The big data challenges facing the current situation range from building low-level processing systems to average high-level analysis. Here, we have described the main challenges of big data.

a. Store large amounts of data storage
b. Share large amounts of data transfer
c. Big data visualization, cleanup, analysis, and search

**RQ 3:** What are the main security dimensions on which researchers are focusing their efforts?

These questions form the basis of most of our research and cover key topics in common safety standards to help identify results, but often safety features or concerns.

RQ 4: What strategies, systems, and models with which to accomplish security in big data exist?

As a result, your system is completely clean and well-organized, and much work is being done on the Hadoop system so that it can be installed.

Similarly, you should make sure you have the right amount and you can't do it. If you do not want to be able to do that, you will be able to make sure that you do not have enough information.

## 10.4 RESULT AND DISCUSSION

In this investigation, 26 articles connected to the protection and security of big data from 2011 to 2021 were examined according to journal names, year of publications, type of research, sector, data collection tool, by using a different type of scale and programs.

Table 10.2 shows the dissemination of articles according to journals names. As shown in the table, the articles were more published in the journals of computer communication, journals of the Internet of things and journals of communication, nature human behavior, International Conference on Consumer Electronics (ICCE), International Conference on Devices, Circuits and Systems (ICDCS), and others.

Figure 10.4 shows the journals' names. It shows the frequency of the different types of journals.

Table 10.2 Distribution of articles according to journal names

| List of journals | Frequency | Percent |
|---|---|---|
| Journal of Communication | 2 | 7.62 |
| Computer Communication | 3 | 11.53 |
| Indonesian Journal of Computer Science | 1 | 3.71 |
| Journal of Interdisciplinary Research | 1 | 3.71 |
| IT Professional | 1 | 3.71 |
| Future Generation Computer System | 3 | 11.73 |
| Communication Survey and Tutorial | 1 | 3.71 |
| ICCA | 1 | 3.71 |
| Diabetes & Metabolic Syndrome Clinical Research | 3 | 11.73 |
| Areas and Communication | 1 | 3.71 |
| ICDCS | 1 | 3.71 |
| Others | 8 | 31.42 |
| Total | 26 | 100 |

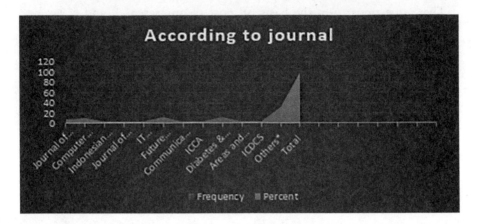

*Figure 10.4* According to the journal.

*Table 10.3* Distribution of articles according to publication

| Year of publication | Frequency | Percent |
|---|---|---|
| 2015 | 2 | 8.01 |
| 2016 | 3 | 12.03 |
| 2017 | 2 | 8.01 |
| 2018 | 2 | 8.01 |
| 2019 | 4 | 16.04 |
| 2020 | 7 | 26.77 |
| 2021 | 6 | 21.13 |
| Total | 26 | 100 |

Table 10.3 emphasizes the dissemination of published investigation, 26 articles connected to the protection and security of big data. In this table, we will observe the security challenges of big data in previous years and current years. In 2000, the big data concept was low but with the speed of time from 2000 to 2021, the concept of big data is increased. This means that with time demand for big data is increased.

Figure 10.5 shows the publication of the article according to table frequency and percentage.

Table 10.4 shows that the dissemination of different articles is correlated to the protection and security of big data according to the countries where the study has occurred. As shown in the table the two or three countries among the maximum article have been occurred in China and Pakistan (26 articles 38.89%). After that most of the study in China, the study occurred in Australia, Lebanon, Qatar, the United Kingdom, and France which are shown in the table.

Here the value is maximum than the paper because some of the papers are published in more than one country; therefore, the total value increased by given papers.

# Frequency

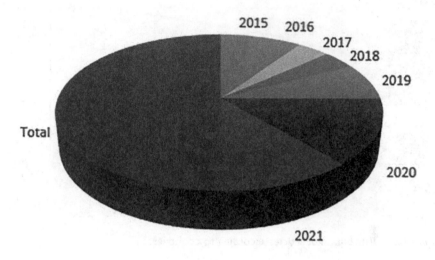

Figure 10.5 According to the publication of the year.

Table 10.4 Distribution of articles according to countries

| Countries | Frequency | Percent |
|---|---|---|
| China | 8 | 29.5 |
| Saudi Arabia | 2 | 7.9 |
| Turkey | 2 | 7.9 |
| Brazil | 3 | 12 |
| India | 2 | 7.9 |
| Pakistan | 4 | 14.98 |
| Australia | 2 | 7.9 |
| USA | 3 | 11.92 |
| Total | 26 | 100 |

Figure 10.6 presents the percentage of the different countries according to publications. In this figure, every country shows a different type of percentage in publication.

Table 10.5 shows the distribution of articles similar to the privacy and security of big data. According to the sector in which the study was regulated. As shown in the table, most of the articles put down the target study in any important sector. The most important is the information and technology sector.

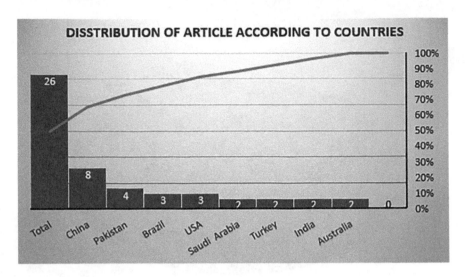

*Figure 10.6* Distribution of articles according to countries.

*Table 10.5* Distribution of articles according to sector

| Sector | Frequency | Percent |
|---|---|---|
| Information and technology | 5 | 19.31 |
| Postal service | 3 | 11.58 |
| Service | 1 | 3.78 |
| Retail and customer service | 4 | 15.45 |
| Education | 1 | 3.78 |
| Regulated industry | 2 | 7.7 |
| No. of specific sectors | 10 | 38.4 |
| Total | 26 | 100 |

Figure 10.7 presents the frequency and percentage of different sectors most of the frequency and percentage of the information technology sector after that the service sector also more frequency and percentage but less than information and technology.

Table 10.6 shows the distribution of articles about the privacy and security of big data according to the research type. Most of the quantitative research is being used in this study the quantitative research is used 53% and qualitative research is 6.67% used in this study shown in the table.

Figure 10.8 shows the different research-type frequencies and percentages. This figure shows the quantitative research is 53% and qualitative research is 6.67%.

Table 10.7 represents the distribution of articles similar to the privacy and safety of big data. According to data collection tools in this table show that

## Distribution of Articles According to Sector

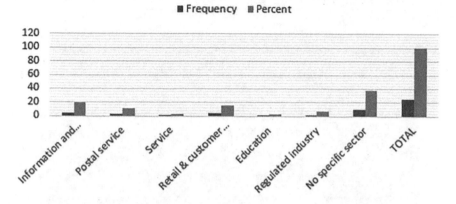

Figure 10.7 Distribution of articles according to sectors.

Table 10.6 Distribution of articles according to the type of research

| Type of research | Frequency | Percent |
|---|---|---|
| Quantitative | 9 | 34.6 |
| Qualitative | 4 | 15.7 |
| Mix method (quantitative and qualitative) | 7 | 26.61 |
| Theoretical | 6 | 23.09 |
| Total | 26 | 100 |

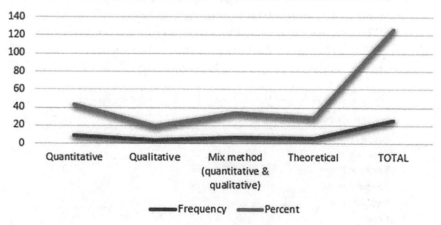

Figure 10.8 Distribution of article according to research type.

Table 10.7 Distribution of articles according to data collection tool

| Data collection tool | Frequency | Percent |
|---|---|---|
| Survey | 12 | 46.32 |
| Secondary data | 8 | 30.89 |
| Interview | 6 | 22.79 |
| Total | 26 | 100 |

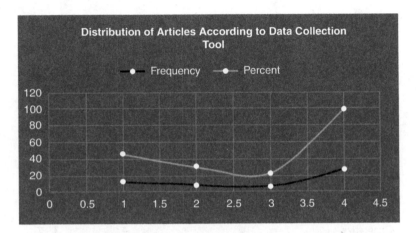

Figure 10.9 Distribution of articles according to data collection tool.

the surveyor secondary data are most used for the data collection in which most of the survey tools are 60% used for the data collection. Secondary data are also helpful in the data collection as shown in this table.

Figure 10.9 shows the different frequencies about the data collection tools in which most of the surveys are most helpful in data collection. It also shows the different percentages and frequencies.

Table 10.8 presents the distribution of an article on the protection and security of big data according to the authorship pattern. The majority are three authors and four author's papers: 19.25% are three author's papers,

Table 10.8 Distribution of articles according to authorship pattern

| No. of contributors | Frequency | Percent |
|---|---|---|
| Single author | 1 | 3.85 |
| Two authors | 3 | 11.55 |
| Three authors | 5 | 19.25 |
| Four authors | 5 | 19.25 |
| Five authors | 2 | 7.6 |
| Others | 10 | 38.5 |
| Total | 26 | 100 |

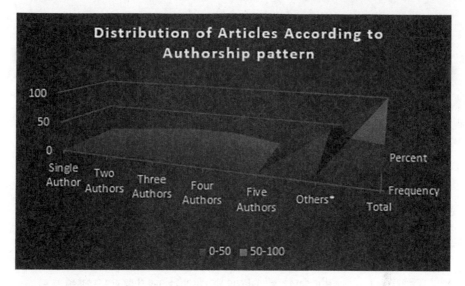

*Figure 10.10* Distribution of articles according to authorship pattern.

19.25% are four author's papers, 38.5% others, single author's papers are 3.85%, two author's papers are 11.55%, and five author's papers are 7.6% as shown in the table.

Figure 10.10 shows the different types of frequency and percentage about the authorship. Most of them (38.5%) are other (move than five authors), three and four authors single author's papers are 19.25% each.

## 10.4.1 Discussion

The basic purpose of **SLR** (Systematic Literature Review) is the examination of similar studies and to approach benefits and future challenges. In the privacy and security of big data seven papers are identified for the final discussion.

This section testified to the different types of results determined in this analysis. We show the total analysis of reactions of the selected process, and after that, the complete research for every type of research question is explained separately. The following questions are answered throughout detail by keeping in mind the objectives of the questions.

**Question 1:** Being referred to they portray a few quantities of exposed problems and upcoming inspection points of view identified with the protection and security of big data. Some of the expected challenges are shown in Table 10.9.

**Question 2:** The big data challenges include the current situation range from building low-level processing systems to average high-level analysis. Here, we have described the main challenges of big data.

Table 10.9 Challenges and explanation

| Sr No. | Problems | Explanation |
|---|---|---|
| 1 | Protection-preserving social network mining | Social organization material is the most dependable wellsprings of genuine big data, because of notable informal organization locales like Facebook, Twitter, and Instagram. Here mining such data is of fundamental interest, nonetheless, the necessity for assurance and security routinely limits the real impact of these tasks. |
| 2 | Security issues of big outsourced database | In cloud frameworks, information bases are frequently reevaluated dependent on the Desktop as a Service paradigm. This offers rise to extremely dangerous security issues as inquiry preparing methods may effortlessly get too touchy informational collections and decide protection breaks. |
| 3 | Security aspects during big data exchange | Data conversation procedures will prove to be more important in the future due to the well-known characteristics of cloud systems. Here applications are likely to exchange large-scale bulks of big data, being this a clear source of security violation risks. |
| 4 | Privacy-preserving big data analytics | Big data are vital and significant since they are treated as a wellspring of data that goes to be useful for dynamic and assumption purposes. |
| 5 | Privacy-preserving big chart study and mining | Enormous Graph examination and mining are among the new wildernesses for logical figuring On account of the comparable idea of consistent tests these diagrams are oftentimes dispersed over fogs. |
| 6 | Enquiring cloud-enabled DBMS | In an average examination motor, information is scattered over cloud-empowered Data Base Management System (DBMS). Here to thwart insurance and security breaks, a despise drive pursues the possibility of exploiting the encryption part to get data. |

a. Save large amounts of data storage
b. Share large amounts of data transfer
c. Big data visualization, cleanup, analysis, search

Question 3: These questions form the basis of most of our research and cover key topics in common safety standards to help identify results, but often safety features or concerns.

Question 4: As a result, your system is completely clean and well-organized, and many pregnant women have no problem with the problem. However, if you don't want to read the information you need to make sure you don't want to read it, you can't get much out of your system. Much work is being done on the Hadoop system so that it can be installed and installed.

Similarly, you should make sure you have the right amount and you can't do it. If you do not want to be able to do that, you will be able to make sure that you do not have enough information.

## 10.5 CONCLUSION

This paper teaches to fix those critical issues which were faced in big data and also teaches about specialist methods to fix those issues. This goal was accomplished by the efficient planning study philosophy which permitted us to find out the papers identified with our primary objective. We found that the foremost issues are identified with the intrinsic qualities of the big data framework and that the privacy problems were not examined at the point when big data at first imagined. Many creators accordingly center their examination around making intends to ensure information especially concerning protection yet protection it isn't the solitary security issue that should be resolved in big data's framework is likewise a colossal worry for the scientists. We have nonetheless likewise distinguished an absence of examinations in the sector of information the board particularly as for governance. We can consider assessment that this isn't adequate since having an administration security structure will permit the quick dissemination of big data innovation. Most importantly, growth of big data is promoting this world's advancement. This is the clarification of researching and developing of big data. At present, it is not far important for this world, as it should so. In further research, the occurred issues probably will be at zero. Moreover, big data can be valuable as a base for the advancement of future things that will change the whole world from our perspective. Big data is considered important for future because of being similar to Internet and request administrator.

## REFERENCES

1. K. Abouelmehdi, A. Beni-Hssane, H. Khaloufi, and M. Saadi, "Big data security and privacy in healthcare: A review," *Procedia Computer Science*, vol. 113, pp. 73–80, 2017, doi: 10.1016/j.procs.2017.08.292.
2. F. L. F. Almeida and C. Calistru, "The main challenges and issues of big data management," *IJRSC*, vol. 2, no. 1, 2013. doi: 10.5861/ijrsc.2012.209.
3. C. A. Ardagna, P. Ceravolo, and E. Damiani, "Big data analytics as-a-service: Issues and challenges," in *2016 IEEE International Conference on Big Data (Big Data)*, 2016, pp. 3638–3644. doi: 10.1109/BigData.2016.7841029.
4. B. Matturdi, X. Zhou, S. Li, and F. Lin, "Big data security and privacy: A review," *China Communications*, vol. 11, no. 14, pp. 135–145, 2014, doi: 10.1109/CC.2014.7085614.
5. C. Sur, "DeepSeq: Learning browsing log data based personalized security vulnerabilities and counter intelligent measures," *Journal of Ambient Intelligence and Humanized Computing*, vol. 10, no. 9, pp. 3573–3602, 2019. doi: 10.1007/s12652-018-1084-9.
6. C. L. Philip Chen and C.-Y. Zhang, "Data-intensive applications, challenges, techniques and technologies: A survey on big data," *Information Sciences*, vol. 275, pp. 314–347, 2014. doi: 10.1016/j.ins.2014.01.015.

7. F. Rahman, S. I. Ahamed, J.-J. Yang, and Q. Wang, "PriGen: A generic framework to preserve privacy of healthcare data in the cloud," in *Inclusive Society: Health and Wellbeing in the Community, and Care at Home*, Berlin, Heidelberg, 2013, pp. 77–85. doi: 10.1007/978-3-642–39470-6_10.

8. N. Chaudhari and S. Srivastava, "Big data security issues and challenges," in *2016 International Conference on Computing, Communication and Automation (ICCCA)*, 2016, pp. 60–64. doi: 10.1109/CCAA.2016.7813690.

9. X. Pei, Y. Wang, W. Yao, J. Lin, and R. Peng, "Security enhanced attribute based signcryption for private data sharing in cloud," in *2016 IEEE Trustcom/ BigDataSE/ISPA*, 2016, pp. 737–743. doi: 10.1109/TrustCom.2016.0133.

10. M. I. Tariq, "Towards information security metrics framework for cloud computing," *International Journal of Cloud Computing and Services Science*, vol. 1, no. 4, p. 209, 2012.

11. M. I. Tariq, D. Haq, and J. Iqbal, "SLA based information security metric for cloud computing from COBIT 4.1 framework", 2015.

12. M. I. Tariq, S. Tayyaba, M. W. Ashraf, and H. Rasheed, "Risk based NIST effectiveness analysis for cloud security," *Bahria University Journal of Information & Communication Technologies (BUJICT)*, vol. 10, no. Special Is, pp. 23–31, 2017.

13. M. I. Tariq, S. Tayyaba, M. U. Hashmi, M. W. Ashraf, and N. A. Mian, "Agent based information security threat management framework for hybrid cloud computing," *IJCSNS*, vol. 17, no. 12, p. 57, 2017.

14. S. Boubiche, D. E. Boubiche, A. Bilami, and H. Toral-Cruz, "Big data challenges and data aggregation strategies in wireless sensor networks," *IEEE Access*, vol. 6, pp. 20558–20571, 2018. doi: 10.1109/ACCESS.2018.2821445.

15. M. I. Tariq, "Analysis of the effectiveness of cloud control matrix for hybrid cloud computing," *International Journal of Future Generation Communication and Networking*, vol. 11, no. 4, pp. 1–10, 2018.

16. M. I. Tariq, "Agent based information security framework for hybrid cloud computing," *KSII Transactions on Internet & Information Systems*, vol. 13, no. 1, pp. 406–434, 2019.

17. S. A. Butt, M. I. Tariq, T. Jamal, A. Ali, J. L. D. Martinez, and E. De-La-Hoz-Franco, "Predictive variables for agile development merging cloud computing services," *IEEE Access*, vol. 7, pp. 99273–99282, 2019.

18. M. I. Tariq et al., "Combination of AHP and TOPSIS methods for the ranking of information security controls to overcome its obstructions under fuzzy environment," *Journal of Intelligent & Fuzzy Systems*, vol. 38, pp. 6075–6088, 2020.

19. B. B. Jayasingh, M. R. Patra, and D. B. Mahesh, "Security issues and challenges of big data analytics and visualization," in *2016 2nd International Conference on Contemporary Computing and Informatics (IC3I)*, 2016, pp. 204–208. doi: 10.1109/IC3I.2016.7917961.

20. S. Kaisler, F. Armour, J. A. Espinosa, and W. Money, "Big data: Issues and challenges moving forward," in *2013 46th Hawaii International Conference on System Sciences*, 2013, pp. 995–1004. doi: 10.1109/HICSS.2013.645.

21. C. Liu, R. Ranjan, C. Yang, X. Zhang, L. Wang, and J. Chen, "MuR-DPA: Top-down levelled multi-replica merkle hash tree based secure public auditing for dynamic big data storage on cloud," *IEEE Transactions on Computers*, vol. 64, no. 9, pp. 2609–2622, 2015. doi: 10.1109/TC.2014.2375190.

22. V. Thayananthan and A. Albeshri, "Big data security issues based on quantum cryptography and privacy with authentication for mobile data center," *Procedia Computer Science*, vol. 50, pp. 149–156, 2015. doi: 10.1016/j.procs.2015.04.077.

23. D. S. Terzi, R. Terzi, and S. Sagiroglu, "A survey on security and privacy issues in big data," in *2015 10th International Conference for Internet Technology and Secured Transactions (ICITST)*, 2015, pp. 202–207. doi: 10.1109/ICITST.2015.7412089.

24. J. Moreno, M. A. Serrano, and E. Fernández-Medina, "Main issues in big data security," *Future Internet*, vol. 8, no. 3, Art. no. 3, 2016. doi: 10.3390/fi8030044.

25. M. I. Tariq, N. A. Mian, A. Sohail, T. Alyas, and R. Ahmad, "Evaluation of the challenges in the Internet of medical things with multicriteria decision making (AHP and TOPSIS) to overcome its obstruction under fuzzy environment," *Mobile Information Systems*, vol. 2020, p. e8815651, 2020. doi: 10.1155/2020/8815651.

26. I. Ahmed, "A brief review: Security issues in cloud computing and their solutions," *Telkomnika*, vol. 17, no. 6, pp. 2812–2817, 2019.

27. N. A. Al-gohany and S. Almotairi, "Comparative study of database security in cloud computing using AES and DES encryption algorithms," *JISCR*, vol. 2, no. 1, 2019. doi: 10.26735/16587790.2019.004.

28. M. I. Tariq, S. Tayyaba, M. W. Ashraf, H. Rasheed, and F. Khan, "Analysis of NIST SP 800-53 rev. 3 controls effectiveness for cloud computing," *Computing*, vol. 3, p. 4, 2016.

29. M. I. Tariq and V. Santarcangelo, "Analysis of ISO 27001: 2013 controls effectiveness for cloud computing," vol. 2, pp. 201–208, 2016.

30. E. Ghazizadeh, M. Zamani, J. Ab Manan, and A. Pashang, "A survey on security issues of federated identity in the cloud computing," in *4th IEEE International Conference on Cloud Computing Technology and Science Proceedings*, December 2012, pp. 532–565. doi: 10.1109/CloudCom.2012.6427513.

31. H. Kupwade Patil and R. Seshadri, "Big data security and privacy issues in healthcare," in *2014 IEEE International Congress on Big Data*, June 2014, pp. 762–765. doi: 10.1109/BigData.Congress.2014.112.

32. M. I. Tariq et al., "An analysis of the application of fuzzy logic in cloud computing," *Journal of Intelligent & Fuzzy Systems*, vol. 38, no. 5, pp. 5933–5947, 2020.

33. M. I. Tariq et al., "A review of deep learning security and privacy defensive techniques," *Mobile Information Systems*, vol. 2020, 18 p, 2020.

34. M. I. Tariq et al., "Prioritization of information security controls through fuzzy AHP for cloud computing networks and wireless sensor networks," *Sensors*, vol. 20, no. 5, p. 1310, 2020.

35. N. Rastogi, S. K. Singh, and P. K. Singh, "Privacy and security issues in big data: Through Indian prospective," in *2018 3rd International Conference on Internet of Things: Smart Innovation and Usages (IoT-SIU)*, 2018, pp. 1–11. doi: 10.1109/IoT-SIU.2018.8519858.

36. M. I. Tariq, S. Tayyaba, H. Rasheed, and M. W. Ashraf, "Factors influencing the Cloud Computing adoption in higher education institutions of Punjab, Pakistan," pp. 179–184, 2017.

37. M. I. Tariq, S. Tayyaba, M. W. Ashraf, and V. E. Balas, "Deep learning techniques for optimizing medical big data," in *Deep Learning Techniques for Biomedical and Health Informatics*, B. Agarwal, V. Balas, L. Jain, R. Poonia, M. Sharma (Eds). Amsterdam, Netherlands: Elsevier, 2020, pp. 187–211.

38. M. Almorsy, J. Grundy, and A. S. Ibrahim, "Collaboration-based cloud computing security management framework," in *2011 IEEE 4th International Conference on Cloud Computing*, Washington, DC, July 2011, pp. 364–371. doi: 10.1109/CLOUD.2011.9.

39. J. Son, D. Kim, R. Hussain, and H. Oh, "Conditional proxy re-encryption for secure big data group sharing in cloud environment," in *2014 IEEE Conference on Computer Communications Workshops (INFOCOM WKSHPS)*, April 2014, pp. 541–546. doi: 10.1109/INFCOMW.2014.6849289.

40. S. Tayyaba, S. A. Khan, M. Tariq, and M. W. Ashraf, "Network security and Internet of things," in *Industrial Internet of Things and Cyber-Physical Systems: Transforming the Conventional to Digital*, P. Kumar, V. Ponnusamy, and V. Jain (Eds). Hershey, PA: IGI Global, 2020, pp. 198–238.

41. P. Adluru, S. S. Datla, and X. Zhang, "Hadoop eco system for big data security and privacy," in *2015 Long Island Systems, Applications and Technology*, May 2015, pp. 1–6. doi: 10.1109/LISAT.2015.7160211.

42. P. Brereton, B. A. Kitchenham, D. Budgen, M. Turner, and M. Khalil, "Lessons from applying the systematic literature review process within the software engineering domain," *Journal of Systems and Software*, vol. 80, no. 4, pp. 571–583, 2007.

# Index